The Significance of Monuments

The Neolithic period, when agriculture began and many monuments were constructed, is an era fraught with paradoxes and ambiguities. Students of prehistory have long found the highly theoretical interpretations of the period perplexing and contradictory. Starting in the Mesolithic and carrying his analysis through to the Late Bronze Age, Richard Bradley sheds light on this complex period and the changing consciousness of the people who lived at the time.

The book studies the importance of monuments, tracing their history for nearly three millennia from their first creation over six thousand years ago. Part I discusses how monuments developed and their role in forming a new sense of time and space among the inhabitants of prehistoric Europe. Such features of the landscape as mounds and enclosures are also examined in detail. Through a series of case studies, Part II considers how monuments were modified and reinterpreted to suit the changing needs of society.

The Significance of Monuments is an indispensable text for all students of European prehistory. It is also an enlightening read for professional archaeologists and all those interested in this fascinating period.

Richard Bradley is Professor of Archaeology at Reading University. Current interests include landscape archaeology and rock art. Recent books include *Altering the Earth* and *Rock Art and the Prehistory of Atlantic Europe*.

The Significance of Monuments

On the shaping of human experience
in Neolithic and Bronze Age Europe

Richard Bradley

London and New York

First published 1998
by Routledge
11 New Fetter Lane, London EC4P 4EE

Simultaneously published in the USA and Canada
by Routledge
29 West 35th Street, New York, NY 10001

First published in paperback in 1998

Typeset in Baskerville by Keystroke, Jacaranda Lodge, Wolverhampton
Printed and bound in Great Britain by Redwood Books, Trowbridge, Wiltshire

British Library Cataloguing in Publication Data
A catalogue record for this book is available from the
British Library

Library of Congress Cataloguing in Publication Data
Bradley, Richard
    The significance of monuments : on the shaping of human experience
in Neolithic and Bronze Age Europe / Richard Bradley.
    Includes bibliographical references and index
    1. Neolithic period—Europe. 2. Bronze age—Europe.
3. Megalithic monuments—Europe. 4. Architecture, Prehistoric—Europe.
5. Europe—Antiquities. I. Title.
GN776.2.A1B73   1998
936—dc21   97–27536

ISBN 0–415–15203–8 (hbk)
ISBN 0–415–15204–6 (pbk)

The cover illustration is taken from a one-person touring exhibition called 'Petrified Garden' organized by An Lanntair Gallery, Stornoway, Scotland. The picture is a photo-montage made by photographing sections of a stone circle and the horizon from a height of 6.5 metres, with the camera on a pole.

Using a flash at night mimics what the stone circle might look like with a central fire, which was one of the curious features of these Aberdeenshire stone circles. Stone circles in the British Isles show enough of a theme and variation in their design to suggest that if we knew the missing elements in each case then the variety of monument types would reduce to a smaller group of pictures on the ground.

Just one of many possibilities is that these circles are an expression of the way Neolithic peoples related to their surrounding landscape. The following text accompanied the exhibition and is my response to a way of seeing unrestrained by the painter's rules of perspective, or the frame of the photograph or television.

In a single photograph, the horizon is a line from one side of the frame to the other. Do we really see our surroundings in this way? No, because we look around, we don't look at. In this way the horizon is a circle, and we are always at the centre of the circle.

Even though we define a circle visually wherever we stand, we need not be conscious of ourselves doing the looking, so we define a circle with a hole in the middle. That is the human condition.

As we look we also unconsciously magnify the horizon. With the discovery of perspective, a painter could convey distance by making objects on the horizon appear very small. But we see the horizon as bigger than that. A photograph never does justice to the 'grand view' to which we aspire because the hills in the distance are smaller than we remembered.

The human mind is easily capable of imagining its surroundings from a vantage point above eye-level. Reality in this sense is more map-like. It makes more sense to imagine things from above because the brain needs less memory to make one useful picture – like a template – from which to infer necessary information as we move about.

It may be the case that our perception and our cosmology are intimately bound together, and that discovering the meaning of lost cultures will require the simple question to be answered: How did they look at their surroundings?

Mark Johnston 1997

For Colin Richards

Contents

Figures

Preface

It is curious how one project can overflow into another. This book is a case in point, having two distinct sources. Its origins go back to a lecture that I gave in 1992 to the Society of Antiquaries of Scotland. A year later it appeared as the first chapter of *Altering the earth*. In it I inverted the usual argument that the building of Neolithic monuments was directly related to the economic surplus provided by farming. I suggested, rather, that agricultural production required a different sense of time and place from hunting and gathering, and may also have involved quite different attitudes to the natural world. Often it was the use of monumental architecture that created the conditions in which farming first became acceptable. The original lecture may have proposed a new way of looking at this problem, but, by its very nature, could not explore such issues in any depth. Part I of the present book attempts to do this.

The other point of departure was a lecture that I gave in Dublin in 1995. I was not satisfied with this paper and never published it, but I suspect that the main problem with the lecture was that it attempted to do too much. The lecture considered the changing character of monuments in Britain and Ireland between the Later Neolithic period and the Later Bronze Age, emphasising the way in which different structures derived from the same circular archetype. This was interpreted and reinterpreted as the character of society changed. At the conference, Barbara Bender suggested that the argument might work better as a book, and to some extent I have followed her advice, dividing the original discussion into four sections. These comprise Chapters 7 to 10 of the present text. Chapter 6, which links the two parts of the book together, is a much-revised version of a paper first published in the Routledge journal *World Archaeology* in 1991 (Bradley 1991).

Some of the other chapters also exist in preliminary versions, either as conference papers or as published articles, but all have been rewritten, some of them so drastically that little remains of the original material. They have also been given new titles. Chapter 2 builds on a conference paper presented at Wassenauer in the Netherlands, and Chapter 5 is distantly related to another, which was first given at a meeting in Glasgow. I am grateful to the organisers for allowing me to publish these here. Chapter 3 is a revised version of an article which first appeared in the *Journal of Material Culture* and is reproduced by permission of the publishers, Sage. Lastly, one section of the final chapter was first given at the annual conference of the Dutch Theoretical Archaeology Group in Leiden, and originally appeared in their journal *Archaeological Dialogues*. It is reproduced here by permission of the editors.

The extracts from 'Of the Builders' and 'Places We Love' are taken from *A Rusty Needle* by Ivan V. Lalic, published by Anvil Press Poetry in 1996. They are reproduced by permission of the publishers.

It will be clear that this book has had a lengthy gestation. One benefit of presenting these ideas in conferences and seminars is that I have been able to profit from the comments of so many people. Among them are Barbara Bender, Bob Chapman, John Chapman, Mark Edmonds, Per Karsten, Torsten Madsen, Colin Richards, Rick Schulting, Julian Thomas, Aaron Watson, Alasdair Whittle and Marek Zvelebil. Other parts of this material have developed during my excavations at Clava, and here my thinking has been influenced by conversations with Gordon Barclay, Andy Jones, Tim Phillips and David Trebarthen, among many others. Howard Williams and Debi Lambert assisted with the editing of my manuscript, and Lyn Sellwood produced all the figure drawings.

The book is dedicated to Colin Richards. It is offered in thanks for a memorable day in Orkney in 1995, when he led my excavation team round the prehistoric monuments. This was our day off from Clava, and it lasted twenty-one hours! We discussed many of these ideas then. I now want to continue that discussion.

Part I

From the house of the dead

But the masons leave
For the lime-pits of time, with flowers, chaff, ashes,
Their plans are spattered with blood, lost,
And the golden plumb-line of sun says: the world is leaning,
Bedded in a base where the fingers
Of ancient waters touch the foundation.
But feel the walls: the glow stays on your hands.

(from Ivan Lalic, 1996, 'Of the Builders',
translated by Francis R. Jones)

Chapter 1

Structures of sand

Settlements, monuments and the nature of the Neolithic

For many years the Neolithic long barrows at Barkaer in Denmark were interpreted as two of the largest houses in prehistoric Europe. The recent report on fieldwork at this site has involved a new interpretation. These were not houses at all but massive funerary monuments, built at the beginning of the Neolithic period. This example serves to introduce a wider problem which runs throughout this book, for it now seems that among the earliest indications of Neolithic activity in north and north-west Europe were enormous constructions of this kind. They played no part in everyday affairs and their prominent place in the prehistoric landscape contrasts sharply with what little is known about settlements and houses at this time. Even the evidence for early agriculture is very limited indeed. This is a situation that is found in many areas during the Neolithic and Early Bronze Age. This chapter sets out some of the problems of studying the archaeology of these periods, and argues that the development of monumental architecture should be treated as a topic in its own right.

THE PROBLEM WITH ARCHAEOLOGY

The practice of archaeology is not as objective as fieldworkers would like to believe; nor is it as subjective as theorists often suppose. Its procedures employ a mixture of objectivity and subjectivity, and it is the business of anyone examining the intellectual development of the discipline to decide where those boundaries were set at different times. The observations made in the field depend on a whole series of assumptions that are not discussed because they are taken for granted. It is only when those ideas are challenged that archaeologists can recognise their own vulnerability. All their primary observations are influenced by their knowledge and experience, but what they accept as knowledge, and what they think of as relevant experience, will change when the assumptions behind them are questioned. The methods used in the field constrain the interpretations formed at the time, and those techniques may not be the best ones for investigating different problems.

Normally, these faultlines in archaeological thinking are concealed from view because the results of an investigation are published while they are fresh. They are more likely to cause confusion where the final report is delayed, so that it appears in a different intellectual climate from the original research. A good example of this problem can be found in Danish prehistory. For nearly thirty years, between 1947 and 1975, it seemed as if two of the largest houses in Neolithic Europe were to be found at Barkaer in Jutland. Excavation had begun even before that period, with a first season of research in 1931. Eighteen years passed before the fieldwork was completed, and another forty-three elapsed before the results were brought to publication. By then the excavator, P. V. Glob, had died and the report was written by someone else (Liversage 1992).

The effect of such a long delay between fieldwork and publication was that Glob's interpretation remained unchallenged until the end of his life, when he became aware of other ways of thinking about the site. It so happened that the intellectual climate in which the work was undertaken remained the same over the greater part of that period. The excavator's interpretation conformed so well to what was thought at the time that there seemed no reason to believe that the results of his work would need to be revised. In any case, since his primary observations had been withheld, it would have been difficult for anyone to feel confident that another interpretation was more appropriate.

The Barkaer excavations are generally acknowledged to have been among the best of their time, and they constitute an admirable programme of research. As early as 1928, Glob had become aware that the site contained Neolithic material, and when he worked there in earnest it was in the expectation that this might be one of the best preserved Neolithic settlements in northern Europe. There seemed to be the remains of four houses on the site, and Iversen's investigation of the pollen in a nearby lake held out the prospect of integrating Barkaer into the early history of agriculture in Scandinavia (Iversen 1941). Becker's account of the pottery found in the first major excavation gave an added impetus to the project, for it suggested that the settlement belonged to the first period of the Danish Neolithic (Becker 1947). More extensive excavation at Barkaer might be expected to shed light on the character of settlement and land use during a formative phase.

Those seem to have been the assumptions with which the main campaign of excavation was undertaken between 1947 and 1949. The work was conducted on an unusually large scale for this time, and an area of nearly 3,000 square metres was investigated. The archaeological deposits were about a metre thick, and were cleared across large areas of the site and recorded in plan at several different levels. The result was the identification, not of four small houses, as Glob had previously supposed, but of two enormous rectangular structures which had been built side by side. Each was just under 90 metres long and approximately 7 metres wide. They were defined by stone walls and by the remains of internal partitions, which could be recognised from sudden changes in the colour of the sand that filled these buildings. These divisions were also marked by lines of stakeholes, while the outer walls of the houses included a number of postholes cut into the subsoil (see Figure 1).

It was not difficult to identify these structures as the well-preserved remains of longhouses, for buildings of that type were already known in earlier contexts further to the south, and most especially on the loess soils of the Rhineland. This was the likely source of Neolithic agriculture in Scandinavia, and it was also the point of origin of some of the artefacts that had already been imported into Mesolithic settlements from across the agricultural frontier. The two houses at Barkaer were later than those excavated on the loess, but they also seemed to be more massive structures. They gained an added significance because of the remarkable conditions of preservation, which allowed individual room divisions to be recognised in a way that could not be achieved with buildings that had been reduced to subsoil features.

Because the structural evidence at Barkaer had survived so well, it was possible to suggest that each of the longhouses had been divided into nearly thirty compartments, separated from one another by light partitions or screens. These compartments extended across the full width of the house, and, as most of the screens that defined them do not seem to have been interrupted by doorways, it was likely that each had its own entrance through the side of the building. On that basis they might be thought of as independent residential units. Each occupied approximately the same amount of space: an area of a little under 20 square metres. These units were long and narrow – just over 6 metres in length and 3 metres in width – and in one of the houses they may have been divided in two by a row of posts running along the middle of the building. Although areas of burnt clay were recognised in the excavation, there was nothing to suggest that each room or pair of rooms was provided with its own hearth.

The outer walls of both houses were apparently of stone, although the roofs were supported by a framework of wooden posts. The buildings were laid out on virtually the same alignment and faced one another across what Glob called a village street. That village was located on a small area of raised ground near to a lake (see Figure 2).

The excavator found other features which were not so easy to fit into this scheme, but none was sufficiently anomalous for him to doubt his interpretation. The first problem was the presence of a stone cist towards the east end of one of the houses. This seems to have been the first feature to be discovered at Barkaer, and, although no bones survived in the acid soil, it seems to have contained two pots and an amber bead: a collection of artefacts which might well have served as grave goods. Glob accepted this interpretation but suggested that this feature was not built until the Late Neolithic.

There were three other features with similar material, each characterised by a pair of upright posts in similar positions to the end stones of that cist. They contained a number of artefacts, which seemed to be of the same date as those associated with the houses, including complete pots, amber beads and copper ornaments. At the eastern end of each of the houses a row of massive posts had

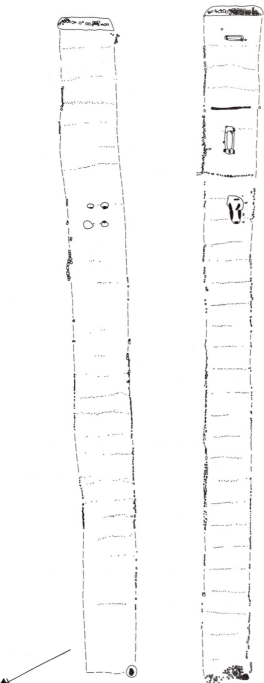

BARKAER

Figure 1. The Neolithic 'longhouses' at Barkaer, Jutland, simplified from Liversage (1992). The drawing also indicates the positions of the mortuary structures and the timber facades at the original ends of the mounds.

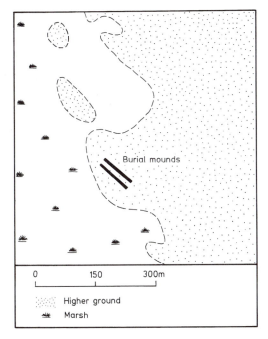

0   150   300m

Higher ground

Marsh

Figure 2. The local setting of the excavated monuments at Barkaer, after
    Liversage (1992).

been bedded in the ground, and each was associated with another decorated
vessel. Glob recognised the exceptional character of such finds and initially
suggested that they had been deposited during rituals associated with the use of
the houses, although he later came to believe that the finds of copper and amber
had been deposited in graves.

That interpretation was almost certainly correct, for, with increasing
excavation on both sides of the North Sea, it became apparent that there were
many Neolithic burials in graves associated with similar settings of posts: stone-
built dolmens were not the only form of mortuary monument in Early Neolithic
Denmark. At the same time, those excavations showed that the long mounds that
were sometimes associated with wooden mortuary structures could be divided
into a series of bays defined by rows of uprights just like those at Barkaer. The
possibility arose that Glob's longhouses might actually be the remains of two
mounds. That certainly seemed to explain some problems that had been identified
since he published his interim report. It was clear that the floors of the houses
could be almost a metre thick, although the same divisions between the
compartments were identified throughout this deposit (see Figure 3). At first, it
was suggested that this material might be windblown sand, filling the inside of
the buildings and causing them to be abandoned, but this could hardly explain
why separate rooms were filled with sand of different colours. The outer walls of

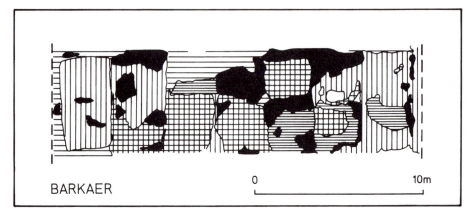

BARKAER

0   10m

Figure 3. The internal structure of one of the monuments at Barkaer, simplified from Liversage (1992). The different kinds of shading represent the separate layers of sand in the filling of the mound.

the houses presented problems too, for they consisted of single rows of boulders, which could be found at quite different levels abutting the 'floors' of the houses. Eventually, Glob himself recognised the difficulties of maintaining his original interpretation and accepted that both structures had been rectangular mounds. Having done so, he held to his original view that the postholes found beneath them were the remains of wooden houses of exactly the same dimensions as the later earthworks. Thus the houses of the living were converted directly into the houses of the dead.

There is no doubt that the site at Barkaer had been occupied before either of these mounds was built. Neolithic artefacts were found throughout the excavated area, but not in particularly large numbers. As we have seen, postholes were also recorded, but these raise many problems, for even on the most optimistic account they do not provide much evidence for buildings in the same positions as the mounds. Moreover, it seems as if the areas thought to be occupied by houses may have been investigated for postholes at the expense of the surrounding area; Glob had already decided that he was excavating two buildings and was looking for their outer walls. This may be why these features seem to cluster in the area covered by the mounds.

The new interpretation of the sequence at Barkaer suggests that a massive structure associated with the dead was built over the ephemeral traces of a settlement of the living. How can that be reconciled with the environmental sequence from the nearby lake? Again, the evidence needs to be reassessed. Iversen's pollen core from Korup Lake lacked any dating evidence, although an outline chronology is now suggested by radiocarbon. This indicates that the episodes of clearance and land use that he recognised there may have been spread over roughly six hundred years. Moreover, the catchment represented by his pollen core could have covered an area extending as far as 10 kilometres from the sample site. As a result, the diagram can only be interpreted in the most general terms. Even accepting these caveats, there is another problem, for Iversen recognised that in the early stages of this sequence the evidence for human activity was actually rather limited. Apart from an elm decline, which may have been the result of natural disease, there was a fall in oak and hazel pollen and a rise in the proportion of grasses. It was only in the following phase that plantain was strongly represented and the increase in the pollen of this plant was matched by the distribution of cereal pollen in the lake. Here we do have evidence of Neolithic farming, although almost 90 percent of the pollen was still contributed by trees. According to the dating evidence currently available, this episode happened some while *after* the building of the barrows at Barkaer. As early as 1941, Iversen was aware of this problem, arguing that the settlement on that site could not belong to the earliest Neolithic period (Iversen 1941: 58–9). The fact that it did so suggests that its occupants had little impact on the local vegetation: they need not have been growing cereals at all. In any case, Liversage comments that the subsoil at Barkaer would not have been suited to cultivation.

THE PROBLEM WITH THE NEOLITHIC

I have considered Barkaer in detail because it epitomises a series of problems experienced in many parts of north and north-west Europe, where long-held preconceptions about the character of Neolithic activity are having to be reconsidered. Glob's excavation strategy was the inevitable outcome of a particular conception of Neolithic life, and so was his interpretation of the results. He assumed that the Neolithic period saw the adoption of stable mixed farming, and for a while the pollen core from Korup Lake seemed to support this contention. He assumed that early farmers would live in permanent settlements, and this view influenced his perceptions of Barkaer. The evidence of the burials on the site was played down; the problem of the metre-thick house floors was overlooked; and he postulated stone walls from a mixture of boulders and loose sand that could never have supported the superstructure of a building. I do not wish to be too critical, for in its time this was a most accomplished excavation. Its shortcomings are simply those of archaeology itself: a subject in which complete objectivity is impossible and in which the extent of subjective interpretations can only be recognised in retrospect.

Glob's confusions were the confusions of an entire generation, faced with a Neolithic that failed to measure up to what was expected of it. Even now archaeologists find it difficult to recognise that, over large parts of Europe, Neolithic activity did not take the form that they had been led to expect. Instead of evidence for stable mixed farming, there are signs of a more mobile pattern of settlement (Whittle 1996a: ch. 7). Instead of the houses of the living, they find monuments to the dead (Bradley 1993: ch. 1). Where they can combine both kinds of evidence, as Liversage has at Barkaer, events might not take place in the expected sequence. It is often supposed that monument building was financed through the surplus created by farming (Case 1969), but in northern Europe the first monuments may be found *alongside* the first domesticates, and sometimes the earliest evidence for more intensive land use does not come until *after* mounds or cairns had been built. The conventional definition of the Neolithic period combines monument building with farming and the adoption of a new material culture, but all too often this association falls apart (Thomas 1993). Beyond the longhouse settlements of the loess, the stereotypes break down.

These problems are shared across most of the area beyond the limits of the Linear Pottery Culture and its immediate successors. They first emerge towards 4000 BC and they are widely shared. Archaeologists encounter virtually the same difficulties across an enormous area extending northwards from the Rhineland into Scandinavia, across the English Channel to Britain and Ireland, and along the rim of the Continent to north-west France. The problems are much the same along the Atlantic coastline, where they extend as far south as Iberia, although in this case domesticated resources were introduced from the Mediterranean (Zvelebil and Rowley-Conwy 1986) In all these areas the same situation arises, although it may be manifested in very different ways. Settlements and houses are difficult to find, although there are a few regions like Scania (Buus Eriksen 1992) or Ireland (Grogan 1996) where this is not always the case. The evidence for economic change may also be difficult to come by, and direct evidence of intensive agriculture can be extraordinarily elusive. Once again, it would be wrong to extend the same interpretation uncritically, for there are some areas, like the west coast of Ireland (Caulfield 1978) or the Shetland Isles (Whittle 1986), with evidence of early settlements and fields, but these are altogether exceptional. For the most part, the same problems continue to puzzle archaeologists studying the Early Bronze Age.

What they find instead of houses are monuments, and these are generally of two kinds. Although there undoubtedly were some fortified settlements during the Neolithic period, the great majority of the enclosures seem to have played a specialised role in a landscape in which the other signs of human activity are dispersed and often ephemeral. They are also likely to encounter a variety of mounds and cairns associated with the remains of the dead. Again, these can take many different forms, but the basic point is that structures of this kind seem to eclipse the dwellings of the living population. Although sites of many different kinds may contain the new styles of artefacts adopted during the Neolithic, there seems little prospect of using this evidence to interpret the patterns of everyday life.

The contrast with the longhouse settlements on the loess could hardly be more apparent, for these were massive structures, accompanied by numerous domestic artefacts and associated with economic residues that allow us to reconstruct their subsistence economies. Some excavations have even revealed traces of what may be associated paddocks or fields (Whittle 1996a: ch. 6). But again there is a paradox, for monuments are virtually absent in these areas. The dead were buried in flat cemeteries outside some of the settlements, and most of the earthwork enclosures found in association with the houses prove to be a late development. As we shall see in Chapter 3, they were first constructed as the domestic buildings were going out of use. Those monuments succeeded the settlements over time, while the distribution of this new kind of evidence extended into completely new areas.

It has often been claimed that the expansion of farming communities across Europe was checked towards the limits of the loess, and that other areas were not affected for a further thousand years (Zvelebil and Rowley-Conwy 1986). That hiatus took place between about 5000 and 4000 BC, and during that time it is appropriate to think in terms of a fairly stable agricultural frontier. On one side were the settlements of the Linear Pottery Culture (Linearbandkeramik) and its successors, the Rössen and Lengyel Cultures. On the other there were groups of hunter gatherers who were clearly in contact with farmers but with minor exceptions adhered to their traditional way of life (see Figure 4). Their lands were not affected by the development of agriculture until that interval was over, and from 4000 BC onwards they seem to have become assimilated into the Neolithic world. That happened at a time when the longhouses of the loess had gone out of use, with the result that the settlement pattern is more difficult to study across most parts of north-west Europe. The focus of interest becomes the areas in which agricultural resources were being employed for the first time. The pattern of settlement is elusive, but it is here that the first major monuments were built (Sherratt 1990).

The apparent hiatus between 5000 and 4000 BC can be viewed in two ways. It may be that the expansion of farming was checked because the most suitable areas had already been settled. Perhaps there was some reluctance to extend the process to areas with less favourable soils. This seems most unlikely, as many of the regions that had remained outside the agricultural frontier provide evidence of productive mixed farming in the later second and first millennia BC (Barker 1985: chs. 7–9). It is far more relevant to observe that, unlike the loess soils of the Rhineland, many of those areas already had a stable population of hunter gatherers. The relationships that had to be negotiated were social, not ecological.

Thus it seems as if we must investigate the ways in which Neolithic culture might have been assimilated by the existing populations in these areas. The process no doubt involved an interchange of personnel, and some regions may have been colonised by farmers from outside. Even so, it seems most unlikely that the native people disappeared.

TWO WAYS OF LOOKING AT THE NEOLITHIC

How have these changes been studied? We can recognise two main approaches, each of which bears the imprint of a different school of archaeology. Both kinds of studies have also been undertaken on two separate scales.

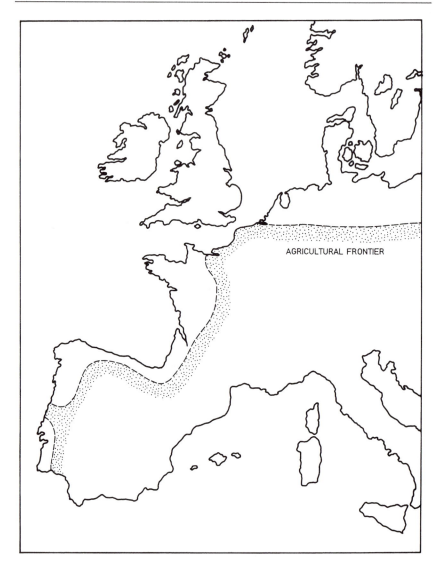

AGRICULTURAL FRONTIER

Figure 4. The agricultural frontier in north and north-west Europe at about 4500 BC. After Sherratt (1990) and Zilhāo (1993).

Those who are more concerned with economic archaeology emphasise the role played by the local hunter gatherers. For a long time they had sustained their traditional way of life by exploiting wild resources. There would be no need to change unless the food supply was in jeopardy. They might be well aware of the potential advantages of farming but they were under no pressures to adopt the same practices as their neighbours. According to this interpretation, the only reason to change must have been an unforeseen crisis in the food supply (Rowley-Conwy 1984). Under no other circumstances would the risks of exploiting domesticates have been worth undertaking at all.

The alternative is to consider the social impact of the new ideas associated with farming communities across the agricultural frontier. Their neighbours would have been a source not only of new kinds of artefacts, like pottery and polished axes, but also of unfamiliar ideas about the world. This approach has attracted a number of writers in recent years (Jennbert 1984; Thomas 1988a). Perhaps the acculturation of hunter gatherers beyond the agricultural frontier was more akin to a religious conversion, and it was the ideas that passed between these different communities that did most to bring about a change in their daily lives. If so, then any developments in the subsistence economy were a secondary consideration.

In recent writing these basic notions have been studied at two quite different scales. There are important general accounts of Neolithic Europe, which place a considerable emphasis on the transmission of a new ideology. That is the approach of Hodder's *The domestication of Europe*, with its emphasis on the changing relationship between the domestic world and the wild (Hodder 1990), and, in a very different vein, it is also true of Whittle's (1996a) *Europe in the Neolithic*, which carries the subtitle *The creation of new worlds*. As he says, 'The Neolithic way of life in Europe was based above all on a set of beliefs, values and ideals, about the place of people in the scheme of things, about descent, origins and time, and about relations between people' (Whittle 1996a: 355). At a more local scale the same approach has been championed by Thomas in *Rethinking the Neolithic*, which is a study of the evidence from southern Britain (Thomas 1991a), and by Tilley's *An ethnography of the Neolithic*, which is concerned with the sequence in southern Scandinavia (Tilley 1996).

The economic approach, which was particularly important in the 1970s and 1980s, is best illustrated by Jarman and his co-authors in *Early European agriculture*, the last chapter of which has the revealing title: 'The megaliths: a problem in palaeoethology' (Jarman *et al.* 1982: ch. 7). This study is typical of the approach that supposes that Neolithic systems of belief were simply a consequence of agriculture. It is a kind of thinking that was very common in the British Academy research project on the origins of agriculture, and for a time it continued to influence the thinking of scholars who had contributed to its work. Among the more influential books by former members of that group are Barker's *Prehistoric farming in Europe* (Barker 1985) and Dennell's *European economic prehistory* (Dennell 1983).

It is sad that, with the exception of Whittle's book, these studies align themselves on either side of an intellectual division which it is hard to bridge. The Neolithic period is studied as either ideology or economy, and the relationship between these two topics is blurred in the course of academic debate. Nor is the chronological setting for these arguments an entirely satisfactory one, for, while the Mesolithic is studied, if only as background to the Neolithic period, the Early Bronze Age is ignored completely. This is understandable but unfortunate, for it was during that period that many of the crucial relationships considered by these authors began to be worked out. There is an inevitable tension between accounts which can do justice to the richness of the available evidence and those which attempt to write a broader history. One runs the risk of ignoring the wider context in the interests of exploring the archaeology of one region, while the other will always be open to charges of superficiality.

An approach that seems to be worth trying is to focus on some of the issues central to these debates, and to make more explicit use of the wealth of information offered by the feature of Neolithic archaeology that is unambiguously new: that is, the monuments themselves. While it is easy to debate the actual importance of farming in many parts of Europe, the presence of these structures can hardly be denied. Rather than treating them as a by-product of more important processes, it is worth studying their significance in their own right. How were these structures related to the other issues investigated in prehistoric archaeology? How did they develop over time – during the Early Bronze Age as well as the Neolithic period? Was their creation related in any way to the development of early agriculture? And how did their presence in the landscape influence the experience of people in the past?

A SUMMARY OF THE ARGUMENT

This book is divided into two parts and is conceived less as a continuous narrative than as a series of linked essays. Part I ('From the house of the dead') considers the Neolithic sequence in Europe in terms of four main issues and introduces the main positions taken in recent debate (see Figure 5), while Part II ('Describing a circle') employs the same ideas in a more detailed account of the sequence in Britain and Ireland that takes the discussion through the Early Bronze Age to the reorganisation of food production from the late second millennium BC onwards (see Figure 6).

Part I introduces a number of themes, using examples drawn from the prehistory of Continental Europe. The first is considered in Chapter 2 ('Thinking the Neolithic'). This is the question of ideology and culture. Why were no monuments built during the Mesolithic period? And what is the link between the creation of these structures and the first experiments with domesticates? It provides a speculative interpretation of the symbolic system expressed by Mesolithic burials and compares that with some ideas put forward recently by Hodder (1990). Rather than opposing the domestic and the wild, Mesolithic people did not consider themselves as separate from the natural world. They did not make any sharp distinction between themselves and the animals that they hunted, and the ideology that found expression in their burial rites was one which emphasised fertility and regeneration. It may have been because these concepts were so well established that it was unthinkable to change the natural world by building monuments. It may have been for the same reason that the first use of domesticated resources proved to be so problematical. Chapter 2, then, is an

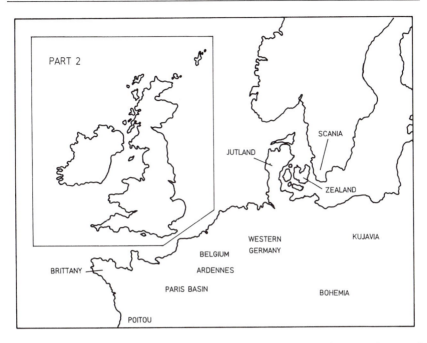

Figure 5. The regions considered in Part I. The inset shows the area discussed in Part II. For details of the latter, see Figure 6.

attempt to consider the *cultural factors* that could have delayed the first adoption of agriculture among Mesolithic hunter gatherers. It is also an attempt to think through the differences of world view that separated those people from their neighbours who had taken up farming.

The following chapter ('The death of the house') is concerned with the problems of agency. The archaeological literature is full of rather abstract reconstructions of how monuments were created and used, and of the ways in which they expressed the basic assumptions of Neolithic society. It is also concerned with the complicated relationship between the development of monuments and the first adoption of farming. Chapter 3 discusses both the main forms of monument to be found in Neolithic Europe: the enclosure and the tomb. How did they originate? And, in particular, why were so many of the funerary monuments originally based on the traditional form of the longhouse? After a discussion of the very different approaches to this problem taken by Sherratt (1990, 1995) and Hodder (1990), it suggests that the explanation may be found in one specific practice evidenced in the longhouse settlements on the loess. Here it seems possible that houses were abandoned and left to decay when one of the occupants died. It was through familiarity with this process and with the decay of the houses that had once been inhabited by the dead that the tradition of long mounds originated. There were also sites where such houses were separated from

Figure 6. Sites and regions considered in Part II.

the others by a ditch, and this may have been another practice that provided the symbolic frame of reference for later developments. Throughout this discussion, I emphasise the experience of people who were living in an environment that was familiar and yet steeped in symbolism. It was out of the routines of their daily lives that the development of these monuments began.

Chapter 4 ('Another time') returns to the problematic relationship between the creation of monuments and the adoption of agriculture, by considering the ways in which archaeologists have discussed the importance of ancestry. Meillassoux's work is fundamental here, for he has suggested that farmers must acquire a different sense of time from hunter gatherers (Meillassoux 1972), which is why they place so much emphasis on their ancestors. My discussion reviews the use that archaeologists have made of these ideas, contending that many of the mortuary monuments that they consider as ancestral tombs may have been nothing of the kind. It was not until new architectural formulae were devised that people were able to express a continuous relationship between the living and the dead; the creation of passage graves and allied monuments made it possible to envisage the same relationships extending into the future. The regular use of such structures may have helped to inculcate the new conceptions of time on which successful farming might depend.

The final chapter in Part I ('Small worlds') takes a similar approach to the importance of place in Neolithic societies by tracing the history of causewayed enclosures in different parts of north and north-west Europe. It discusses the role of earthwork monuments as a new and quite distinctive form of material culture that could be interpreted across the generations in a way that would hardly be possible with portable artefacts. It shows how these particular enclosures were originally created in a domestic setting. As the way of life changed, they took on an increasingly symbolic role and seem to have been used in a much more specialised manner – for the treatment of the dead and for rituals of various kinds. Those enclosures assumed an ever-more stereotyped groundplan and may have become the symbolic centre of the landscape for groups of people whose settlements were widely dispersed. By tracing the distinctive organisation of these monuments back to their point of origin, we can argue that they were regarded as the ancestral homes of communities who were bound to one another through their connections with places of this kind.

By the end of Part I, then, the basic materials are in place for a more detailed discussion. Chapters 2 to 5 trace the changes of attitude that characterise Neolithic culture towards the outer margins of Europe, and discuss the role played by monumental architecture in helping to inculcate a new sense of time and place. Part II examines a single sequence in Britain and Ireland from the later part of the Neolithic period to the reorganisation of food production which took place during the Bronze Age. It considers how one way of organising sacred space – the creation of a circular enclosure – was manipulated over the generations and how the changing forms of such monuments may reflect more basic processes in society.

The pivot of this discussion comes in Chapter 6 ('The persistence of memory') and builds upon the interpretations put forward in Part I. This chapter considers the relationship between ritual, time and the history of individual monuments, and suggests a way of thinking about their development. They present an image of massive continuity in a world which may actually be changing, but beneath the surface, and in often subtle ways, they are adapted to conform to the new concerns of society. Chapter 6 contends that the extended time scale of public ritual makes it particularly well suited for study by archaeologists and illustrates this proposition with an account of the famous monument at Stonehenge. This was a structure which conformed to the same basic groundplan for 1,500 years, yet at the same time it was altered in ways that referred to the developments that were taking place in the surrounding landscape.

The same framework is employed in the remainder of Part II, which consists of a series of studies of circular monuments in Britain and Ireland. Here there are two major themes. The first is the relationship between the form of different types of monument and more basic principles of order which may have their roots in a shared cosmology. The second theme is the way in which these same principles were expressed in a succession of quite different contexts. It discusses the relationship between the forms taken by the monuments and the experience of those who used them. Thus Chapter 7 ('The public interest') is a study of the transformation that came about as passage graves went out of use and large circular arenas were created for the first time. These could accommodate a different kind of audience from the closed spaces of the tomb.

Some of the implications of this development are considered in Chapter 8 ('Theatre in the round'), which compares the ways in which henge monuments and stone circles might originally have been used. These are generally considered together, as if they were the same kind of monument, and they were often placed in the same relationship to the surrounding landscape. In many cases their distinctive outline mirrors the structure of the local topography, but henges were closed off from the surrounding area while stone circles were completely permeable. This may be connected with the kinds of audience that used the sites, but it also provides evidence for two quite different relationships between these monuments and the landscape.

Chapter 9 ('Closed circles') traces the later history of both types of monument during the Early Bronze Age. It was at this time that some of these open arenas were taken over as the burial places of a small section of society. This discussion follows that process at a number of well-known sites and reflects on the implications of this development for any attempt to categorise such monuments on the basis of their surface remains. The appropriation of these different monuments marks one stage in a process by which particular people became more closely identified with particular locations in the landscape.

Taken together, the effect of all these developments was to create profound changes in human perceptions of place and time. That development is followed to its logical conclusion in Chapter 10 ('An agricultural revolution'), which reflects on the ways in which land use was finally reorganised around the needs of settled agriculture. Although it is commonly supposed that monuments played little part in that process, it suggests that these developments adhered to a symbolic scheme which was already well established. By that means the effects of sudden changes might have been easier to assimilate. On a more abstract level, the creation and use of monuments had another effect too, for by creating such subtle changes in people's perceptions of place and time it made a commitment to intensive mixed farming much easier to contemplate than it had been in the Early Neolithic.

The argument turns full circle, and the book ends.

Chapter 2

Thinking the Neolithic

The Mesolithic world view and its transformation

Recent interpretations of Neolithic society have been based on different ways of reading its material culture. By contrast, Mesolithic material culture is normally treated as evidence of food production. At Dragsholm in Denmark two graves were found side by side; one was late Mesolithic in date and the other was early Neolithic. This chapter explores the contrasts between the artefacts associated with these burials, broadening the discussion into a general review of the symbolism of Mesolithic graves in Europe. It suggests that Mesolithic people, like some hunter gatherers today, made no clear distinction between culture and nature or between the animal kingdom and the human population. There were many sacred places in the landscape, but none of these was constructed for the purpose. It was only when that ideology broke down during a prolonged period of contact with neighbouring farmers that agriculture became thinkable at all. It was in the same situation that some of the first monuments were built.

INTRODUCTION

Thomas's (1991a) *Rethinking the Neolithic* was published in 1991 and was among a number of studies that questioned the conventional interpretation of that period (Hodder 1990; Barrett 1994; Whittle 1996a). On one level it was an attempt to investigate some of the assumptions on which Neolithic archaeology had been based. Thus different chapters provided novel interpretations of artefacts and their deposition, mortuary rites, monuments and even the Neolithic economy. On a more abstract level, however, Thomas argued that the distinguishing feature of the Neolithic was a new understanding of the world: 'The idea of a way of life which separates humanity from nature may have been more important than the material reality. The appropriation of nature may have been conceptual as much as it was physical' (1991a: 181). Although this particular account was concerned with the archaeology of the British Isles, in an earlier paper (Thomas 1988a) he had taken the same approach to the prehistory of southern Scandinavia.

I am not sure whether the title of Thomas's book was intended to have a double meaning, but it is certainly true that it identifies the Neolithic way of life as the outcome of a particular kind of thinking in the past. This is a refreshing approach, but it is also one which raises a number of questions. If we can characterise a Neolithic way of thinking about the world, how did it differ from the ideas that were already current among hunter gatherers in the same parts of Europe? Why did any changes occur? How rapidly were they accomplished? Was the Neolithic view of the world an entirely new one or did it incorporate some beliefs that were already well established?

Here we face a curious paradox, for Thomas and other writers have felt that it is possible to reconstruct Neolithic ideology from the remains of burials and material culture (Criado 1989; Hodder 1990; Thomas 1991a; Whittle 1996a). The same approach has had little or no impact on the archaeology of the Mesolithic period where similar material is available for study. Instead specialists in either field have engaged in a rather polemical debate with one another which might suggest that they have entirely different interests (Mithen 1991; Thomas 1991b). This is not quite true, yet when they turn their attention to the earlier period, Neolithic specialists are more concerned with identifying those features which are supposed to explain the adoption of domesticates than they are with other aspects of Mesolithic life. Mesolithic specialists, on the other hand, have a severely restricted set of information at their disposal, in which monuments are virtually absent and even burials are rare. On most sites all the surviving artefacts are made of stone, setting considerable limits on the ease with which they can discuss the roles that material culture played in social life. What they do have are numerous carefully excavated collections of food remains – a source of information which is surprisingly uncommon on Neolithic settlements.

As a result of these differences it is hard to discuss the transition between the two periods. In some ways the issues were easier to understand when Neolithic material culture seemed to be introduced by colonists from another region, but over much of the north-west margin of Europe this interpretation seems unlikely. It is in just these areas that the two traditions of research come into conflict. True to their commitment to a social archaeology, students of the Neolithic explain this particular transition in terms of the strategies employed by specific groups of hunter gatherers drawing on unfamiliar elements as a source of power in their own societies (Jennbert 1984; Thomas 1988a). Mesolithic specialists, on the other hand, have always placed more emphasis on the practicalities of maintaining a food supply. As we have seen, both groups of scholars agree that for a substantial period of time farmers and hunter gatherers were to be found in adjacent areas of Europe, and that there must have been regular exchanges between the two populations. Those who study the Neolithic period emphasise the social impact of new practices and a new material culture (Thomas 1996: ch. 5; Whittle 1996a). Mesolithic specialists, on the other hand, sometimes suggest that domesticates were adopted in hunter-gatherer societies to offset a crisis in the food supply. They distinguish between a prolonged 'availability phase', in which such resources were known but hardly used, and a 'substitution phase', when they were adopted because the supply of wild resources was no longer dependable (Zvelebil and Rowley-Conwy 1986).

These limitations owe as much to different traditions of archaeological research as they do to any real differences in the past. Yet there are cases in which we can take the same basic approach to the archaeology of both periods. This allows us to characterise not only the 'Neolithic' way of thinking considered by Thomas, but also those 'Mesolithic' views of the world from which it may have departed in significant respects. Although the material record of Mesolithic societies is often quite impoverished, recent discoveries of burials and even whole cemeteries suggest one area in which we can compare like with like. This chapter provides a new analysis of that evidence.

THE EVIDENCE OF MESOLITHIC BURIALS

I would like to begin my discussion with one specific discovery. This was at Dragsholm in Zealand, where, in 1973, two prehistoric graves were found side by side (Brinch Petersen 1974). Both have radiocarbon dates, and these confirm the impression provided by the associated artefacts that the earlier burial belonged to the end of the Mesolithic period and the other grave to the beginning of the Neolithic. Although they were located together on a slight knoll, each appears to have been deposited in complete isolation. Both burials were of almost entire bodies. Two women had been placed together in the Mesolithic grave and a man was buried in the Neolithic grave alongside it, but there were important differences of material culture between these separate deposits (see Figure 7). The Neolithic burial was accompanied by a pot, an axe, a battle axe, ten flint arrowheads and a series of amber pendants. Apart from the presence of amber and a single arrowhead, the older grave contained a completely different assemblage, with a decorated bone dagger, a bone awl, and numerous pendants made from the teeth of wild pig and red deer. There were beads formed out of the teeth of cattle and elk, and the grave also contained red ochre. The evidence of bone chemistry shows that the women in the Mesolithic grave had consumed marine resources, but this did not apply to the man.

There is much to be gained from comparing these graves directly, but, as we have seen, to do so cuts across two distinct traditions of research. The Neolithic period is interpreted through a detailed reading of the archaeological record, with the result that there are almost as many models as there are burials. When it is considered at all, Mesolithic society is interpreted by analogy with the ethnographic record. As a result, social interpretations tend to be extremely generalised.

Had the Neolithic burial at Dragsholm been associated with a mound or a stone-built chamber we would feel entitled to connect it with a wider cultural phenomenon: either with the tradition of long mounds in northern Europe

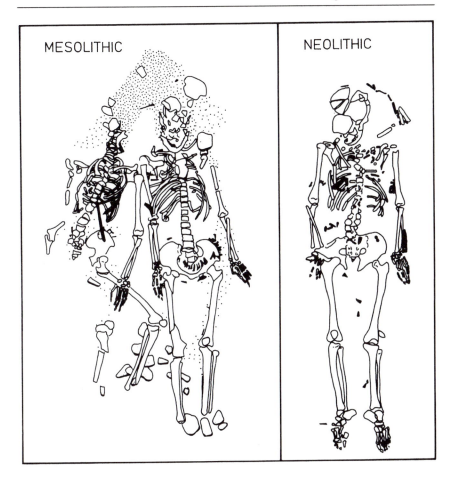

Figure 7. The Mesolithic and Neolithic burials at Dragsholm, Zealand, after Brinch Petersen (1974).

considered in Chapter 1, or with the still more extensive distribution of mega-lithic tombs that provides the subject matter of Chapter 4. In either case, we might interpret that structure as a symbolic transformation of domestic architecture. Yet faced with the Mesolithic burials from the same site – and still more with entire cemeteries dating from that period – we engage in a completely different kind of discussion. Drawing on general statements based on modern ethnography, we link the existence of such graves with changes in the pattern of settlement, with economic intensification or with control over critical resources (R. Chapman 1981). More ambitious studies have looked for differences of status between the various individuals buried in the same cemetery (Clark and Neely 1987; O' Shea and Zvelebil 1984; Jacobs 1995; Schulting 1996), but in every case the argument depends on generalisations derived from social anthropology. In contrast to Neolithic burials, the symbolism of the Mesolithic graves is largely ignored.

This seems strange, and it does so for two reasons, one theoretical and the other empirical. The empirical reason is that the dominant symbols of Mesolithic burials are actually shared across large geographical areas. Such areas are just as extensive as the spread of megalithic tombs (Kayser 1990), yet we appear reluctant to come to terms with such similarities. The theoretical reason for my unease is that this is precisely the kind of evidence that might allow us to assess the models that we have drawn from ethnographic sources. Was there really a Mesolithic world view? Had it much in common with the ethic of sharing found among modern hunter gatherers? And did that perception change between the creation of the earlier grave at Dragsholm and the placing of the Neolithic burial beside it?

If we widen the discussion from those two graves to other Mesolithic burials in north and north-west Europe we begin to recognise a number of persistent features. Some of them originated in the Upper Palaeolithic, but it is noticeable how few of them persisted into the Neolithic period. Not all of these features are present on every site, nor were they all used simultaneously, but beneath these local variations a number of more general patterns do stand out.

Let us begin with two of those elements identified in the Mesolithic grave at Dragsholm. Perhaps the most striking feature was the use of red ochre. This is a widely distributed practice and one which has a lengthy history. It is evidenced during the Upper Palaeolithic period and continued to be followed in the Neolithic. It is not limited to burial sites, and red ochre is recorded from settlements in Norway which belong to the same period as the establishment of cemeteries further to the south (Bang-Andersen 1983). Even after the intro-duction of domesticates to southern Scandinavia, red ochre continued to be deposited in graves, although these were generally located on or beyond the agricultural frontier (Wyszomirska 1984). A popular interpretation of such deposits is that they may have symbolised life-blood.

Another striking feature of the Dragsholm Mesolithic burial was the presence of a set of grave goods made almost entirely from organic materials. The most elaborate artefact was a decorated bone dagger, and the only tool in the grave was also made of bone. The assemblage was dominated by a great array of beads and pendants, formed from animal teeth (Brinch Petersen 1974). The common element among these finds is that all originate in the animal kingdom. In that sense they refer both to the natural world and to important components of the food supply. Such a connection is often evidenced by bone or antler objects from Mesolithic graves, but the distribution of these deposits overlaps with that of another related artefact, for perforated shell beads also occur in European Mesolithic cemeteries. Again, these objects have a lengthy history and, like the use of red ochre, they can be traced back to the Upper Palaeolithic. By contrast, in the Neolithic period there was a much stronger emphasis on the deposition of stone artefacts. The distinction between the two assemblages might be expressed by saying that in these Mesolithic graves objects associated with the natural world were modified very little, so that their original source was still apparent. The creation of stone artefacts, and of ground stone axes in particular, obscured the original form taken by the parent material. A useful point of comparison is provided by those cases in which we can compare the funerary assemblage with the objects that were used in everyday life. Although stone artefacts are by no means absent from Mesolithic graves, they can form a much higher proportion of the domestic assemblage. The contrast is perhaps most apparent at Oleneostrovski Mogilnik, where 'organic' artefacts are most frequent in the women's graves (O'Shea and Zvelebil 1984). The same seems to be the case with some of the burials at Skateholm (L. Larsson 1989).

Related to this is another pattern, which is not represented at Dragsholm itself. This is the provision of antlers in the grave (see Figure 8), which is a feature that links Mesolithic burials in widely separated areas of Europe, from north-west France to southern Scandinavia. Some of the unworked antlers have been shed and for this reason they do not seem to be a by-product of hunting expeditions. Others were converted into artefacts, and in both these areas a number of them were decorated. Their main function, however, seems to have been to provide a kind of framework for the body in the grave. In such cases they can also be found together with deposits of red ochre.

It would be easy to suppose that these finds emphasise the importance of deer in the subsistence economy, but that would not explain the significance of shed antlers in these burials. Nor does it provide a reason why the antlers should be favoured rather than other parts of the body. On the other hand, the fact that antlers could be shed and replaced every year makes them a potent source of symbolism. The mature stag offers a powerful metaphor for fertility, as we know from later rock art, and the annual growth of its antlers provides an ideal symbol of regeneration (Bradley 1997: ch. 13). That may be why they occur in Mesolithic graves over such a wide area. A comparable practice is recorded in the British Neolithic, where ceremonial monuments are also associated with large accumulations of red deer antler.

The same emphasis on antler is found in the mobile art of southern Scandinavia (Tilley 1996: 43–8). Before pottery was adopted, a significant number of artefacts were decorated with incised motifs, depicting fish, deer and human figures, as well as a variety of abstract designs. Nearly all of these were carved on antler, and other kinds of bone were little used, although rather similar images of animals were made from a second material with unusual properties – amber. The antler artefacts were sometimes hafted, while the smaller examples were perhaps used as pendants. They show little sign of wear, in spite of evidence that some of them had been decorated on more than one occasion. There was a decorated dagger in the Mesolithic grave at Dragsholm.

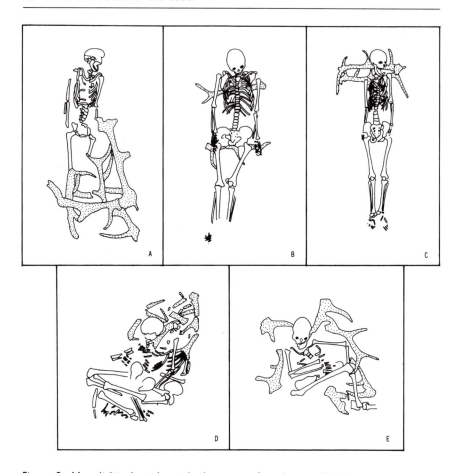

Figure 8. Mesolithic burials with deposits of antler at (A) Skateholm, Scania, (B) and (C) Bogebakken, Denmark, (D) Téviec, Brittany, and (E) Hoedic, Brittany. Modified from Kayser (1990). For clarity, the cist accompanying the burial at Téviec is omitted. It is illustrated in Figure 10.

There are gifts of meat and fish in a number of the burials, but it is uncertain how we should interpret the appearance of dogs in the same contexts. It is worth emphasising the distinctive ways in which these particular animals were treated. Some appear to have been sacrificed in the graves of members of the community, while others were buried separately within the cemetery at Skateholm, and were even provided with red ochre and with offerings in their own right. In one of the graves at Skateholm these were arranged in the same configuration as in the human burials (L. Larsson 1990), and on another site, at Bredasten in southern Sweden, a puppy may even have been buried inside a specially constructed building (M. Larsson 1986).

As Hayden (1990) has observed, the domestication of the dog is a widespread phenomenon among late hunter gatherers, although not everyone is agreed on the reason for this practice. In some cases dogs may have played an essentially economic role, used in hunting wild animals or even as a supplementary source of food, but the special treatment paid to the dogs at sites like Skateholm suggests something else as well. Here they not only accompanied their owners to the grave, they seem to have been treated as individuals in their own right and were buried with at least as much formality as the humans found in the same cemetery. It would be wrong to invoke a specific ethnographic model, but one reading of this observation would suggest that the inhabitants of Skateholm made no clear distinction between the human and animal populations of the site.

This might also provide a reason why isolated human bones could be treated in the same ways as isolated animal bones. Occasional beads were fashioned out of human teeth, and there is also some evidence for the circulation of human bones during the Mesolithic period. This evidence is of two kinds. First, there are graves in which only parts of the body were buried, most probably after they had lost their articulation. In other cases, the remains seem to have been rearranged. There is comparable evidence from other sites where isolated human bones are found (Larsson *et al.* 1981). There seems to be evidence that certain parts of the body were selected deliberately, as the representation of these bones does not seem to result from differential preservation. Two examples perhaps illustrate this point. The famous nests of skulls at the west German site of Ofnet are now known to be of Mesolithic date (Meikeljohn 1986), while recent excavations in the shell middens on the island of Oronsay in Scotland show that it was mainly the extremities of the body that remained in the settlement (Mellars 1987: 9–16). The more substantial relics were presumably taken away. The same might have been the case at Dragsholm, where the Mesolithic burials lacked their feet.

This is one practice that certainly survived into the Neolithic period, when it forms a major feature of the mortuary ritual at megalithic tombs and other sites. There is another characteristic of the later Mesolithic which endures for an even longer period of time. Some years ago I commented on the way in which Neolithic votive deposits seemed to be most apparent around the agricultural frontier (Bradley 1990: 43–75). I now believe that my interpretation was not radical enough and that the practice of making offerings in natural locations was actually a Mesolithic development. A number of clues point to this, although none is of particular significance when taken in isolation. There are occasional hoard finds. Two recent examples are particularly revealing. A remarkable group of decorated bone and shell artefacts were buried together in a pit at the Breton settlement site of Beg-er-Vil and the position of this feature was marked by a deposit of antlers (Kayser and Bernier 1988). In the same way, a group of ground stone axes was found in another settlement in south-west Ireland, near to a small group of cattle bones (Woodman and O'Brien 1993). In Scandinavia, Lars Larsson has already pointed to possible hoards of Mesolithic artefacts and to what seem to have been deliberate deposits of antler placed in shallow water

(1983: 78–81). There is evidence that complete animal carcasses might be treated in the same fashion (Møhl 1978). More important, a systematic study of votive deposits in southern Sweden has shown that some of the stone axes imported into northern Europe before the adoption of agriculture are also found in rivers and bogs (Karsten 1994: ch. 12). The same is true of some isolated Ertebølle pots which should belong to the same period (Benike and Ebbesen 1986). Decorated bone and antler artefacts are also found in bogs, and again this anticipates a practice that increased in importance during the Neolithic. Karsten (1994) has suggested that the composition of such offerings could have changed over time, from entire animals to pieces of decorated bone and antler, and then to stone axes and pottery.

A new site in Scania, Bökeberg III, lends weight to these suggestions. This lies on the former shore of Lake Yddingen and is being excavated by Mats Regnell and by Per Karsten, to whom I owe this information. This site dates from about 4000 BC and, although undoubtedly a settlement, it does have a number of features that stand out from the normal range of activities. There are two lengths of shallow ditch, one of which contains an imported axe, while the other included an axe, which had been set upright in the ground and burnt. In the edge of the lake two antler picks were discovered together with a large stone. One of these antlers had anthropomorphic decoration, while fragments of human skull, again accompanied by a stone, were found in a similar position. Elsewhere on the edge of the refuse layer an antler point was found in direct association with a mint-condition axe. Karsten has also observed that the more elaborate flake knives seem to have been discarded towards the limits of the occupied area. Some of the same features occur among the graves at Skateholm.

So far, I have highlighted five recurrent features in the archaeology of Mesolithic Europe, none of which is related in any obvious way to the practicalities of food production. Four of them form a regular feature of the Mesolithic grave assemblage from Karelia to Portugal, although not all need be present at the same sites or even in the same regions. These features are: the importance of red ochre; the use of what we can call 'organic' grave goods; the deposition of antlers with the dead; the significance of domestic dogs in the mortuary ritual; and the circulation of isolated human bones. To this we can add increasing evidence for the creation of votive deposits in natural locations. The material found in these places overlaps with the contents of the graves. Given the wide distribution of so many of these elements, it is perhaps less surprising that these finds share features with Lepenski Vir (Srejovic 1972). Here we find deposits of human crania, together with offerings of fish and animal bones. There is evidence for the circulation of human bones and also for the use of red ochre in the burial rite. Still more striking is the emphasis placed on deposits of antler. Similar practices are evident on other sites in the same region. Figure 9 illustrates a series of burials in the settlement at Vlasac (Srejovic and Letica 1978), which again have features in common with those in northern Europe.

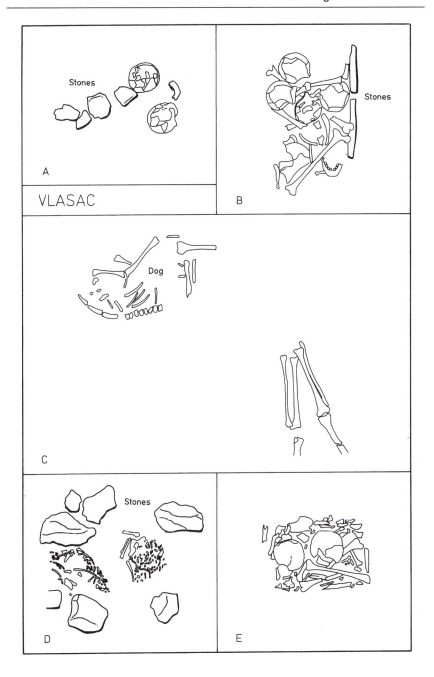

Figure 9. Mesolithic burials at Vlasac, Serbia, after Srejovic and Letica (1978), emphasising the variety of different mortuary practices on the site. No scales are provided in the original drawings.

Of course, there are other features of Mesolithic sites on the Danube that are not found anywhere else, in particular, the monumental sculptures at Lepenski Vir and the curious buildings with which they are associated. Whether these were houses or altars, they stand out from the evidence in other parts of Mesolithic Europe, where there are no structures of this kind. Indeed, they may have been built at a time when the local population was already in contact with Neolithic farmers (Whittle 1996a: 44–6). Elsewhere there is even less evidence of monument buildings. At present there are only the slab-lined cists of Brittany (see Figure 10; Schulting 1996), the tiny cairns associated with human burials in southern France (Rozoy 1978: 1,115–26), and the small ritual buildings at Skateholm and possibly at Bredasten (L. Larsson 1988; M. Larsson 1986). The very rarity of such constructions may be one of the features that marks a difference between the Mesolithic and the Neolithic.

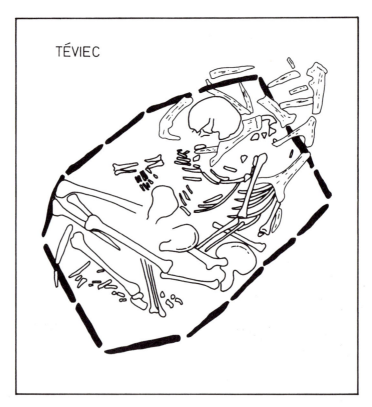

Figure 10. Cist burial at Téviec, Brittany, after Kayser (1990).

THE HUNTER GATHERER'S VIEW OF THE WORLD

Having emphasised this distinction, we need to appreciate the extremely long history of a number of these practices. Few of them may have originated during the Mesolithic period and some certainly extend well back into the Upper Palaeolithic. That makes the transition to the Neolithic appear even more abrupt.

There are two main groups of Upper Palaeolithic burials in Europe. The earlier dates from between 26,000 and 21,000 BP, while the second concentration is found at the very end of this period (Gamble 1986; Binant 1991; Bernaldó 1995). In many ways these anticipate the finds from the Mesolithic cemeteries. The earlier group already includes a number of familiar elements. Among the grave goods there are artefacts of antler and mammoth ivory, as well as animal carvings. The dead were accompanied by perforated shells or by necklaces of deer teeth. One of the burials, at Cueva Morín in Spain, had been covered by the body of an ibex or possibly a roe deer, and other graves of this period have produced deposits of fish bones. Red ochre also occurs in this group. As well as single burials there were multiple deposits. The best known example of this practice was at Predmost in Moravia, where eighteen individuals were found together in a pit capped by stones and mammoth bones. Another case may be a triple grave at Dolní Vestonice, which contained perforated teeth, red ochre and shells.

Much the same range of evidence comes from the Late Upper Palaeolithic period. One burial in northern Italy was associated with two slabs bearing animal carvings, while another grave in south-west France was associated with a cattle skull. Again, this burial was accompanied by a necklace made of the teeth of reindeer and red deer, but this time the body had been placed inside a small stone chamber rather like those in the Mesolithic cemeteries of Brittany. A double grave of this period from Italy shares some of the same characteristics, and here the bodies of two children were covered by another substantial deposit of shells.

This evidence suggests that at least three distinctive elements recognised in the Mesolithic burials were already present in the Upper Palaeolithic period. There is the same emphasis on organic grave goods: a pattern strongly reinforced by the occasional carvings of animals. There are offerings of food, and there is convincing evidence that some of the bodies had been treated with red ochre. At a more detailed level, there is the regular association between the burials and necklaces of perforated deer teeth.

Other elements do not seem to be represented in Palaeolithic graves in Europe. It is hard to discuss the transport of human relics because of the taphonomic problems which beset the interpretation of such early material. There is no evidence for the use of unworked antlers to furnish the grave, nor is there an emphasis on the dog, although it had been domesticated by the end of the Palaeolithic period (Clutton-Brock 1984). Despite these differences, the evidence is sufficient to suggest that certain preoccupations were widespread among European hunter gatherers and that those concerns were expressed in symbolic form over a considerable period of time.

How are we to understand these patterns? First, it is clear that Mesolithic ritual placed considerable emphasis on the natural world. We see this through the importance attached to organic grave goods, as distinct from the wider repertoire used in the domestic assemblage. It is particularly obvious when we consider how much of this material was based on bone and antler. The same attitudes may be evidenced by the cemetery at Skateholm, where some of the dogs appear to have been buried as if they were human beings. This emphasis on the natural world is also consistent with the provision of votive deposits in locations such as rivers and lakes.

Second, this material seems to emphasise the importance of fertility and regeneration. There is the pervasive symbolism of the red ochre, which appears to stand for human blood. There is the equally powerful symbolism expressed by the use of antlers at sites as far distant from one another as Skateholm, Téviec and Lepenski Vir, and there is a more tentative suggestion of the same emphasis on fertility in the association between organic artefacts and the burials of women. Again, it seems that the natural world was perceived as a creative principle rather than a source of danger. That is what Bird-David (1990) means when she refers to the 'giving environment'. Some hunter gatherers do not distinguish sharply between their own fortunes and the character of the world around them, and they may refer to the environment in which they live in terms of metaphors such as procreation and kinship (Bird-David 1993).

This is very different from the interpretation of the excavated material from Lepenski Vir that Hodder proposes in *The Domestication of Europe* (Hodder 1990: 24–31). For the most part he discusses the same symbolic elements as my account of the Mesolithic burials found in other parts of the Continent, but he sees them in quite another way. Lepinski Vir is characterised by an unusual combination of houses, altars, burials and sculptures of composite figures, half-human, half-fish. Hodder suggests that there:

> death . . . is closely associated with the wild. Stag antlers occur in the graves and as 'offerings' behind the hearths. Fish remains also occur here and in relation to the 'altar'. [The] . . . boulder art links humans, death and fish. The two main wild resources exploited at Lepenski Vir thus both seem closely associated with the main symbolic metaphor used within the house – death.
>
> (1990: 27)

He extends this interpretation to the orientation of the houses with their entrances facing east towards the sunrise, for it is at their darker western ends that most of the burials are found. As a result he argues that the site had been organised around a complex symbolic scheme. The back of the house was

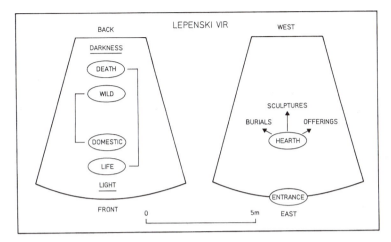

Figure 11. Hodder's interpretation of the structures at Lepenski Vir and their symbolism.

opposed to the front, just as darkness is opposed to light. The same contrast expresses the distinction between death and life and between the wild and the domestic (see Figure 11). Hodder himself acknowledges that this is probably too schematic, but he does place considerable emphasis on a reading of this evidence that opposes the domestic and the wild. He also favours a clearcut distinction between the living and the dead. These basic concerns, he argues, pervade the subsequent prehistory of Europe.

If my argument is correct, we might need to consider a different reading of this symbolism. The distinctive character of Mesolithic burials in north and north-west Europe suggests that instead of this antagonism between culture and nature we might think in terms of a reciprocal relationship, more akin to the animistic beliefs so often reported among hunter gatherers. The dead were accompanied by the symbols of fertility and regeneration, and Mesolithic communities may not have recognised a categorical distinction between the human and animal kingdoms. For them, any simple division between culture and nature might have been meaningless. Within northern Europe an appropriate comparison would be with the beliefs of the modern Saami (Ahlbäck 1987).

THE IMPLICATIONS OF THE ARGUMENT

If this argument has any merit, it might help to explain why northern Europe has no Mesolithic monuments. It could also have some light to shed on the problems posed by the adoption of farming. It is not simply a matter of subsistence and nutrition. In my interpretation this form of partnership with nature is inconsistent with the direct ownership of resources, which is, of course, the social meaning of domestication. It also seems likely that in a world in which human identity was not felt to lie outside nature – a world in which natural places could take on a special significance – monuments would have little part to play. The same applies to the creation of a new range of grave goods based, no longer on bone and antler, but on the complete transformation of the raw materials; the obvious examples of this are pottery and ground stone axes.

I mentioned earlier that Zvelebil and Rowley-Conwy (1986) have discussed the reluctance of some hunter gatherers to take up farming even when the techniques and materials were available to them. They suggest that in such cases economic change may have been very gradual. No doubt, some of that reluctance did have its roots in the subsistence economy. I would add that it may also have been based on ideology. During the period of contact between 'Mesolithic' and 'Neolithic' communities that these authors describe as the 'availability phase', there would have been many different kinds of exchanges, but until local hunter gatherers had modified their own views of the world – views which may have remained much the same since the Upper Palaeolithic period – it is hard to see how they could envisage the radical changes of attitude that would accompany the adoption of farming. Until 'Mesolithic' belief systems lost their force, as they may have done through day-to-day interaction between different communities and their neighbours, domestication may have been literally unthinkable.

Having said this, I shall make one last suggestion. Both the ownership of resources and the building of monuments reflect the eventual breakdown of such inhibitions, and both involve the development of different attitudes to the natural world: the adoption of new beliefs as well as the adoption of new techniques. If Mesolithic communities had engaged in a reciprocal exchange with nature, the metaphor certainly changed. The new idiom was concerned with power. Monuments were constructed to dominate the landscape and to withstand the process of natural decay. The domestication of plants and animals was another form of control, and the creation of arable and pasture involved a still more drastic modification of the natural terrain. In that sense both processes were really rather alike, and, once traditional beliefs began to lapse, both could be found together.

That may be why those models which trace a direct succession from complex hunter gatherers to the first farmers in Europe have raised some chronological problems. The earliest Neolithic monuments in Brittany and Portugal may have been created while Mesolithic cemeteries were still in use, but this is not the case in the region with the largest number of these graves, for in southern Scandinavia nearly all the Mesolithic burials of the kind discussed in this chapter disappear before there is any evidence for the adoption of domesticated resources. The earlier grave at Dragsholm is exceptional in this respect, as it lies at the very end of the local sequence.

The graves that I have discussed emphasise the continuity between humans and the animal kingdom. Such ideas have little place among farmers. Perhaps such perspectives had to be modified before new forms of food production could be contemplated, and in Scandinavia that may be why these mortuary rituals lapsed before the beginning of the Neolithic period. The process of ideological change was as drawn out as the process of economic change, and the two reinforced one another.

The graves at Dragsholm represent different stages in that process. They were 2 metres apart in space and less than three centuries apart in time, but the people who were buried there had lived in quite different worlds.

Chapter 3

The death of the house

The origins of long mounds and Neolithic enclosures

Many writers have recognised that two traditions of monuments – long mounds and enclosures – seem to have their prototypes in Neolithic settlements on the loess, but there have been few suggestions as to why this should be so. This chapter provides an analysis of the settlements of the Linear Pottery Culture, contending that the symbolic dimension of such sites has been largely overlooked. A detailed examination of their structure and chronology reveals that many houses were abandoned while they were structurally sound and were replaced on an adjacent site as the original building decayed. Occasionally, entire groups of abandoned houses might be enclosed by a ditch. Perhaps this happened because it was necessary to relocate the dwellings on the death of one of the occupants, so that the distinctive sequence on such sites relates to the social lifespan of the household rather than the structural stability of the buildings. Settlements might consist of a mixture of 'living' houses and 'houses of the dead', laid out on the same alignment and sharing the same spacing across the site. The decay of the longhouses could have provided the prototype for the long mounds on the agricultural frontier, and the enclosure of recently abandoned houses could have led to the more general creation of enclosures in Neolithic society.

In 1993, a conference was held at Glasgow University concerned with 'Social life and social change in the Neolithic of north-west Europe'. One might have supposed that the theme was wide enough to encourage many prehistorians to contribute, but in fact the great majority of the speakers came from just three areas: Britain, France and Scandinavia. Why was this?

To a certain extent the situation reflects the existence of quite separate traditions of research in different parts of Europe. German archaeology, for example, has always been more concerned with detailed documentation than with theoretical issues (Härke 1995), but it would be quite wrong to suppose that the existence of such divisions supplies an entirely satisfactory answer. The distinctive character of Neolithic material culture must also be considered.

As we saw in Chapter 1, there are two basic traditions of research in the

Neolithic of north-west Europe, each with a different geographical focus. These reflect the existence of significant contrasts in the character of the evidence being studied. At the risk of over-simplification, we can say that archaeologists working in central Europe, and in particular in the Rhineland, have usually investigated settlement patterns. They have based their work on the discovery of timber longhouses on the loess and have interpreted their evidence in terms of the colonisation of the most favourable land by farmers (Lüning 1982; Whittle 1988a: ch. 3; 1996a: ch. 6). Their studies have operated on the assumption that the prehistoric landscape was structured by practical considerations. Although a number of cemeteries have been investigated in this area, local archaeologists have shown surprisingly little interest in the interpretation of ancient social life. This may also be why the earthwork enclosures found among these settlements have not been discussed as fully as the houses.

Beyond the limits of the area in which settlements with longhouses are found, we can identify a different tradition of research, and it was this tradition that was so well represented at the Glasgow conference. It places less emphasis on the importance of the subsistence economy and is more prepared to entertain questions of ritual and ideology (Thomas 1988a; Hodder 1990: chs. 6–9). This reflects a distinct change in the material available for study. In this region the settlements leave little or no trace, there is rather less evidence for the character of food production, and it is by no means certain that Neolithic material culture was introduced by settlers from outside. Quite possibly, elements of the new way of life were assimilated by native populations who had previously depended on the use of wild resources. One feature of these regions dominates all the others, for these are where large monuments – both mounds and enclosures – are the main components of the landscape. It is the presence of earthworks like the two long barrows at Barkaer that has encouraged so many archaeologists to consider the nature of Neolithic society.

These contrasts must not be exaggerated, for the two systems were closely related to one another. In chronological terms, the creation of landscapes with prominent monuments seems to have happened as the colonisation of the loess was reaching its limits. The agricultural settlements were associated with the Linear Pottery Culture and its immediate successors, the Lengyel and Rössen Cultures. They span a period beginning about 5500 BC and ending about 4000 BC. Many of the monuments were built later and in adjacent areas. These are associated mainly with the TRB or Funnel-necked Beaker Culture or with the Michelsberg tradition, and they probably developed during the fourth millennium BC.

Perhaps the most important point is that these two kinds of pattern had complementary distributions. This is illustrated in Figure 12, which compares the distribution of three quite different features: longhouses, long mounds and megalithic tombs. Only in one part of Poland, Kujavia, can we be certain that the distribution of longhouses coincided with that of long barrows (Midgley 1985), yet ever since the work of Gordon Childe (1949) archaeologists have recognised

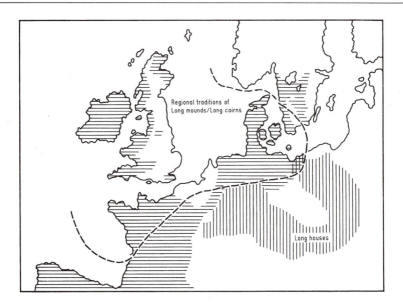

Figure 12. The distribution of longhouses, long mounds and megalithic tombs (horizontal shading) in north and north-west Europe. The distributions of longhouses and chambered tombs are modified from Hodder (1984).

the similarities between the different kinds of structures built in these two zones. Long mounds, which are normally associated with the dead, seem to copy the ground plan of the older longhouses. It is still not clear to what extent their chronologies also overlapped, but, as the excavations at Barkaer demonstrate so clearly, the visual cross-reference between them is very striking indeed. Ian Hodder has suggested eight specific connections between these two phenomena (1990: 149–56). These include their shape, their alignment, the positions of their entrances, and what slight evidence there is for their internal organisation.

Figure 13 emphasises some of these points. It compares a fully excavated longhouse of the Linear Pottery Culture (Hensel and Milisauskas 1985) with a much later long mound belonging to the British Earlier Neolithic period (Manby 1976). Although the mound is more extensive than the house, both were defined by a massive outer wall of posts, and both were almost precisely the same shape. Each was entered at one end and both structures were flanked by pits or ditches. On the Polish site these were borrow pits, dug to provide clay daub for the walls, while the earthwork monument was flanked by considerable quarry ditches, excavated to supply material for building the mound. Not all these features need be shared by both classes of structure – some of the houses and mounds are trapezoidal rather than rectangular, by no means all the long barrows were flanked by ditches, and the later houses often lacked borrow pits – but their relationship is close enough to demand an interpretation.

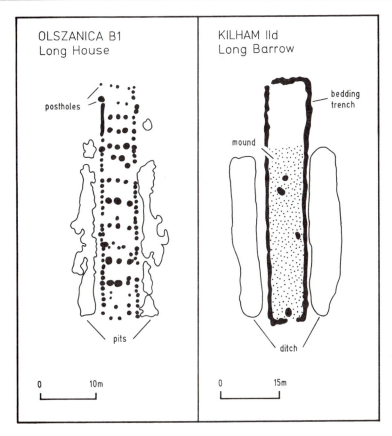

Figure 13. The plan of a Linear Pottery Culture longhouse at Olszanica, Poland, after Hensel and Milisauskas (1985), compared with that of Kilham long barrow, England, after Manby (1976).

It is here that most of the difficulties arise. We can identify two basic approaches in the work of recent authors. One epitomises the functionalism that has afflicted so much archaeological writing in this field, whereas the other owes a greater debt to structuralism. What they share is an inability to come to terms with human agency. Another reason why both methods fail to provide a satisfactory interpretation is that they take little account of the fine detail of the material that they are discussing.

For Andrew Sherratt, the creation of long mounds is a feature of the agricultural margin. He accepts that these constructions were intended to copy the traditional form of the longhouse and he retains the link between the building of these monuments and the process of agricultural colonisation. In his view, long mounds *represented* longhouses, and in France, he argues, they were built by immigrant farmers. He also suggests that the round mounds along the Atlantic seaboard were constructed by local hunter gatherers and reproduced the form of their circular houses, even though these domestic structures are almost entirely hypothetical.

Why were such monuments ever built? In different papers Sherratt has suggested a variety of reasons. In 1990, he argued that the building of mortuary mounds was a way of celebrating the cohesion of the agricultural workforce:

> It can . . . be argued that these tombs . . . were as basic a feature of early cereal agriculture as the hoe and axe; the material infrastructure of the organisation of labour was as crucial in the establishment of horticulture as the more obvious elements of technology. . . . In a society where labour was the most important commodity, moving large stones symbolised the workforce that could be assembled at any one time.
>
> (1990: 150)

There is a problem here, as very little is known about the subsistence economy during the period when these mounds were first constructed, and there is still less to indicate any relationship with intensive farming.

Five years later Sherratt argued that the same structures were 'instruments of conversion': corporate projects intended by incoming farmers to engage the interest of local hunter gatherers as a means of recruiting a labour force: 'Monumentality was an essential element of the cultural rhetoric whereby . . . indigenous groups were converted to a Neolithic way of life' (1995: 245). Again the same objections apply, but with the additional problem that Sherratt does not explain why that process should have involved the building of these particular structures. He suggests that in areas where longhouses were no longer being built, people may have created replicas in order to retain their sense of community, when in reality they lived in a more dispersed pattern of settlement. That may well be true, but for the argument to proceed any further we need to know how and why the long mound was thought to be an acceptable substitute for the longhouse. Appeals to an ancestral past may supply part of the answer, as Sherratt himself suggests, but the weakness of his approach is his insistence on relating these developments to the needs of farming when its actual importance is never established in the first place. The same problem affects the interpretation of long mounds as territorial markers in areas where resources were scarce (Renfrew 1976).

It is the role of human experience that supplies the missing term of the equation. Hodder claims that his account of the same evidence takes this into account, but it does so by considering the abstract ideas carried in people's heads. To explain these ideas, he has coined three terms, each based on a common element in Indo-European languages. The *domus* is not just the home, as the Latin word might suggest, rather it:

> involves practical activities carried out in the house, food preparation and the sustaining of life. . . . Secondary, symbolic connotations are given to the

practical activities, leading to the house as a focus for symbolic elaboration and to [its] use . . . as a metaphor for social and economic strategies and relations of power. . . . The domus . . . is the concept and practice of nurturing and caring, but at a still more general level it obtains its dramatic force from the exclusion, control and domination of the wild.

(1990: 44–5)

He refers to the wild as the *agrios*. This describes 'a . . . set of concepts concerning individual display, hunting, warring, death and males' (*ibid.*, p. 85). The agrios is associated with exchange and hierarchy, and therefore it is directly opposed to the ideas represented by the domus. 'Agri-culture', then, is the taming of the wild – its 'domestication'. The boundary between these two worlds Hodder describes as the *foris*. This term indicates a threshold, like the door of a house connecting the domestic space to the world beyond.

How were these concepts related to the transition from houses to tombs? In Hodder's interpretation the long mound provided a successful synthesis of these competing elements (1990: ch. 6). Its importance was that it could draw upon so many powerful images. It evoked the concept of the domus by the way in which it was modelled on the external form of the longhouse. The entrance of these tombs was often the focus for architectural elaboration. Thus it provided a monumental version of the foris, the boundary between the domestic space and the wild. Yet the mound also reconciled the antagonistic tendencies in Neolithic society. The competitive strains that characterise the agrios resulted in the burial of only a few individuals beneath these monuments, often men, but their remains were contained within an ideal version of the house. As the pattern of settlement became more fragmented, the domus was recreated through communal labour and its significance was reaffirmed by the scale of the finished earthwork. At this point Hodder's structuralist interpretation finds common ground with Sherratt's functionalism.

There are problems with Hodder's presentation too, for the division of experience on which it depends is much more clearly evidenced in south-east Europe than in other areas, and his most plausible arguments are based on the use of a range of symbolic elements, like wall paintings and figurines, which are hardly found in the north-west. His account of Neolithic culture traces the spread of those same ideas across vast reaches of space and time but the material record is hardly sufficient for us to feel confident that the same dualities were equally important where he first identifies them, in Anatolia in the late seventh millennium BC, and in the Rhineland over a thousand years later.

There is also a problem that Hodder's interpretation shares with the structuralist approach by which he is influenced, for it is difficult to see quite how such changes were effected. Who devised them, and why did they come to mind? The subtitle of his book *The domestication of Europe* provides something of an answer, speaking of 'structure and contingency in Neolithic societies'. It suggests that such developments arose out of chance combinations of symbolically charged elements, but that is still too abstract. Hodder says very little about the distinctive practices that pervaded social life. As a result, it is difficult to establish why the ideas that dominated Neolithic thought should have led to the creation of the earliest earthwork monuments. Nor is it obvious why those constructions took the form that they did. Is another approach likely to be more productive?

The built environment is not simply a representation of a set of abstract ideas. It is through their engagement with that environment in the course of daily life that individuals learn how to become members of society (Giddens 1984; Bourdieu 1990). They do so through the routines of living with other people in a cultural setting that is permeated with symbolic meanings. But buildings are often more durable than other forms of material culture and this allows their significance to be interpreted and reinterpreted over considerable periods of time. The conscious creation of monuments often takes that process towards its limits. If long mounds were meant to evoke the past significance of the longhouse, surely it is with those houses that any new analysis should begin.

LONGHOUSES

There are two sites which sum up changing perceptions of the settlements built during the Linear Pottery Culture. The first is Köln-Lindenthal, which was excavated on a large scale before the Second World War (Buttler and Haberey 1936). All the characteristic features of these settlements were found there, as well as the remains of as many as four enclosures, but the sheer abundance of material at first proved to be deceptive. The post-built structures seemed to be so massive that they were initially interpreted as barns. The subterranean features that we would now recognise as borrow pits were originally mistaken for houses, an error which was all the easier to make because they contained so many artefacts. It did not take long to realise that this interpretation was unsatisfactory and it soon became accepted that the settlement had consisted of a large number of timber buildings. Now the earthwork enclosures presented more of a problem, but, true to the prevailing emphasis on such sites as farming settlements, it was supposed that these features were intended as stock compounds. Where there were houses inside these earthworks the enclosures were regarded as a form of defence.

My second example is Bylany in Bohemia. This was an equally influential excavation, which began in 1953. Again it was conducted on a very large scale, and in this case fieldwork extended to other sites in the surrounding area. There was no difficulty in identifying the basic components of the settlements at Bylany: the houses, the borrow pits and a number of subsoil features which were thought to have been used for storing grain. In this case the interpretation which was favoured after the first fifteen years of excavation was coloured by the basic assumption that the surrounding land had been farmed by slash-and-burn cultivation, and that cereal yields from recent agriculture might provide some indication of the length of time over which this activity could have been sustained (Soudsky and Pavlu 1972).

Such evidence was combined with two main forms of chronological analysis. The pottery from the Bylany complex was examined using complex statistical procedures which anticipate the use of seriation on similar sites today (Soudsky 1973). The length of occupation of individual houses was also worked out by considering how many times the grain storage pits had been relined. Soudsky and Pavlu assumed that this would have been an annual event and on that basis they suggested that each house had been occupied for about fourteen years. Their estimates of the productive capacity of the surrounding land provided rather similar figures: it would require two fields, used in alternation, to provide enough food for the inhabitants of a settlement of the size of Bylany and these would only be worth cultivating for between fifteen and eighteen years. After that, the settlement might be abandoned in favour of another site and would not be reoccupied until sufficient time had elapsed for the agricultural soil to recover. That would have taken about thirty years, which was long enough for two more sites to be settled in succession to one another.

Again, this analysis makes a number of assumptions, all of which are founded on entirely practical considerations. It supposes that the houses were used and abandoned simultaneously, and the entire reconstruction depends on the use of shifting cultivation. Although there is still some evidence that Bylany was used discontinuously, it no longer seems that the changes in the settled area were particularly abrupt (Pavlu et al. 1986). Moreover, recent studies of Bandkeramik settlements suggest that land use could be sustained for much longer than Soudsky and Pavlu supposed (for a summary of this literature see Whittle 1996a: 160–2). Many sites were occupied over considerable periods of time. If so, it becomes even more of a problem to reconcile the unexpectedly brief lifespan of individual houses with the continuous use of the settlement as a whole.

In fact, it has always been very difficult to analyse such complex settlement plans. Their main features, however, are easy to identify (Whittle 1988a: ch. 3). The massive timber longhouses are normally laid out on a common axis and their positions rarely overlap. On some sites they may be spaced at roughly the same intervals over a large area. There is no stratigraphy except in the fillings of sub-soil features and, because so few of the houses were built in the same places as one another, the best way of working out the sequence of development is through detailed seriation of the pottery. This suggests that some of these sites underwent numerous phases of construction and that relatively few houses were in use at the same time. A new analysis of the excavated material from Köln-Lindenthal suggests that the occupied area went through as many as sixteen phases of activity (Bernhardt 1986). At Bylany there were no fewer than twenty-five (Pavlu et al. 1986).

Where sufficient excavations have been undertaken within the same area, it is possible to construct a finely calibrated sequence (Lüning and Stehli 1994: 122–35). In the Merzbach region in west Germany, for instance, a detailed artefact sequence has been devised which runs between about 5300 and 4850 BC, and this can be used to work out the lengths of the different phases identified at the excavated settlements. Similar problems arise to those encountered by the excavators of Bylany, for this work suggests that each house may have been used for only quarter of a century; the settlement at Laurenzberg 7, for instance, was occupied for two centuries but the mean length of any building phase was only twenty-seven years. That is a rather short period for such massive buildings to remain habitable, and the problem becomes even more apparent as the excavated evidence from Linear Pottery Culture settlements provides few indications that these structures had ever been repaired. These buildings were rarely destroyed by fire, yet where the excavation record is sufficiently detailed there is no indication that the timbers were salvaged and reused. Unless we follow the model developed by Soudsky and Pavlu (1972) at Bylany, this implies that the buildings were abandoned while some of them were structurally sound, and that they were left to decay. One way of reconciling this evidence with the pottery sequence at these sites is to suggest that the abandoned buildings no longer provided a focus for the deposition of artefacts.

These observations can be combined with some other ideas suggested by Hodder (1994). He points out that in south-east Europe houses were regularly burnt down with their contents inside them, and that normally they were replaced in a different position. This is unlikely to be fortuitous (Tringham 1991; J. Chapman 1994). It seems much more probable that the decision was taken deliberately and that the houses were destroyed when one of the inhabitants died. The obvious reason for this practice may have been a fear of pollution. Hodder suggests that rather similar considerations might account for the distinctive way in which Bandkeramik longhouses were very rarely replaced in the same positions, but he does not take this idea to its logical conclusion.

LONGHOUSES TO LONG MOUNDS

It seems as if the history of these buildings was determined not by the physical lifespan of the longhouse but by the social lifespan of the household. After these buildings were abandoned they were probably replaced on another site. The implication of this argument is that at any one time a Bandkeramik settlement might consist of a whole variety of buildings, only some of which were currently inhabited. Others were in various stages of decay and in certain instances the empty spaces that could not be reoccupied would show where similar buildings had once been. Such a settlement, then, might consist of a series of 'living houses', interspersed with 'dead houses' or, more precisely, the houses of the dead. The two groups would be laid out on the same alignment and would conform to the same spacing across the occupied area (see Figure 14). Eventually, as the process of decay increased, each of the houses would collapse, leaving a gap in the distribution of buildings marked by a long, low mound, much of it

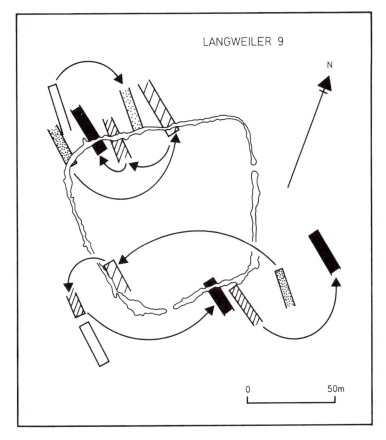

Figure 14. The changing locations of the longhouses at Langweiler site 9, western Germany. The houses were eventually replaced by a ditched enclosure. Modified from Kuper *et al.* (1977).

contributed by the daub which had covered the walls. The erosion of the barrow pits might even give the impression of side ditches. The very process of decay in the heart of the inhabited area might have given rise to the basic idea of the long barrow.

This is not to suggest that the dead were actually buried in their houses, as was the case in south-east Europe. The human remains associated with these buildings are mainly those of children, and there is no evidence that they were placed there when these structures were abandoned (Veit 1993). Adult burials are found in flat cemeteries located close to some, but not all, of these sites. These were accompanied by artefacts, which probably reflect the existence of quite simple divisions based on age and gender (Whittle 1988a: ch. 5; Farrugia 1992). The growth of these cemeteries runs in parallel with the structural history of the houses, suggesting that the evidence from these two locations may result from quite different processes. The burials in the cemeteries were concerned with individual identities, whereas the decaying buildings, and ultimately the low mounds that might have taken their place, would have commemorated the history of the household.

I have suggested that a detailed reading of the field evidence from Bandkeramik settlements adds weight to the suggestions put forward in Hodder's article. It also provides a more direct source for the idea of the long mound than his emphasis on the abstract ideas that influenced Neolithic perceptions of the world. The everyday experience of living in a settlement where many of the houses had been abandoned might have been enough to create an association between the form of the longhouse and the celebration of the dead. The link with an earthwork monument would be even easier to conceptualise if the cycle of decay had ended in the creation of a mound. In the beginning it would only be necessary to imitate the results of that natural process.

Where did that first take place? On present evidence this was most probably in modern Poland, the one region in which the distributions of longhouses and long mounds overlap (Midgley 1985; Bogucki 1988: chs. 4 and 7). The precise character of this transition remains controversial. The two kinds of structure are not found on the same sites, although it seems possible that some of the earthwork monuments were built over earlier settlements of some kind. Nor is there any agreement on whether the two kinds of structure were exactly contemporary with one another or whether they belong to successive phases. The most recent account, however, favours a period of overlap (Midgley 1992: ch. 5).

Why should the crucial transition have taken place in this area? One possibility is that the practice of leaving longhouses to decay had gone out of favour. A characteristic of the settlement sites found in this region is that the house plans often overlap (Bogucki 1988: ch. 4). There is no longer the same evidence that new buildings respected the positions of their predecessors. Instead, it seems that they were replaced in exactly the same locations. As a result it is sometimes difficult to work out the history of individual settlements. If this interpretation is correct, it would no longer have been possible to treat an abandoned longhouse as a memorial to its inhabitants, although individual burials were certainly deposited within the settlement area. Perhaps that is why new practices were adopted. In this case the former existence of the house was marked by the construction of a mound of very similar proportions, but at another location. As many writers have argued, this first generation of long barrows shows greater similarities with the organisation of the longhouses than many of their successors (Midgley 1985). More important, the newly built earthworks were not constructed in isolation, but are found in groups. The mounds may be approximately equally spaced and they conform to the same very general alignment. As a result, their spatial organisation is virtually the same as the organisation of the houses within a settlement. Figure 15 illustrates this point, comparing the groundplan of a series of excavated houses with the layout of one of these cemeteries. If the long mounds can be thought of as the houses of the dead, these cemeteries recall the

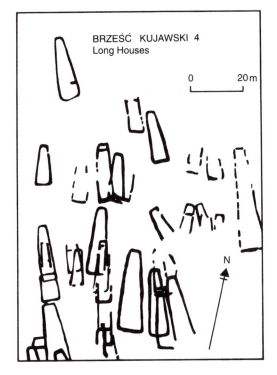

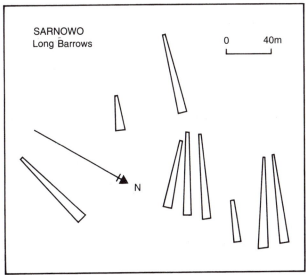

Figure 15. The layout of the longhouses at Brześć Kujavski, compared with that of the long barrows at Sarnowo, Poland. Information from Bogucki (1988).

existence of entire settlements. As different households or their members were extinguished, fresh mounds may have been created until the domestic buildings were replaced entirely by specialised monuments to the dead.

LONGHOUSES AND EARTHWORK ENCLOSURES

Having suggested a mechanism by which longhouses might have given way to long mounds, we need to address the problem of the enclosures. The evidence is less compelling, but once again it is worth returning to the excavated site at Köln-Lindenthal. This was one of the first places where earthwork enclosures were identified, and it is still quite difficult to establish how they were related to the houses. Recent analysis of the excavated material favours the view that all four of these features should be attributed to a late period in the occupation of this site (Bernhardt 1986). A similar sequence has been recognised at other settlements in west Germany (Boelicke *et al.* 1988: 417–28). It is harder to decide on the relationship between the enclosures and the successive houses on these sites, and at Köln-Lindenthal the preferred interpretation presents an intriguing problem. It had always been supposed that such earthworks would have protected the houses, but in two of the phases of occupation this does not seem to have happened. Instead the enclosure abutted the position of these buildings and bounded an apparently empty space. But the sequence is not as straight-forward as this outline would suggest, for in each case that 'empty' space was where a building or buildings had stood during the previous period. In the light of my earlier arguments, it seems more likely that such earthworks contained what I have called the 'dead houses': buildings that had been abandoned by their inhabitants and left to decay.

A similar situation has been recognised at Langweiler site 9 (see Figure 14; Kuper *et al.* 1977). The end of the sequence of building at this site sees a quite new development. Throughout the history of this settlement there were two distinct groups of structures, separated from one another by an open space which may have been used for communal activities. After the last longhouses had gone out of use, it was precisely this part of the site that was enclosed by a ditch. It seems as if one function of that earthwork was to emphasise the importance of an area which no longer formed an integral part of any settlement. Similar developments are known elsewhere in the region as ditched enclosures and were apparently created towards the end of a long succession of houses.

This is not to argue that every enclosure was built to emphasise the positions of buildings that had already been abandoned. There are certainly cases in which the traditional interpretation is likely to be correct, and in central Europe there are even enclosures which are surrounded by houses of exactly the same date as the earthworks. Such enclosures adopt a particularly formal groundplan. They are generally circular and have four entrances which may be aligned on the cardinal points. Some of them contain placed deposits of fine artefacts and groups of human remains (Trnka 1991). In these cases the central part of the settlement is distinguished as an area devoted to ritual activities. It may be significant that earthworks of very similar form and function continued to be built after the pattern of settlement had changed. There are other regions in which enclosures with an equally stereotyped groundplan were closely associated with houses. Work in Belgium has identified a number of late Bandkeramik enclosures, defined by interrupted ditches and palisades, with domestic buildings inside them (Keeley and Cahen 1989). Thus the idea of creating such earthworks was current over a large area and the monuments themselves played several different roles.

That said, it is certainly true that their association with settlements became less important over time. Some of the central European enclosures were created in virtual isolation, and others are certainly known in later contexts than any of the longhouses. In north-west Europe too, enclosure building increased in importance as settlements took a less obvious form. These enclosures were increasingly separated from the living sites and, as we shall see in Chapter 5, they played a significant role in ritual life. Their contents include deposits of fine pottery or axes, meat joints and human remains. As this happened, they also assumed the distinctive groundplan encountered at the enclosed settlements in Belgium. They were commonly provided with interrupted ditches or palisades and are characterised by a considerable number of entrances (Bradley 1993: ch. 4).

If the tradition of long mounds involved a reference to the distinctive history of the household, it seems quite possible that some of these enclosures referred to the past importance of whole communities. In certain cases such earthworks may have surrounded a group of abandoned buildings, and in others, like Langweiler site 9, they may have come to stand for a recently deserted settlement or the activities that had once been carried out there. There are further possibilities. The late Linear Pottery Culture earthworks in Belgium seem to have enclosed entire settlements, and in this case there is no reason to suppose that the buildings inside them had gone out of use before these features were built. Such enclosures are among the earliest to be provided with causewayed ditches and they may have been among the sources of inspiration for a large number of monuments created during later phases. Few of those monuments appear to have been inhabited, but, because of the circumstances in which they first came into being, their creation and use may have played an important role in the affairs of a wider community. Just as the long mound evoked the form of a domestic building that had existed in the past, the ditched enclosure may have provided a metaphor for entire settlements of a kind that were no longer encountered in daily life. Again, I shall take this argument further in Chapter 5.

SUMMARY

I began this chapter by observing that Neolithic material culture is studied according to two broad traditions of enquiry. In those regions where settlements provide the main source of information the emphasis is upon food production and the colonisation of farmland. Archaeological writing tends to be descriptive rather than analytical, and where theoretical issues are mentioned at all they are concerned with adaptation to resources. In other parts of Europe those empirical patterns give way to a distribution of earthwork monuments, and settlements are more difficult to study. Here, archaeological writing places a greater emphasis on ritual and ideology. The division between these two approaches to the past obscures the basic point that one of these systems was a transformation of the other.

In order to understand this development, it has been necessary to question the conventional portrayal of the settlements as ruled by functional considerations. A more detailed study of the life cycle of Neolithic longhouses revealed a whole series of anomalies, from their initial siting within these settlements to the processes leading to their abandonment. That distinctive sequence helped to account for their relationship with the first enclosures and long mounds and even suggested some new ways of interpreting the transition from domestic landscapes to monumental landscapes that characterises the Neolithic sequence.

On one level, this analysis emphasises a point that is already familiar in social anthropology: that a house is far more than a machine for living in, and that no settlement will ever be understood if we assume that all its elements play a practical role (Carsten and Hugh-Jones 1995). At another level, this chapter suggests that Neolithic specialists have treated symbolism and ideology at such an abstract level that these issues hardly bear on the experience of people in the past. It was out of the routines that those people followed and the conventions that they accepted as second nature that their history was made. It was a history that could take unexpected turns. One of those was the first appearance of earthwork monuments in Europe.

Chapter 4

Another time

Architecture, ancestry and the development of chambered tombs

The emphasis on mortuary mounds in Neolithic Europe is often connected with the importance of ancestry in farming societies. The presence of the ancestors in a particular place helps to establish a community's claim to agricultural land, while the practicalities of farming a particular landscape over a lengthy period involve a new awareness of time. But it is not at all clear that the first mortuary mounds were associated with such basic changes. Often they covered a single individual, whose bones were no longer accessible to the living. It was at a later stage in the development of Neolithic tombs that the remains of more people were deposited. Only then did the form of the monument permit continuous access between the living and the dead. This change occurred very widely, and it was under these circumstances that relics were often moved between the tomb and other kinds of monument. Using the distinctive sequence in north-west France, this chapter puts the case that only these later monuments were really associated with the exploitation of ancestry. It is these sites, rather than their predecessors, that epitomise a new conception of time, and it was not until they had been built that the environmental evidence from the same areas reveals any significant traces of agriculture.

TIME AND THE TOMB

One of the main influences on the archaeology of the 1980s was the work of Meillassoux and in particular his essay 'From reproduction to production' (Meillassoux 1972). In that paper he distinguished between the conception of time found among hunter gatherers and that shared by farmers. Hunter gatherers, he said, acquire their food through a series of short-term transactions. They do not invest in a particular area of land and their fortunes do not depend on the work of earlier generations. Farming, on the other hand, requires a different perception of space and time. It involves a long-term commitment to a specific territory, and its success may depend on the outcome of decisions that reach back into the past. That is why Meillassoux suggested that farmers have a stronger sense of genealogy than hunter gatherers do, and it also accounts for the importance that they attach to ancestry.

No doubt, such contrasts were over-simplified, but they had an appeal for archaeologists who were studying equally general processes. They offered a way of coming to terms with the appearance at about the same time of the earliest domesticated resources and the first monumental tombs. As we have seen, such structures were generally found around the limits of agricultural colonisation, where, it seemed, land suitable for farming might have been in short supply. This was an observation discussed by Renfrew in his paper 'Megaliths, territories and populations', in which he suggested that these monuments could have been constructed as communities established their claims to agricultural land (Renfrew 1976). Influenced by Meillassoux's scheme, later writers extended this argument, proposing that territorial claims were in fact legitimised by the physical presence of the ancestors (R. Chapman 1981; Bradley 1984: ch. 2). In contrast to the archaeology of hunter gatherers, with its emphasis on the subsistence economy, Neolithic studies placed more weight on relations between the living and the dead.

Meillassoux's model was of course a product of its time and no one would any longer talk of hunter gatherers as an ideal type. Studies of Neolithic Europe have involved equally fundamental changes of perspective, and it is with these developments that this chapter is chiefly concerned. Is there any merit in the view that the creation of monumental tombs reflects a new sense of time and place in prehistoric Europe? And is it still helpful to equate their construction with the adoption of an agricultural economy?

There have been three major developments during the last few years, each of them involving a much closer study of the local sequence of development. First, there has been a reappraisal of agricultural origins in north and north-west Europe, the very areas in which the earliest tombs are found. This has revealed a striking paradox, for, as I argued in earlier chapters, these constructions seem to have been built in precisely the areas where agriculture was adopted late and perhaps by local hunter gatherers. The case for economic change was actually rather tenuous, but some authorities were so convinced of a link between farming and monument building that the first appearance of stone-built tombs seemed enough in itself to indicate a new economic regime. At the same time, Case (1969) argued that the building of such large structures could only have been supported by an agricultural surplus, and Sherratt (1990) suggested that it would have required a labour force which owed its very existence to the demands of an agrarian technology.

In fact, there is little independent evidence of the subsistence economy at this time. There is no doubt that the earliest domesticates are found at virtually the same date as the first monuments to the dead, but it remains to be seen whether the use of these new resources played a decisive role in the creation of the tombs. It is just as likely that farming was adopted only gradually and that wild plants and animals retained some of their original significance. There is also the very real problem that stone and earthwork monuments seem to have occupied a more prominent place in the landscape than the settlements of the living population. Indeed, they may have been among the few fixed points in that landscape, for one shortcoming of the territorial model in its original form was that for some time people may have adhered to a mobile way of life (R. Chapman 1995). Nor is it by any means clear that agriculture was adopted at the same pace in every region.

Similarly, it is no longer acceptable to treat the tombs as a unitary phenomenon. As we shall see, there are at least two distinct styles of architecture, with their own sources and their own distributions, and some writers have even suggested that tomb building developed spontaneously in several different areas. (Renfrew 1973). More important, several studies have investigated their character as buildings that would have played an active role in the rituals that were conducted there. The tomb plans that seem to have obsessed prehistorians for generations reflect quite basic differences in human behaviour and experience (Fleming 1972, 1973; Bradley 1989; Thomas 1990).

Examples of these contrasts abound. For instance, the builders sometimes provided a special area from which onlookers could view the ceremonies conducted in front of the burial chamber, and this forecourt might be more or less extensive in relation to the size of the tomb. At other monuments the audience was apparently kept at a distance. The remains of the dead might be readily accessible, close to the entrance to the monument, or they might be held in chambers beneath the heart of the mound, where they could not be seen by many people. Access to the chambers might be restricted by special barriers. Some sites were decorated by paintings or rock carvings, and again their placing within the structure reveals an obvious order, suggesting not only that certain images might have been restricted to certain viewers but also that those features had to be experienced in a specific sequence. Although these monuments are often treated like portable artefacts, as clues to a wider pattern of communication, it is clear that they played a vital role in the lives of Neolithic people. Such monuments helped orchestrate a series of public and private experiences that were absolutely central to the ways in which the living approached the dead.

The third area in which there have been new developments concerns the remains of the dead. For many years archaeologists had been aware of certain broad patterns in the distribution of bones inside these monuments. Sometimes these were burnt, but this is not particularly common. Elsewhere, bodies retained their articulation, or the unfleshed bones of a number of different individuals were mixed together or rearranged according to age, sex or body parts. There may also be cases in which human remains were translated from one monument to another, and it is sometimes observed that any one individual is represented by only a few fragments of bone. The remaining parts of the body may have circulated as relics of the deceased, and it is becoming increasingly obvious that such items may be found at other kinds of Neolithic field monument, including settlement sites and the specialised enclosures which are considered in Chapter 5.

One consequence of this analysis has been to reveal the limitations of our terminology. If bones could be taken in and out of these monuments and could also circulate between other kinds of site, it hardly seems appropriate to maintain the conventional description of all these monuments as 'tombs'. At best, we can suggest a close association with the rites of passage of the dead. A more neutral term is to describe these constructions as 'mortuary monuments'.

Even then, that revision does not capture the full complexity of the situation, for there is a very real difference between those sites where intact bodies were deposited and left in place and other monuments, which were more like charnel houses where human relics could be added, reorganised or even taken away. Barrett (1988) has discussed some of these observations, arguing that there is a significant contrast between the practice of human burial and the circulation of human relics. The first he describes as a funeral rite in the traditional sense of the term, whereas the second he sees as part of a more geographically extensive set of ancestor rituals. As he says, 'ancestor rituals establish the presence of ancestors *in rites concerned with the living*' (my emphasis). 'Among the places and symbols used may be funerary architecture and the bones of the dead'. Funerary rituals, on the other hand, 'are specifically concerned with human burial' (*ibid.*, p. 31). What we usually think of as tombs or burial mounds were often used in ancestor rites.

ARCHITECTURE AND ANCESTRY

In fact, there is a close connection between different kinds of architecture and different ways of treating the dead. The two are considered together in Thomas' study of the megalithic tombs on the Cotswold hills of southern England (Thomas 1988b). He distinguishes between two main kinds of monument, each associated with one particular way of dealing with human remains. In both cases the monuments consist of elongated mounds or cairns similar in plan to the long-houses discussed in Chapter 3, but in one group the chambers are found in the sides of these monuments and in the other they occur at one end (see Figure 16). Although the side chambers contain an apparently chaotic mass of bones, it seems that wholly or partially articulated corpses were first deposited at the entrances to these sites. As those bodies lost their flesh, they were transferred through to the heart of the monument, where the relics assumed their final configuration.

The other kind of monument considered in Thomas' paper has the internal structures at one end, and these often assume a modular plan, with pairs of chambers ranged on opposite sides of a central path. These 'transcepted tombs' are sometimes approached through a monumental forecourt. The separate chambers played a distinctive role in the treatment of the dead, for although there is evidence for the abstraction of relics from these buildings it seems that the remains were organised according to basic distinctions of age and sex. These

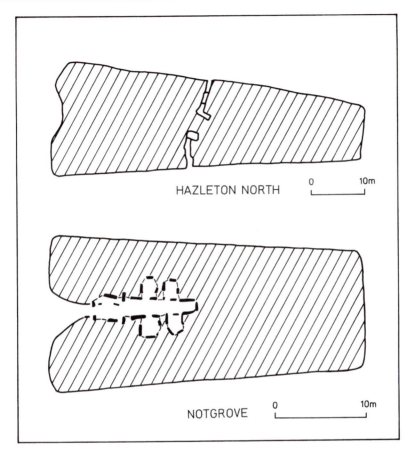

HAZLETON NORTH

0   10m

NOTGROVE

0   10m

Figure 16. Alternative groundplans of Severn Cotswold tombs, modified from Thomas (1988b).

monuments may be later in date than the others, suggesting that the dead came to be classified in more complex ways.

That does not exhaust the potential variety of such monuments. A still more striking contrast is illustrated by those found in Brittany. Here, the modern visitor undergoes a confusing experience, for one of the largest and best known of these constructions, Tumulus-St-Michel at Carnac, must be entered by a modern tunnel (Le Rouzic 1932). At its centre are two rectangular chambers and a series of smaller cists. These were covered by a circular cairn buried beneath the principal mound, but none of these could have been reached from the exterior once either monument had been built. On leaving the tumulus, however, the visitor sees that another stone chamber has been constructed against the flank of the mound. In contrast to the cists at the centre of the site, this has a clearly defined entrance (see Figure 17).

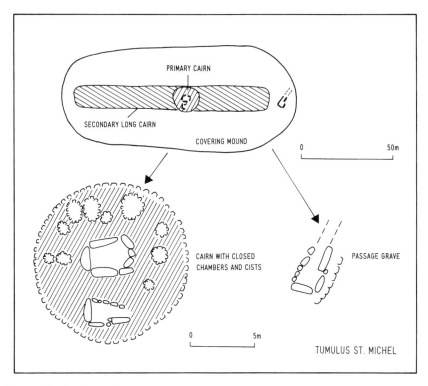

PRIMARY CAIRN

SECONDARY LONG CAIRN

COVERING MOUND

0   50m

CAIRN WITH CLOSED
CHAMBERS AND CISTS

PASSAGE GRAVE

0   5m

TUMULUS ST. MICHEL

Figure 17. Outline plans of Tumulus-St-Michel, Carnac, Brittany, based on the illustrations in Le Rouzic (1932).

The character of the successive structures at Tumulus-St-Michel may never be established in detail, but fortunately another major monument in the Carnac region has recently been excavated. This is Le Petit Mont at Arzon, where a far more distinctive sequence has been established (Lecornec 1994). This began as an oval earthwork mound approximately 50 metres long and 1.5 metres high. Towards its south-western end there were the remains of what may have been the socket for an upright stone (see Figure 18). This is one of a number of mounds in Brittany whose form seems to have been influenced by that of earlier long-houses; I discussed the beginning of this tradition in the previous chapter. The example at Arzon dates from approximately the middle of the fifth millennium BC.

It was succeeded by a much more massive construction of stone, but the newly built cairn had several features in common with the older mound. It was rectangular rather than oval, but it was built on top of that monument and conformed to its alignment. This cairn was little more than half the length of its predecessor but it was very much higher. In places it was supported by three stepped walls and reached a maximum height of 5 metres. Like its predecessor, it lacked any

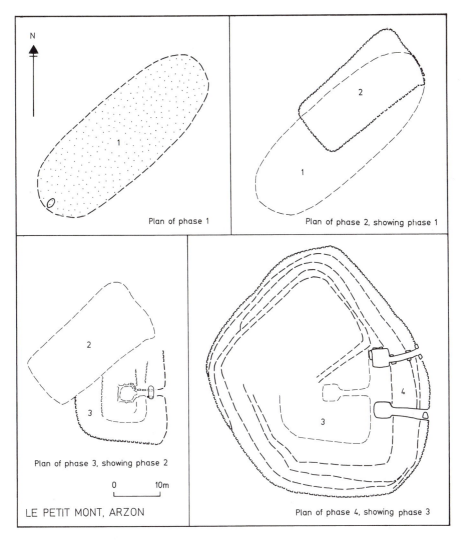

Figure 18. The excavated sequence at Le Petit Mont, Arzon, Brittany, in the light of recent excavation. Only the later monuments have entrance passages. Information from Lecornec (1994).

evidence of a passage or a burial chamber, although parts of this structure were not investigated by excavation.

In this respect, the first two monuments at Le Petit Mont differ radically from those that followed them. In a third phase of construction on the site the cairn was extended and a major addition was abutted on to its south wall. This involved a departure from the regular outline of the two previous monuments, but it did allow the creation of a stone-built chamber approached by a passage which was originally about 5 metres long; this type of structure is known as a *passage grave*. It incorporated broken fragments of at least three statue menhirs, and the filling of the chamber contained a series of hearths as well as two axes and a quantity of pottery. Radiocarbon dates suggest that the addition to the monument was built about 4000 BC and that the chamber and passage remained accessible for perhaps another 500 years.

In its final phases, Le Petit Mont was enlarged again. The composite stone-built monument was entirely encased in a massive pentagonal cairn, supported by as many as five revetment walls. The precise configuration of this monument is uncertain because of modern damage, but it seems that this new construction would have cut off access to the chamber and passage established during the previous period. The new cairn itself contained two passage graves, the surviving example of which included more pieces of carved stone.

Despite this long history of activity, each successive structure seems to have respected the remains of its predecessor. The first stone monument followed the axis of the original long mound, and when it was extended the builders took care that the newly built chamber and passage did not impinge on the original construction. The same was also true during the final phase. In each case the passage grave(s) were integral with the extension of the cairn. The excavator has also suggested that the reused stonework was taken from statue menhirs which had originally stood on or around the first two monuments on the site. As we have seen, there is a possible socket for one of these uprights at the end of the long barrow.

Not only does this sequence shed light on the poorly recorded Tumulus-St-Michel, similar contrasts can be recognised elsewhere in the Carnac region (Boujot and Cassen 1992). At their simplest they concern two elements: the character of the mortuary deposit and the form of the covering monument.

SEQUENCE AND CONSEQUENCE

Generally speaking, the first oval or rectangular mounds found in this area cover a series of deposits which would not have been accessible after those monuments were completed. These included small stone cists, at least some of which contained artefacts and human bones; there were also tiny cairns which marked the positions of similar deposits. These were not found at Le Petit Mont, where only limited parts of the first two monuments could be investigated, but even on fully excavated sites there might be only one or two of these features underneath the mound. It seems likely that some of the early long mounds were incorporated into a group of exceptionally large monuments near Carnac known as Grands Tumulus. Both types of structure may have been associated with decorated stones which were erected in the open air, although in many cases they were taken down and reused in a subsequent phase. It seems that the deposits beneath these mounds were inaccessible after the earthworks were constructed, although the decorated menhirs may have provided the information needed to understand their significance.

The sequence at Le Petit Mont, and most probably at a number of the Grands Tumulus, shows that a new type of structure – the passage grave – was built during a later stage in the history of these monuments. It marks a new departure in two respects. The chambers were larger than the cists found under the long mounds and the existence of a passage allowed continued access to the interior of the site after the covering monument had been built. Despite the poor survival of human bone in this region, it is clear that some of these structures were associated with the remains of a number of individuals (Patton 1993: 91–8). Some of them also incorporated fragments of carved stonework, which presumably belonged to the 'idols' of the previous phase (L'Helgouac'h 1983). Thus the dead became more accessible to the living as the statues that had originally stood in the open air were broken up and concealed.

In fact, the archaeology of Brittany illustrates two quite different aspects of Neolithic mortuary practice, both of which extend well beyond the monuments found in this particular area. The first is an important change in the character of the mortuary chamber. As we have seen, in north-west France there is a striking contrast between the closed cists created beneath the early mounds and the more accessible chambers constructed when such monuments were rebuilt. Closed chambers of this general kind have a wide distribution in time and space, but they are a particular feature of the Late Mesolithic and Early Neolithic periods. They are found mainly on the Atlantic coastline, where they first appear in Mesolithic cemeteries. Like those of Neolithic date, such cists may originally have been associated with small mounds or cairns (Scarre 1992).

Their later history takes various forms. Sometimes the basic module may have been recreated on a much larger scale. This may well account for the massive closed chambers (*portal tombs*) found along the Irish Sea coast, while in other cases those chambers were provided with an obvious entrance, or even with a distinct passage leading out of the monument altogether. We have seen examples of this development in Brittany, but much the same sequence is sometimes found among the first stone-built monuments in parts of Iberia (Da Cruz 1995) and south Scandinavia (Midgeley 1992: ch. 9).

The second major change is also illustrated by the sequence at Le Petit Mont, where two linear monuments were succeeded by a massive pentagonal cairn. At other sites, and particularly those constructed in a single phase, passage graves are found in precisely circular monuments.

The changing form of the cairns is surely significant. As I argued in Chapter 3, long mounds had a most distinctive history in other parts of Europe, although they were always associated with the dead. We saw how the form of the mound probably echoes the distinctive appearance of Neolithic longhouses, even though the two types of structure were only in use together over a limited area. Long mounds, however, came to be built much more widely until their distribution extended from Poland to the Atlantic coastline. With only limited exceptions, the oldest of these monuments were associated with individual burials in graves (Midgley 1985; Duhamel and Prestreau 1991). Although there could be several such graves beneath any one mound, *the burials were inaccessible once that earthwork had been built.*

Later, long mounds or cairns often took a different form (see Figure 19). In some areas a stone-built passage provided access to a chamber deep inside the monument, while in other instances the entrance might lead directly into such a chamber. At times there could be several of these structures, and that is an arrangement that we find on many sites. Although that general sequence conceals many local variants, it has one important point in common with the development of the round cairns, for once again the dead were no longer cut off from the living. Now their remains were accessible from the world outside.

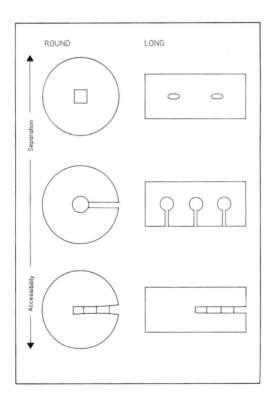

Figure 19. Alternative groundplans for megalithic tombs, emphasising the choice between long and round mounds or cairns. The diagram also illustrates the variable distance between the living and the dead in both series of monuments.

At Petit Mont the original long cairn was gradually rebuilt until it assumed a roughly circular groundplan. The tradition of creating round mounds and cairns probably originated along the Atlantic coastline of Portugal, Spain and France, and may be a later development in Scandinavia. Its origins are quite uncertain, although it is true that some of the closed cists that were created at the start of the sequence had been covered by tiny circular cairns (Scarre 1992). The distribution of larger monuments of this form might be more consistent with Mesolithic antecedents than with an ultimate origin in the heartlands of Neolithic Europe. Sherratt (1995) suggests that their creation was a response to the introduction of long mounds by the first farmers. Although the distributions of the two types could encourage this idea in western France, it is hard to use the same explanation in Iberia, where the first domesticates were introduced from regions which lacked a tradition of either longhouses or long mounds. It may be simpler to follow the hypothesis outlined in Chapter 2 and to suppose that the adoption of new resources in that area accompanied a far wider change in ways of thinking about the world. Monumental architecture became imaginable for the first time, and round cairns may have developed through the embellishment of local mortuary practices.

These developments among the megalithic tombs of north-west France concern some of the fundamental properties of such monuments. Their outward appearance reflects two quite different symbolic systems, one of them based on the houses of an ancestral past. The contrasting forms taken by their chambers illustrate equally basic differences of access between the living and the dead. These distinctions cut right across the more local styles of tomb plan established by prehistorians and may offer one point of departure for a more radical analysis.

That is suggested by the sequence of deposits, for some of the earlier sites contained the body of only one person, whilst the later cairns might have housed the bones of significantly more individuals. This applies to both the eastern tradition of long mounds and to the circular monuments that originated along the Atlantic seaboard. In the case of stone-built monuments we have already seen that this development ran in parallel with structural changes that permitted continuous contact between the living and the dead.

There was another important development in the treatment of human remains, although this must be expressed more cautiously as the chronology of Neolithic 'tombs' is so controversial. It seems as if some of the early single burials had been those of intact bodies, while the human remains associated with the later monuments consisted of unfleshed bones. That same pattern is echoed right across the distribution of megalithic monuments. The origins of this practice may be found among late hunter gatherers, for, as we saw in Chapter 2, a number of isolated human bones have been discovered on Mesolithic occupation sites while some of the cemeteries of the same period contain bodies that are incomplete.

There are exceptions to all these statements, but what is very striking is how

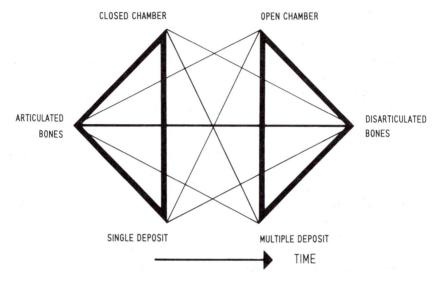

Figure 20. The changing relationship between tomb plans and human remains.

often these patterns can be identified. Figure 20 summarises these different tendencies, distinguishing between those links that are found persistently and other connections that occur less often. Although there are few sharp divisions, it does illustrate two general trends. First, it seems as if basic differences in the treatment of the dead are reflected by the use of different kinds of architecture. For the most part, monuments that housed individual corpses lacked any means of access from the world outside. On the other hand, those sites where the remains of the dead underwent a more complex history often allowed direct communication with the chamber where the bones were housed. That 'burial chamber' frequently contained the remains of a larger number of people, and in such cases we sometimes find that the bones themselves were reordered.

The second point is even more important, for it seems as if these two ways of dealing with the dead are often found in succession. If we follow Barrett's argument, that would imply a gradual change of emphasis from burial rites to ancestor rites. In the burial rite the body was consigned to the ground and it was left undisturbed (Barrett 1988). That corpse might already have undergone a sequence of primary and secondary funerals, but from the time of its deposition it was cut off from the world of the living. That separation was achieved symbolically by building a chamber without any entrance. In ancestor rituals, on the other hand, the human remains themselves would provide a resource that could be used by the living. Those remains might be visited, inspected, augmented or rearranged, or they might be taken away and circulated over a wider area. The dead were continuously accessible and the remains of the ancestors might even be distributed between different kinds of field monument.

IMPLICATIONS

Each system has implications for Neolithic conceptions of time and place. Both involved the creation of a conspicuous monument that established the importance of a particular location. Such buildings provided a focus for later mortuary rites, but only those structures which allowed access to the ancestral remains expressed a clear continuity between the past and the present. This continuity was symbolised by the passage communicating between the outer world and the world of the ancestors within the monument. Such structures also allowed the possibility of further use in the future. Thus the forms of different kinds of 'tomb' may have epitomised different notions of time.

This analysis forces us to reject any simple equation between the first appearance of mortuary monuments and the increasing significance of ancestry. There are two reasons for taking this view. Although the scale of these constructions was new, the practice of individual burial was already present before the appearance of domesticates. At the same time, the creation of more complex monuments, in which human relics were continuously accessible, was a later development and need not have happened alongside the first experiments with farming.

I mentioned that the adoption of agriculture in the areas with megalithic tombs has been very difficult to document. There is no doubt that the first monuments originated at about the same time as we find the first evidence of domesticates, but there is little to indicate their impact on the subsistence economy. The problem is made worse because we know so little about the settlement pattern at this time. But there are two areas, Denmark and north-west France, in which we can compare the changing form of the mortuary monuments with direct evidence of food production. Both sequences have points in common, but they took place independently and at different times. In Brittany the sequence starts about 4500 BC and runs for about 1,500 years. In Denmark it starts 500 years later, with the main period of change occurring from about 3400 BC.

Recent publications have placed the sequence of mortuary monuments in Brittany on a reasonably secure footing (Boujot and Cassen 1992; Patton 1993). The first structures were probably the cists associated with Mesolithic cemeteries. We have seen how similar structures are found beneath early long mounds. Passage graves were apparently a rather later development, and these are the first type of monument to allow access to the remains of the dead. Although human bones are rarely preserved, it seems as if these structures housed a limited number of bodies, both articulated and disarticulated. In the latter case the remains might be ordered according to body parts, with a special emphasis on the skull and the long bones.

At a still later stage the tomb plans became more varied, although there is much more evidence for the building of chambers that could be approached directly from the exterior; these structures have been described as *gallery graves*. Few bones survive on the Breton sites, but analogy with well-preserved sites in

Normandy and the Paris Basin suggests that these structures could have served as charnel houses, holding the remains of many more people (Masset 1993: ch. 6). Some had been brought to the site as entire bodies, but in other cases only certain parts of the skeleton are represented, suggesting that other bones had been removed.

This distinctive sequence can be compared with the results of pollen analysis in Brittany. In the Early Neolithic period there is little evidence of farming. Only two sites out of the seven studied by Marguerie (1992) show any signs of cultivation, but during the currency of passage graves the proportion rises to half the locations investigated. All these were near to the coast, and inland areas apparently retained their original forest cover. It is not until the period of the gallery graves that we find evidence for more intensive disturbance of the natural vegetation. On all the sites considered, the vegetation had been modified by human activity, and now it seems that settlement extended into the interior of the country. That is particularly striking, since this is the first period in which megalithic monuments are sufficiently widely distributed to have acted as territorial markers. This suggestion was recently put forward by Patton (1993: ch. 6).

The Danish sequence is even more detailed. There are three lines of evidence to consider here (Madsen 1982; Midgeley 1992: ch. 9; Skaarup 1993). There are the long mounds discussed earlier, which are normally associated with individual graves. These are found from the beginning of the Neolithic period, and their development runs in parallel with a tradition of rather similar graves which are sometimes grouped in cemeteries. We know rather less about the earliest megalithic tombs, although it is usually suggested that they exhibit a sequence from closed chambers to more extended chambers which were accessible from outside. Some of these early 'dolmens' are associated with individual deposits, although in other cases the bones appear to have been mixed, perhaps through later reuse.

By the Middle Neolithic period we find the construction of a large number of passage graves, whose distinctive architecture formalised the connection between the chamber and the world outside (see Figure 21). These contained many more bodies than the earlier monuments, and once again it seems that their bones had been thoroughly mixed. Although this evidence is often difficult to interpret, there are certainly sites where the remains had been rearranged and organised according to body parts.

These developments ran in parallel with important changes in the landscape. The earliest Neolithic settlements seem to have been rather ephemeral. Not all of them may have been used throughout the year, and some sites were dedicated to the exploitation of wild resources (Madsen 1982). Pollen analysis suggests a similar picture. Lime was cleared for pasture and areas of birch woodland were burnt and cultivated, but the cleared areas were small (Andersen 1993). In the Middle Neolithic period the situation changed. Much larger settlements became established and these may have been used over longer periods. Use-wear analysis

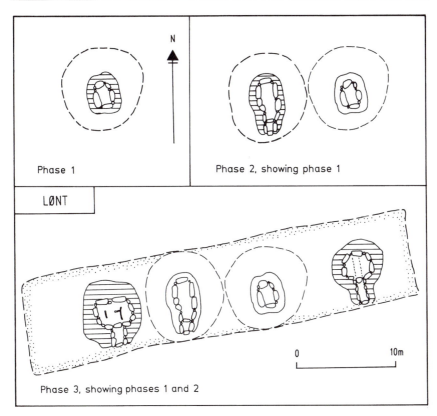

Figure 21. The sequence at the megalithic tomb of Lønt, Jutland, based on
information in Skaarup (1993). Note how the later chambers are
more accessible than the first one on the site and how they were
eventually brought together within a single monument.

on flint sickles suggests a considerable increase in the harvesting of plants (Juel
Jensen 1994), and at the same time we find more evidence for the exploitation of
domesticated cattle and sheep. Pollen analysis again reinforces these impressions.
There seem to have been major changes in land use and far larger areas of
secondary woodland were created during this period. Andersen suggests that
there was considerably greater demand for agricultural products. At the same
time there is more evidence of cultivation, shown by the first plough furrows
preserved beneath burial mounds (Thrane 1989). Some of these may result
from the construction of monuments on disused farmland, but in certain cases
the relationship is so close that another interpretation seems likely. On a
metaphorical level the dead may have been associated with the fertility of the soil
(Tarlow 1994). That idea remains controversial, yet it would be wrong to confine
the argument entirely to practical considerations, for it was at this time that the

number of megalithic tombs increased so sharply that they could have supported territorial claims (Madsen 1982).

The two sequences have many points in common, and if these findings are at all representative, they would suggest that the real impact of farming was not felt until a developed phase of the Neolithic period, and that it was during the same phase that ancestor rites became fully established. These took over from simpler funerary rituals, some of which may have had their ultimate origins among local hunter gatherers. This sequence is most revealing, for it suggests that we must contemplate a significant realignment in our attitudes to the Neolithic period. It is no longer acceptable to postulate a direct equation between the introduction of domesticates and the development of ancestry, and still less to suppose that the first monumental tombs need have been closely related to the definition of agricultural territories. They may have helped to establish the lasting importance of certain places, but closer attention to the architecture of those buildings, and to any human remains that still survive within them, suggests that they are related to a rather different conception of time.

The attraction of Meillassoux's (1972) work for archaeologists was the way in which it suggested that hunter gatherers and farmers might have possessed a different sense of time and place from one another, but it now seems that it was much too simple to infer those new conceptions from the adoption of mortuary monuments. Such an approach paid too little attention to the detailed design of those structures or to the treatment of the dead whose remains were deposited there. But that does not mean that his basic point was incorrect or that it no longer has any implications for our reading of the archaeological record. Farming demands a quite distinctive conception of space and time if it is to be undertaken effectively. In the same way, there is no doubt that eventually Neolithic society was permeated by ancestor rituals. My point is very simple. The most convincing evidence of early farming does not come from the early Neolithic, but is significantly later in date. Exactly the same is true of the archaeological evidence for ancestor rituals. Neither plays a particularly significant part at the beginning of this period, but there is some chronological evidence that the two developed in parallel. This does not oblige us to think in terms of cause and effect, for the relationship between these processes was surely a reciprocal one. What it does suggest is that Neolithic ideologies and Neolithic economies were subtly intertwined and that both emerged after a period of gradual change.

Those changing perceptions may have made the adoption of agriculture easier to contemplate, but they do not, and cannot, tell us why the decision was taken. That surely lies in the realm of ideas, for, as I argued in Chapter 2, it was only as the 'Mesolithic' world view broke down that the ownership of domesticates became conceivable at all. The same could be true of monument building. Long mounds may represent a symbolic recreation of the longhouse, round mounds may result from the elaboration of burial rites along the Atlantic coastline, but in either case for their creation to have been socially acceptable new attitudes had to develop. Megalith building runs in parallel with the beginnings of agriculture because both processes result from the same way of thinking about the world. Like civilisation, domestication was really a state of mind.

Chapter 5

Small worlds

Causewayed enclosures and their transformations

Although the first Neolithic enclosures were often associated with houses, such earthworks were eventually to take on a life of their own. A few sites were used for defence, but many of the enclosures adopted an increasingly stereotyped groundplan and were the focus for specialised deposits of artefacts and of human and animal bones. In a landscape where the settlements took an increasingly ephemeral form such enclosures may have symbolised the ideal community of the past, just as the long mounds sometimes found near them reproduced the form of longhouses that were no longer being built. Such monuments endowed particular places with a lasting significance at the same time as their strikingly uniform layout expressed the links that seem to have existed between these sites and a wider area around them. This chapter traces the part played by such earthworks in establishing a new sense of place and new kind of sacred geography.

MONUMENTS AS MATERIAL CULTURE

In Chapter 3 I suggested that two major traditions of prehistoric monuments developed out of the distinctive practices found on settlements of the Linear Pottery Culture. Long mounds were not only copies of an earlier tradition of longhouses; their creation recalled the way in which apparently serviceable buildings had been abandoned on the death of the occupants. I applied a similar argument to the first enclosures too, for there are a number of cases in which these earthworks were built after similar houses had gone out of use. At Köln-Lindenthal it even seemed likely that they surrounded the houses of the dead as well as those of the living. If the long mounds recalled the significance of individual longhouses, might some of these ditched enclosures have symbolised the past importance of entire settlements?

Chapter 4 expanded on these ideas by tracing the changing character and significance of mortuary mounds in different parts of Europe, but in doing so it raised a new kind of problem. Such traditions were very volatile and quite extraordinarily long-lived. Thus the earthwork mounds or cairns might very well evoke the appearance of the longhouses that had been constructed in the past, but their actual roles appear to have changed over time. Such mounds were first associated with individual graves, or with the burials of people whose remains were no longer accessible from the world outside. The later monuments, on the other hand, may have been ancestral tombs, involved in a far more flexible system in which the living were able to visit the dead and to redistribute their remains. The history of circular cairns may have taken a similar form, although the first stimulus for their building might have come from 'Mesolithic' communities living on the Atlantic seaboard.

There is an inevitable tension between the fine-grained analysis of individual monuments and the development of the same architectural forms over the *longue durée*. That tension has two sources. First, it arises because no single analysis, however compelling in its own terms, can capture the essence of the sequence as a whole. At best it illustrates a moment in time within a history that was by no means preordained. Second, we must be aware that the distinctive character of stone or earthwork monuments makes them very different from other forms of material culture.

As Whittle has noted (1996a: 269–70), it is not easy to trace a continuous sequence from the first Bandkeramik enclosures found on the loess to those constructed during subsequent phases. That is not just a chronological question, for the later enclosures have a remarkably uniform groundplan, which is hardly represented among the earliest earthworks. Their most distinctive features are easily summarised. They involve a restricted space, encompassed by one or more ditches. These ditches are more often curving than straight, and they are either set close together or are separated by areas of open ground. The earthworks are accompanied by internal banks, and sometimes by palisades. The element that seems to unite these enclosures can be described as segmentation. The ditches around these monuments are interrupted at regular intervals by causeways (although continuous earthworks may also be found in some of the same cultural contexts). It is a moot point how often the banks had been broken, but at times the earthworks follow the same course as interrupted palisades (see Figure 22). On a few sites there was one major entrance flanked by a more considerable earthwork, which formed a kind of facade (Evans 1988). Elsewhere a number of separate causeways were enhanced by complicated structures interpreted as gateways (Boelicke 1976). The distribution of these enclosures is enormous. Examples are known as far north as Sweden and as far south as Languedoc (Larsson 1982; Vaquer 1990: 294–6). They also extend the whole way from Ulster to the Danube (Mallory and Hartwell 1984; Lüning 1988).

The role played by these monuments has always been difficult to decide, but in each part of their distribution there has been the same temptation to adopt one particular reading of the evidence and to apply it to the category as a whole. Such theories have tended to oscillate between their role as domestic sites and an alternative version that sees them as ceremonial centres (Whittle 1988b).

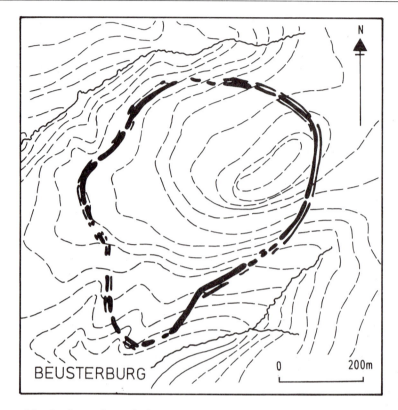

Figure 22. Outline plan of the causewayed enclosure at the Beusterburg, western Germany, after Tackenberg (1951). The contours are at 5-metre intervals.

That ambivalence was widespread. It characterised much of the discussion of causewayed enclosures in this country during the 1970s and 1980s (Whittle 1977; Mercer 1980: ch. 1), and it can also be traced in the French and German litera-ture (Beeching *et al.* 1982; Boelicke *et al.* 1988: 417–26). This uncertainty has had unfortunate consequences, for particularly plausible explanations of individual sites or groups of sites have been extrapolated from one cultural context to another, while the evidence from any one area could be used to rebut the pre-vailing interpretation of the enclosures in another region. Often this has involved drawing comparisons between earthworks that were built at different times. Such appeals to distant comparanda resulted from the desire to fix the 'right' interpretation of these monuments. The views of British prehistorians illustrate this point, for ever since the work of Stuart Piggott in the 1950s there has been a feeling that if they were to discover the correct interpretation of Continental enclosures they would be able to use the same ideas in their own research (see Piggott 1954: 17–32).

Such an appeal to authority is bound to fail. It depends on the existence of traditions of very great antiquity, but these are wedded to an inadequate conception of material culture: one that treats its categories as closed. The work of recent years has shown quite clearly that material culture cannot be studied in this way. Such research stresses its unstable character, its mutability from one context to another (Shanks and Tilley 1987a: ch. 6; Hodder 1991: ch. 7). The self-same elements could be interpreted and reinterpreted through time and space. Thus a portable artefact like an axe might carry quite different connotations according to the ways in which it was obtained and the cultural conditions under which it was used (Bradley and Edmonds 1993). In the same way, pottery styles have lost their neutral character, for they may have played a special role in social transactions in the past (Thomas 1991a: ch. 4). Much the same argument applies to earthwork monuments. Thus Thomas talks of 'reading' such monuments (*ibid.*, ch. 3), and Hodder suggests that Neolithic enclosures had something of the character of texts, to be interpreted by different people in different ways (1988: 69–71).

Discussions of this kind do not go far enough, for they treat several different kinds of material culture in much the same fashion. This procedure does not do justice to the special properties of monumental architecture. Monuments have certain features which make them quite unlike the objects or styles of decoration on which so much discussion has been based.

Their most obvious characteristic is that they are extremely durable, so that some form significant features of the landscape even today. Earthwork enclosures would last for a very long time unless they were levelled deliberately, and that would be difficult to achieve. Thus they might be present in human consciousness whether or not those sites were in active use. They are not like portable artefacts which can be deposited or destroyed; a construction like a megalithic tomb might assume new roles after it had apparently been closed. Such monuments were constantly visible, and in this respect they differ still more radically from other forms of material culture which can be displayed or concealed according to the occasion. Of course, there could be restrictions on who was allowed to visit particular monuments, or on when they could be used, but their scale and resistance to decay mean that for many people they would have posed special problems of interpretation.

The second point applies mainly to the larger monuments. Unlike ceramics or lithic artefacts, it seems likely that their production involved a considerable number of workers. Even though we do not know how long it took to build these sites, practical considerations allow us to estimate the approximate size of the labour forces necessary to create them (Startin and Bradley 1981; Abrams 1989). That does not mean that they need have remained accessible to everyone once their construction was finished; in any case the very idea of 'completion' may be inappropriate, for some earthworks witnessed so many episodes of renewal and modification that it is probably better to think of them as *projects* (see, for example, Pryor 1984: 8–12; Whittle 1988a). It is a familiar argument that the task of building such monuments helped create a sense of group identity: the construction of Neolithic enclosures certainly required more people than most productive activities.

Taken together, these distinctive features of earthwork monuments would give them a special place in human experience, and would also tend to provide them with a lengthy history. Ideas about their origin and significance may have changed quite radically, but it would be difficult to remain innocent of their very existence. The fact of their survival meant that they had to be incorporated in any understanding of the world.

This process of thinking about monuments was not straightforward either, for these constructions could not travel: it was the concept of that monument which passed from one cultural setting to another. Kopytoff (1986) suggests that portable artefacts carry their own histories with them, but in the case of an earthwork enclosure only the ideas behind its creation might have moved. This is utterly different from most forms of material culture. Again, we need to appreciate the special problems of studying the monumental.

FORMS AND TRANSFORMATIONS

There are two ways of taking this discussion further: by reflecting on the distinctive character of individual enclosures and by tracing their transformations over time. They epitomise the two approaches that I have already taken to Neolithic long mounds. Thus in Chapter 3 I discussed their origins among the specific practices taking place in Bandkeramik settlements; and in Chapter 4 I considered the changes that characterise their later history.

It is easier to appreciate the stereotyped character of the enclosures than it is to interpret them, but several elements feature prominently in most discussions, and they are worth mentioning here. As Jan Harding has suggested, on sites with several circuits of earthworks the effect is to emphasise the depth of the passage leading from exterior to interior (Harding 1995; see also Hodder 1990: 160). At the same time, the sheer number of breaks in the perimeter also indicates the openness of the site to people from the surrounding area. It may be possible to combine both those ideas with the suggestion that the segmented groundplan expressed the participation of different groups in the creation of the monument.

It is difficult to assess these arguments, but in a way it may not be necessary to do so, for the point that I wish to stress is how that characteristic groundplan was interpreted and reinterpreted in the past itself. I take my cue from a recent paper by Johnson (1989), in which he argues that one way of incorporating a concept of agency in archaeological research is to contrast very local developments with the long-term structures out of which they arise. As he says:

> Agency is a manipulation of an existing structure that is external to the individual . . . and appears to the agent . . . as something to be drawn upon.

. . . Such a normative outline is not necessarily a repressive, prescriptive one. While to the social agent it appears to be a coherent set of values, *it is one to be drawn upon selectively, manipulated and even inverted.*

(Johnson 1989: 206–7; my emphases)

How can this approach illuminate the history of causewayed enclosures? One of the most widespread practices in Neolithic Europe was the building of earthworks with interrupted ditches. At one level, this seems to have been a process attended by very strict rules, and that may be why enclosures that were built in different periods and different areas followed virtually the same groundplan. At the same time, those monuments appear to have been used in radically different ways from one context to another. If we are to understand these developments we must trace the basic idea of the causewayed enclosure, from its origins at the end of the Linear Pottery Culture through to the Late Neolithic period. As we shall see, this history crosses two important thresholds, and by defining these in some detail it will be easier to reflect on the nature of the sequence as a whole.

In doing so, we must not take advantage of hindsight. We must not suppose that these earthworks were created with some ultimate goal in view: that after a long enough period of experiment causewayed enclosures would assume a definitive form. Rather, the same elements were deployed in different configurations from one cultural setting to another according to local inventiveness and the needs of particular groups of people. Instead of masking so much variation in the interests of a straightforward sequence, we should pay more attention to the contexts in which these enclosures were created. We must also understand the ways in which they were changed. There was always a complicated relationship between tradition and invention, and that is precisely why we can never discover *the* purpose of causewayed enclosures. It is a kind of archaeological research that must be abandoned.

CAUSEWAYED ENCLOSURES IN CONTEXT

As we saw in Chapter 3, the first appearance of enclosures seems to have taken place late in the Linear Pottery Culture (Lüning 1988). Some of these earthworks were closely associated with houses and were found in regions that had already experienced a substantial history of occupation (Boelicke *et al.* 1988: 417–26). The enclosures were usually constructed within a broader concentration of settlements and cemeteries, but at the larger, regional scale they tend to occur most frequently towards the edges of the Neolithic landscape.

There are not many common elements to be found among these early enclosures. Although a few examples were associated with abandoned houses or even with entire settlements, there are other cases in which the same elements appear to have been in use together. There are also earthworks which seem to have been completely isolated. Nor do the sites assume a common form, for the nature and scale of these constructions is by no means consistent. They may be defined by one or more ditches, sometimes backed by palisades, but they do not conform to any single design, although Van Bergh (1991) has suggested that the plans of different examples were laid out according to a system of basic proportions that was shared quite widely. For our purposes, an equally important observation is that segmented earthworks are rare.

The one clear exception is the extensively excavated enclosure at Darion in Belgium (Keeley and Cahen 1989). Like the others, it belongs to the late Bandkeramik, but in this case the site is defined by a segmented ditch and by several lengths of fencing. There were four houses within its interior, as well as distinct areas which may have been used for growing cereals, pasturing livestock and for craft production (see Figure 23). It would be all too easy to treat such a coherent layout as a model for interpreting sites which are less well understood, but while this may be valid for neighbouring sites in Belgium, any extension of the argument to a wider area falls into the trap that this chapter has attempted to expose.

The excavators' interpretation of Darion operates on several different levels. They observe that, like other ditched enclosures in the vicinity, it lies on the outer edge of the area of Bandkeramik expansion. Beyond these sites there are a significant number of Mesolithic settlements, which appear to be of the same date as these earthworks. Keeley and Cahen (1989) observe that there appear to have been few contacts between their inhabitants. The material found on the Mesolithic sites shows very little evidence for exchanges with their neighbours and the same applies to the finds from the monuments themselves. Several of the longhouses, however, had been burnt down during the period of occupation. Two of the excavated enclosures in this area were built as soon as the sites were occupied, while the third was added to an existing settlement. Keeley and Cahen suggest that this could be explained by the uncertain conditions prevailing on the agricultural frontier. Perhaps these earthworks were defences against attack, for colonisation of this region may not have taken place unopposed.

This is a plausible argument, and it is certainly one which accounts for a number of observations. The earthworks are found close to one another on the outer edges of the Neolithic landscape. Two of these settlements had been enclosed from the outset, and, rather unusually, several of the houses had been destroyed by fire. But there are also problems with this interpretation, for, despite the presence of several lengths of palisade at Darion, it is hard to see how the settlement could be protected by a ditch with so many causeways. For our purposes it may be more important to emphasise a different point. At Darion we have a residential site which was obviously defined by a segmented ditch towards the end of the Linear Pottery Culture. Although it is not quite like the earthworks found in west Germany, it forms a vital link with subsequent developments in north-west Europe.

From the end of the Linear Pottery Culture the key feature of the enclosures seems to have been an emphasis on providing a permeable perimeter. This was

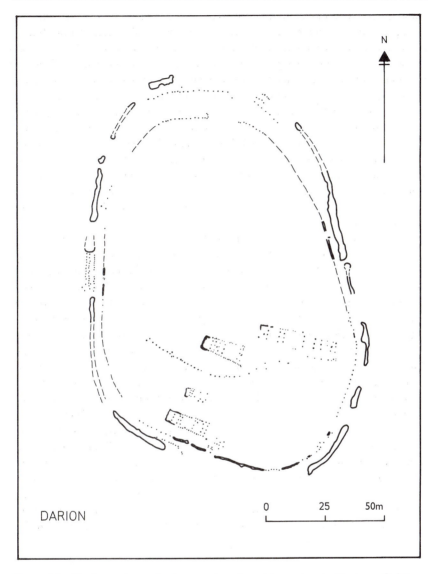

N

DARION

0   25   50m

Figure 23. Outline plan of the enclosed settlement at Darion, Belgium, simplified from Keeley and Cahen (1989).

particularly obvious at the well-known site of Urmitz, where an interrupted palisade existed before any earthworks were built (Boelicke 1976). In some cases the causeways in the ditch were enhanced by wooden gateways (Raetzel-Fabian 1991). There were houses inside a number of these enclosures, but with the demise of flat cemeteries certain of these earthworks seem to have taken on additional roles, and we find evidence of human remains within their area. For example, at Menneville in northern France an enclosure dating from the Rössen period may have enclosed a settlement (Coudart and Demoule 1982), but in this case the excavation also provided evidence of a series of structured deposits including articulated animal bones and the burials of two children covered by red ochre: a practice that recalls the evidence from older graves. At the same time, the enclosure ditch was broken by a series of causeways and shows the sequence of filling and recutting that becomes increasingly common on later sites. Similar evidence is associated with the Michelsberg phase. A good example of this is the enclosed settlement at Mairy in the Ardennes (Marolle 1989). Like Darion and Menneville, this contained a number of houses, but also included a series of pits. These had a complex filling and contained articulated animal bones, as well as elaborate artefacts and complete pots. There seems little doubt that they were formal deposits.

I mentioned the idea advanced by the excavators of Darion that the first enclosures might have been defensive sites. The same interpretation has been suggested for some of the later examples, and with rather more reason, for at a number of sites, particularly in eastern France, there are indications that these possessed substantial stone-faced ramparts not unlike the structures created during later prehistory (Nicardot 1974). Again, there is a danger of framing the argument too rigidly. Not all these enclosures are associated with houses, and in some cases they may have been located in marginal areas of the landscape some distance away from the major settlements of this period. We would be wrong to assume that these earthworks were limited to a single role. For example, at Boury in northern France there is evidence that an enclosure with a considerable rampart had been levelled, and yet overlying the remains of its defences there was an extraordinary series of animal burials, ranged symmetrically on either side of a causeway in the ditch (Lombardo et al. 1984). At a still later stage in the history of this site the same area was used for the deposition of human bones. This sequence is a reminder of how misleading it can be to assume that the range of activities taking place on those sites must have remained constant over time. At Boury we have an enclosure which had apparently been attacked and destroyed, and yet one of the causeways in its ditch provided the focal point for a series of placed deposits.

That particular sequence is also important because it epitomises a significant development in the history of causewayed enclosures. So far, I have followed the changing articulation of enclosures and settlement sites, suggesting how some of the later earthworks assumed additional roles after the Linear Pottery Culture. At the same time, some of the major enclosures were never used as settlements at all. This is a particular development of the Michelsberg phase, and it is found very widely. Some of the recently excavated enclosures are especially elaborate affairs, with multiple ditches, palisades and complex entrance structures (Biel 1991). These ditches contain deposits of human and animal bones, while similar material can be found in pits within their interior. A good example of this practice comes from the type site at Michelsberg itself (Lüning 1967: 113–19 and 297–332).

A particular feature of such finds is the discovery of disarticulated human bones in some of these deposits, for this recalls the evidence from other monuments of this date (Lichardus 1986). Again, there is no uniformity. In north Germany the distribution of enclosures overlaps with that of megalithic tombs (Raetzel-Fabian 1991), yet in northern France deposits of human bone may be associated with enclosures in regions which seem to be without other kinds of mortuary deposit. In such cases human skull fragments are the commonest find and tend to be associated with the upper levels of the enclosure ditches (Mazingue and Mordant 1982). It is especially important to recognise that these sites may also have been set apart from the main areas of domestic occupation. Figure 24 illustrates a completely excavated example in northern France. It may be significant that its earthwork overlies the sites of two earlier longhouses.

A good example of the same transformation of causewayed enclosures is provided by Noyen-sur-Seine (Mordant and Mordant 1977). At different times this was enclosed by an interrupted palisade and by a causewayed ditch, but inside the excavated area there was no convincing evidence of houses. The

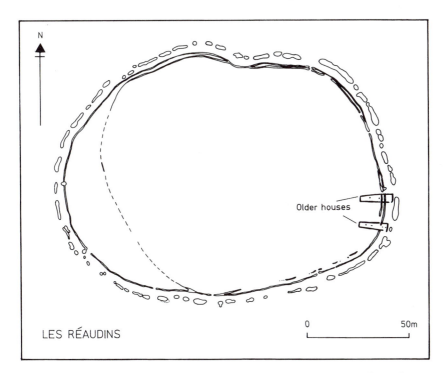

Figure 24. Plan of the causewayed enclosure at Les Réaudins, northern France, simplified from Blanchet (1993). Note how the enclosure overlies the positions of two earlier houses.

excavators recognised local areas of cobbling and also a line of hearths, but their report gives the impression that this was principally a place where artefacts were deposited. Some of these objects had concentrated distributions within the excavated area, including animal bones, quernstones, pottery and a group of axe fragments. There were also ceramic figurines and a perforated human skull. Taken together, such finds seem to suggest that by this stage there may have been a wider range of deposits on these sites and perhaps more concern with the relics of the dead.

It is no accident that the Michelsberg enclosures were the group that Stuart Piggott compared with those in the British Isles (1954: 17–32). There are striking similarities in the forms taken by the earthworks and in the character of the associated material, but once again it is quite misleading to select one version of the causewayed enclosure and to suppose that it represents the entire phenomenon, for even these 'ceremonial' enclosures did not remain entirely unaltered. A second important development took place in widely separated areas around the margins of Neolithic Europe. In western France, for instance, we find further earthworks with interrupted ditches, and once again they contain concentrations of human skull fragments and groups of non-local artefacts (Joussaume and Pautreau 1990: 159–61, 246–90). Here, a new development took place, for some of these sites were rebuilt with large stone-walled ramparts and complicated outworks, which resemble nothing so much as the defences of Iron Age hillforts. These sites continued to form a focus for specialised deposits, but the outward appearance of the enclosures was altered completely.

A number of the same observations apply to the enclosures of south Scandinavia (Madsen 1988). Again, these have a very stereotyped groundplan and seem to have contained placed deposits of exotic and unusual artefacts. Some of these sites are situated near to mortuary monuments. In Scandinavia there may have been another basic change, but one which differed in some respects from developments in Atlantic France. A number of Danish sites seem to have seen a final phase of activity as large open settlements after their earthworks had gone out of use. These settlements were more extensive than those of earlier phases. The development of domestic sites in and around existing enclosures may be shared between Denmark and western France, but again the details are different. In the French example they were turned into hillforts, but in Scandinavia their earthworks were superseded as these sites became unenclosed settlements.

It is less of a surprise, then, that occasional sites in the British Isles should show a rather similar sequence, with a late phase of domestic activity in which enclosures were rebuilt with considerable defences. This is not especially common and very little of the evidence has been published in final form. Even so, it is clear that their earthworks were sometimes recut with continuous ditches and that the ramparts were rebuilt. The entrances to these sites were also modified so that they presented more of a challenge to intruders. The houses found inside a few of these sites perhaps date from this final phase.

The British sequence has one distinctive feature of its own: it was abruptly curtailed. Where enclosures were provided with defences their period of use was much shorter than that of sites in western France, and some of these earthworks seem to have been attacked and destroyed (Mercer 1980). After that, they do not seem to have been maintained. There is some evidence of Later Neolithic activity on the sites of causewayed enclosures in Britain, but the associated material has a rather specialised character; it has close counterparts in the secondary levels of other kinds of Neolithic monument (Thomas 1991a: Figure 5.9), but it is too soon to say whether any of these finds reflect a similar development to the sequence identified in Denmark. The last rather anomalous enclosures in Britain – earthworks like Flagstones (Healy 1997), Stonehenge 1 (Cleal *et al.* 1995: ch. 5) or the inner ring at Briar Hill (Bamford 1985) – were precisely circular structures, which resemble the Late Neolithic monuments that I shall discuss in Part II (see Figure 25).

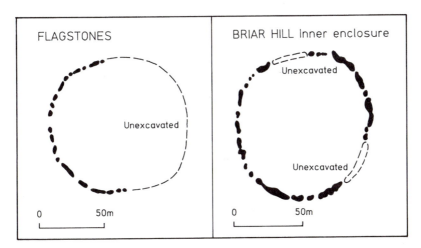

Figure 25. Plans of the causewayed enclosure at Flagstones, after Healy (1997), and the inner earthwork at Briar Hill, after Bamford (1985).

IN RETROSPECT

I have considered the first Neolithic enclosures in north-west Europe and the ways in which their roles were transformed from one area and one cultural setting to another. In the beginning, they were closely integrated into the pattern of settlement and many of these sites were associated with groups of houses. The relationship between these elements was by no means consistent. Sometimes, the enclosure was built after the houses had gone out of use, but in other cases the earthwork marked the boundary of the settlement and may even have offered protection against attack. Yet, with time, all these elements were to change. The earthworks were increasingly constructed towards the margins of the settled land-scape rather than its centre, and the link between these sites and everyday activities became increasingly tenuous. At first some of the domestic enclosures provided an arena for specialised deposits, but eventually these earthworks played a more obvious role in ritual activity. They were no longer occupation sites and become more closely associated with the consumption of special kinds of artefacts. They were apparently used for feasting well outside the domestic arena, and seem also to have been associated with animal sacrifice and with the rites of passage of the dead. As that happened, they assumed an increasingly stereotyped groundplan in which the numerous gaps in the ditches might be echoed by the layout of the banks and fences found inside them. The causeways became an important focus for intentional offerings and their locations were often emphasised by the provision of gateways. On some sites these features may have been levelled between major episodes of use and renewed at regular intervals when the sites were brought back into commission. Minor differences in the ways in which different sections of these barriers were constructed suggests that they were built by different groups of workers drawn from the surrounding area (Edmonds 1993).

These developments are very distinctive, and they are also widely distributed. Although there were differences of detail between the enclosures from one region to another, it seems as if the general trend was away from a domestic role towards a more specialised function as ceremonial centres. One reason why they have received so much attention from archaeologists is because this transition took place as the pattern of settlement changed. Occupation sites became far more ephemeral and, in contrast to the situation during the Linear Pottery Culture, houses are increasingly difficult to identify. For a while it looked as if the cause-wayed enclosures might be the 'missing' settlement sites, but this interpretation has not stood up to scrutiny. Now there seem to be signs of a more mobile pattern of exploitation. Larger areas of the landscape were used, and cereal agriculture may have lost some of its importance to the exploitation of animals (Whittle 1996a: ch. 7).

The first causewayed enclosures seem to have been integrated into the pattern of settlement, and certain sites like Darion and Menneville are among the places where the remains of substantial houses have been found. Enclosures adopted the same groundplan when such settlements were no longer built and, if anything, they followed a still more formal layout. Certainly, there was a greater emphasis on the segmentation of the earthwork perimeter, as if to symbolise the relation-ship between these places and the landscape that extended away from them on every side. It was also at this stage that they became more closely associated with the remains of the dead, whether or not specially built mortuary monuments existed in the same area.

Perhaps these features are linked in a significant way. It seems possible that the continued construction of enclosures in the traditional form was actually intended as a reference to the settlements of the past, in the same way that the newly constructed long barrows referred to the longhouses of a distant age. It may not have been the settlement itself as a group of residential buildings that such monuments were meant to recall, so much as the wider community that had lived together there. The enclosure might act as a testimony of people's attachment to place and to their relationships with one another, even though in practice they may no longer have come into contact on a day-to-day basis. It may be this fusion of history and myth that made it so appropriate that ancestral relics should be deposited at these sites.

If that is true, then the later use of some of the enclosures becomes rather easier to understand. At this point the entire sequence could be reversed so that ceremonial enclosures might be chosen as the sites for settlements or could even be rebuilt as hillforts. In Britain, these places were not particularly suited for domestic activities, for the sites had initially been selected precisely because they were so remote – that is why some of them were originally located in woodland (Edmonds 1993). Maybe they were converted into defended settlements because in the minds of their occupants they were settlements already. Their defenders would be sustained by their knowledge of that mythical past.

One last development should be considered here. Not only did the earthwork boundaries of these enclosures assume a more formal layout with time, the groundplan of some of the enclosures also changed. The earlier enclosures often followed an irregular outline, and many made use of topographical features as well as banks and ditches. That is why so many earthworks were constructed across promontories. This development runs through the entire sequence of causewayed enclosures, but at the same time we find that an increasing proportion of these sites assumed a more regular configuration. The most common form was a circle.

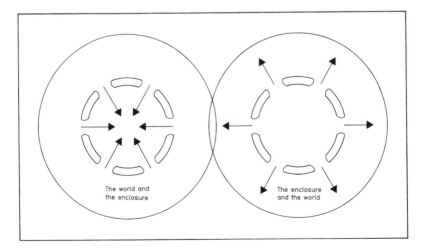

Figure 26. The relationship between causewayed enclosures and the wider landscape.

The circle is the ideal outline for an enclosure of this kind, for its many different entrances would face in every direction, perhaps emphasising its role as the centre of a dispersed community (see Figure 26). It does not matter whether that arrangement reflected the actual distribution of people in the wider country: it would have been more important that this symbolism be understood by those who came to visit these sites. Their presence within this enclosure could have had another meaning too, for this was a specialised arena which stood for the land-scape as a whole. It was the mythical settlement from which they had departed many generations before, and on their return it was the small world that linked them to their past. As the Yugoslav poet Ivan Lalic once wrote, 'Space is only time visible in a different way' (from 'Places we Love', Lalic, 1996). His words provide the conclusion of this chapter and sum up the first part of this book.

Part II

Describing a circle

See how the arched earth does here
Rise in a perfect hemisphere.
The stiffest compass could not strike
A line more circular and like,
Nor softest pencil draw a brow
So equal as this hill does bow.
It seems as for a model laid
And that the world by it was made.
(from Andrew Marvell, 'Upon the Hill and Grove at Bilbrough')

Chapter 6

The persistence of memory

Ritual, time and the history of
ceremonial monuments

Ritual often employs a distinctive notion of time, which stands apart from
the pace of everyday events. It draws its potency from this feature, and
that is why the assumptions that it enshrines are so difficult to challenge.
At the same time, the settings in which supposedly timeless rituals take
place may actually change considerably. Thus it is that on one level the
famous monument at Stonehenge retains essentially the same layout over
a period of fifteen hundred years, while at another its structural history
summarises in monumental form the changing concerns of the societies
who built it. That interplay between the apparently fixed forms of ritual
monuments and the more varied ways in which they were interpreted and
used provides the main theme for the studies in Chapters 7 to 10.

INTRODUCTION

The first part of this book has been concerned with transitions. It has considered
the changes of ideology that seem to have accompanied the first adoption of
domesticates, traced the emergence of long mounds from an origin among the
houses of the Linear Pottery Culture, and has also considered how the changing
form of mortuary monuments might illustrate a growing concern with ancestry.
The last chapter analysed causewayed enclosures, charting a rather similar development to the history of the long barrows. The kinds of earthwork boundary that
had originally been associated with settlements were still being built after the
character of domestic activities had changed, and in this case the enclosures
assumed largely new roles in ritual and the treatment of the dead.

Such changes are easy to recognise, even if they are difficult to interpret. They
can be identified because certain structural principles, like building a rectangular
mound or digging a segmented ditch, were translated from one kind of context
to another over a considerable period of time. There are much greater problems
in addressing the issues considered in Part II. So far, my discussion has focused
on selected monuments distributed over an extensive area: Chapter 2, for
instance, extended from Russia to the Danube, and Chapter 3 from Bohemia to

Brittany. I also discussed monuments with a very long history: from about 4500 to 3000 BC for the enclosures and even longer in the case of burial mounds. Now we should consider the understanding of monuments at an altogether more detailed level.

To do so raises a whole series of new issues. We need to focus on a smaller area and on sequences calibrated at much finer intervals. We can no longer treat particular forms of monument separately from one another, and we must also consider how far these 'types' were ever truly distinct. To do so means that Part II must also address more detailed questions than the earlier chapters of this book. Having suggested some very general changes in the ways in which people perceived time and space, we need to define them more exactly. How far do the changes in the character of monuments reflect corresponding changes in the ways in which they were used? How sensitive was prehistoric architecture to changes in the audience to whom it was addressed? How were these monuments related to the landscapes in which they were built? And how far can that relationship be used to identify developments in the political life of the community?

In Part I it was possible to make some progress because the discussion was conducted at such a general level. The emergence of particular types of monuments took place alongside equally gradual changes in the pattern of settlement. But can any progress be made when we are studying changes that happened over a much shorter period, or is our chronology simply too coarse to allow this approach? I do not doubt that the dating of many monuments could be improved by a more refined analysis, but to a large extent the answer to this question depends on how we can resolve a number of abstract problems. Quite simply, we have to decide whether the chronological resolution of this kind of study allows such an ambitious approach to the evidence.

I shall begin by attempting to resolve this problem, and in the course of doing so I shall suggest how the history of monumental architecture might be studied at a more detailed level. Then I shall attempt to illustrate this proposal with an account of the well-known monument at Stonehenge. Chapters 7 to 9 will build on the same ideas by discussing different aspects of other British and Irish monuments dating from the same period, before Chapter 10 takes us full circle by reconsidering the relationship between farming and monument building. This time the discussion is not concerned with the Early Neolithic, when the first of these constructions were built, but with the Later Bronze Age, when many of these sites were transformed.

TIME AND HISTORY

We must begin with the problem of *time*. Over the past hundred years archaeologists have found many ways of working out a time scale. From typology to radiocarbon dating, they have emphasised the importance of establishing a sequence, for, as Lévi-Strauss once said, 'there is no history without dates' (1966: 258). But dates are only a way of measuring time. This chapter contends that, without a clearer conception of time itself, it may be difficult to make the transition from chronological studies to interpretation.

How should we think of the relationship between chronology and time? The answer seems self-evident, but in fact it raises a significant theoretical problem. The conception of time used by archaeologists is of quite recent origin. It is a time that can be measured and divided precisely: the time scale of the modern economy. Shanks and Tilley, who make this observation, believe that in their unreflecting use of this idea archaeologists are lending legitimacy to a modern, Western view of the world (1987b: ch. 5), yet the creation of chronologies – especially those founded on absolute dating – must be one area in which material originating in the past actually constrains interpretations in the present.

These authors offer a series of useful distinctions between the conceptions of time used in chronological studies and the experience of people outside the modern world system. The difference is between 'human' or 'substantial' time and chronological or 'abstract' time. Substantial time is marked by human experience; in abstract time it is measured. In one case people submit themselves to the passage of time; in the other, time is managed. As they say, human time consists of many recurrent moments, but abstract time is broken into equal segments, which are endlessly repeated. More important for the present discussion, human time can also be backward looking; people live their lives in relation to the past, and they understand their world by referring to tradition. Abstract time, on the other hand, involves rational calculation and can be used to plan the future.

Shanks and Tilley are not alone in emphasising different kinds and perceptions of time (Adam 1990; Gell 1992; Gosden 1994). It was the great French historian Fernand Braudel who suggested that the past could be considered on several levels (Braudel 1969). Time could be measured at three different scales, and each would allow us to study a different kind of history. There was the *longue durée*, which we can think of as 'geographical' time; this operates at the scale of environmental change. There was 'social' time, which measured out the history of particular groups of people; and there was individual time, which Braudel called 'the history of events'.

All these time scales contribute to the archaeological record, but each is studied in a different way (Bailey 1983). Geographical time is perhaps the time scale closest to our chronologies. In particular, it is the time scale of environmental archaeology, and those who work at this level often see social developments as minor interruptions to the broader pattern of change. Post-processualists, on the other hand, emphasise the role of the individual, and sometimes they operate on a very short time scale indeed. This is best compared with the practice of social anthropology, where most of the classic texts discuss observations made during brief periods of fieldwork. That leaves 'social' time, which should be a major focus of interest for archaeology, and it is here that we are faced with difficulties.

The historian can choose the time scale at which to work, but archaeologists face the problem of chronological resolution. Even on the most optimistic estimate, it seems unlikely that prehistorians will be able to work with blocks of time of much less than fifty years; often these units are longer, like the successive phases defined by Bronze Age metalwork in Europe. The deposition of a hoard, for example, may be a single event, whereas the hoard itself can only be dated to the nearest century. How can we measure the development of particular societies when the intervals between our observations are set so far apart?

Social changes can happen through a whole series of short-term events, but, as we have seen, they can only be recognised by archaeologists working at a longer time scale. Numerous individual acts may be apparent, from making an artefact to building a monument, but they are set against a very coarse chronology. Consider the question of prehistoric economies: archaeologists can recognise environmental changes at one scale and the behaviour of individuals at another, but they lack the chronological precision that will permit them to investigate human intentions. Without that information, Ingold argues, '*the object of prehistory must be cultural adaptation rather than social evolution*' (1984: 12, my emphasis).

TIME AND RITUAL

But is it true that archaeology cannot find its way between these two extremes? Although our chronologies will never be exact, something may be wrong with this conception of time. Even at an empirical level, there do seem to be objections, for many features of the archaeological record which can hardly be described as 'cultural adaptation' are very long-lived indeed. Among the most obvious examples are styles of public monuments of the kind considered in Chapters 4 and 5. Like art styles or the deposition of hoards, these extend into the *longue durée*.

Public monuments, art styles and the deposition of hoards have one feature in common, for all three phenomena provide evidence of ritual rather than subsistence. This is important not only because ritual plays such a central role in studies of prehistoric archaeology, but because it may involve a rather different conception of time from everyday affairs. 'Human time' is by no means monolithic. Bloch (1977) makes the point in his famous essay 'The past and the present in the present'. Although this idea has been criticised (Gell 1992: chs. 9–11), it seems that more than one sense of time can often be found in the same society. Everyday activities may be conducted according to a practical understanding of time, but there are many cases in which ritual may uphold a different view of the world. To some extent, the distinction is that between 'habit' and 'public time' (Gosden 1994), but this difference should not be overemphasised, as they represent the opposite ends of what is usually a continuum.

Bloch's concern is with the distinctive nature of ritual communication and the ways in which it operates in society. He has studied these in a number of publications (1974, 1977, 1985, 1986). Taken together, they suggest another way of viewing archaeological chronologies. For Bloch, public rituals communicate through very specialised media. They follow a set pattern, and their contents are formalised to an extent that allows little modification. That is why they may communicate through song or dance, or employ forms of language not in everyday use. The texts may be accompanied by prescribed postures, gestures and movements, and they can be characterised by a restricted vocabulary. There may be further rules that determine how the texts are to be performed, and these may include specialised forms of utterance – a good example would be plainchant. These are all features by which rituals come to be memorised, so that they are transmitted from one generation to the next (Connerton 1989). Most important of all, the texts of such rituals may not vary and employ archaic forms of language that are carefully preserved. As Bloch says, the effect is to protect the contents of such performances from evaluation or challenge. Ritual is a special form of human communication, and by its very nature cannot be discussed by the participants. Barrett (1991a) likens this distinction to the difference between holding a conversation and reading a text.

It is the contrast with everyday communication that informs the notion of ritual time. Bloch distinguishes between mundane conceptions of time which govern the conduct of everyday affairs, such as the sowing and harvesting of crops, and ritual time, which involves the merging of the past in the present. We see this in the use of archaic language, but it is also a way in which the ritual expression of fundamental values is distanced from everyday experience. Because the basic beliefs of society lie outside the passage of time, they cannot easily be challenged. Bloch goes on to suggest that there is a direct relationship between the existence of these two ways of perceiving time and the presence of social distinctions which can be protected by means of ritual. In that sense, rituals maintain social divisions by making them part of a timeless natural order.

The fact that public rituals retain so much stability does not mean that such societies stay the same. If ritual helps to preserve the social order, it can be manipulated with a different end in view, and this is of particular importance to the archaeologist. Bloch (1986) traces the history of one public ritual used by the Merina of Madagascar. Documentary research shows clearly that this ceremony has maintained the same form over more than 200 years. The words and actions remained virtually unaltered, as did the different roles played by the participants, but the scale of the ritual has changed, and so have the locations where it is performed and the number of people taking part. What had once been a smallscale local ritual was used to support the growth of a royal dynasty. Later, it was employed as one of the focal points of opposition to French colonial rule. There were very real political changes during those 200 years, but some of those changes were more effective because they preserved an appearance of stability.

This is not to say that public rituals of this kind are found universally. They characterise what Sahlins calls *prescriptive* rather than *performative* structures – societies 'with bounded groups and compelling rules that prescribe in advance much of the way people act and interact' (1985: 28). In such groups 'nothing is new, or at least happenings are valued for their similarity to the system as constituted. What happens, then, is the projection of the existing order. . . . All is execution and repetition' (*ibid.*, p. xii). In performative structures, on the other hand, 'the cultural order reproduces itself in and as change. Its stability is a volatile history of the changing fortunes of persons and groups.' Again, these are ideal types and elements of both may be found in the same society. Sahlins acknowledges this point, and much the same observation is made by Bloch (1985: 35–6).

Rowlands (1993) has drawn attention to a similar contrast, which is relevant to any account of prehistoric monuments. This concerns different ways of transmitting memory. The first is the transmission of culture through the creation of structures which are intended to endure: 'Remembering is . . . a form of work and is inseparable from the motive to memorialise. . . . Building memorials and monuments are part of the material culture of remembering' (*ibid.*, p. 144). These are *inscribed practices*, because they leave a lasting trace behind them; the comparison with an inscription is particularly appropriate in this case. *Incorporated practices*, on the other hand, take a completely different form:

> In contexts where objects are destroyed or taken out of circulation through burial or some other form of intentional symbolism, *such objects become a memory in their absence*, and therefore the essence of what has to be remembered. The opportunities for manipulating the possibilities of repetition are . . . abolished in an act of sacrifice or destruction that severs connection with its original status.
>
> (*ibid.*, p. 146, my emphases)

The two processes are incompatible with one another, and for that reason we might expect them to be found in different periods of prehistory. A good example of this contrast is the sequence in Bronze Age Europe in which a widespread tradition of burial mounds containing grave goods went out of use at just the time when similar objects were deposited in rivers (Bradley 1990). In Sahlins's (1985) terminology this transition may also have marked the change from a prescriptive to a performative structure.

If this suggestion is correct, Bloch's ideas would seem to be more helpful in studying societies that built lasting monuments. Perhaps some of the fundamental rituals responsible for the maintenance of prehistoric society really can be recognised, despite the imperfections of our chronology. This is possible precisely because in certain societies it is the nature of public ritual to maintain its stability over long periods. Archaeologists are capable of recognising some of the elements in such ceremonies: monuments whose special forms may have influenced the movements of the participants; art styles that could have reinforced the traditional messages enshrined in ritual; even the artefacts deposited in the course of such performances. At the same time, Bloch's work provides a warning against taking such signs of 'continuity' too literally, for, at one level, the maintenance of ritual systems seems to have played an essentially political role. We can best understand how the past was deployed in a changing present by seeing how far such evidence altered its contexts through time. Is there archaeological evidence that the scale or setting of traditional practices was changing? And, more important, under what circumstances were these traditions eventually rejected? By playing off ritual time against the archaeological evidence of sequence, we may be better equipped to explore the nature of social evolution.

So far, I have suggested that Braudel's three time scales cut across the fundamental division between ritual and mundane time which is so central to the operation of traditional societies. It is the fact that ritual can operate in the *longue durée* that means that archaeologists are not limited to studying adaptation. Instead of Braudel's concern with geographical, social and individual time – a scheme which demands more chronological precision than we possess at present – we should concern ourselves with the contrasts described by Bloch. How far can archaeological chronologies provide a commentary on the growth and dissolution of ritual systems in prehistory? By observing the interplay of ritual and mundane time, we can practise a form of contextual archaeology, but one which makes a proper use of sequence. In doing so, we can investigate some of the fundamental changes that took place in prehistoric society. Our long time scale is no longer a disadvantage; in this context it could even be a strength.

RITUAL, TIME AND HISTORY

I referred earlier to Ingold's (1984) assertion that the prehistorian can investigate cultural adaptation, but is prevented from studying social evolution because of the generalised character of archaeological chronology. That may be too pessimistic. In particular, this limitation need not extend to those societies with what Sahlins (1985) calls 'prescriptive' structures, for some of the social changes that are missed on a year-to-year basis can still be identified by archaeologists because of the slower pace of ritual time. I shall illustrate how this can be done, using the history of one famous monument whose role in public ritual has never been disputed.

That monument is Stonehenge, in southern England (Cleal *et al.* 1995). The site was used for practically 1,500 years, yet elements of every successive phase of construction and reconstruction are still visible to us today. They would have been even more obvious in the past, when each of these features could have carried a significance that is now lost. The surviving monument encapsulates an extraordinary history, but its layout also maintains a striking continuity from its earliest use to its final phases. Throughout that time it was defined by the same circular earthwork, with just two entrances controlling access from outside. After its initial construction, the bank and ditch were respected but no longer maintained, yet in virtually every phase the central area was occupied by circular settings of uprights, of stone and quite possibly of timber. In more than one period the same parts of the monument provided a focus for intentional deposits of artefacts and bones, while the landscape visible from the centre of the site contained a series of monuments dedicated to the dead. Even when the site was abandoned, the remains of the first Stonehenge could still be identified: the bank and ditch survived intact, and shallow hollows containing offerings of human bone and other material could still be recognised on the surface. The monument remained the pivotal point of a landscape in which the distribution of human activity was constantly changing.

Modern visitors find it confusing when they are told that the visible monument – apparently such a unified conception – is actually an amalgam of many different phases of construction and reconstruction. On the other hand, this may be its essential feature. The monument illustrates wider changes so effectively because so much was retained from the past. This account follows a recent reassessment of the sequence at Stonehenge – the first to be based on a proper study of the results of excavation at the site – and does not suggest any radical departures from that account (Cleal *et al.* 1995). It does, however, replace my own interpretation of this evidence published four years earlier (Bradley 1991). For our purposes, the value of this sequence is that it illustrates very clearly the interplay between the apparently continuous use of one ceremonial monument and changes in its character that shed light on more general developments in prehistory. We can divide that sequence into four basic phases.

The earliest phase of monument building at Stonehenge took place between about 3000 and 2900 BC and resulted in the construction of a precisely circular earthwork enclosure defined by an internal bank and an external ditch (see Figure 27; Cleal *et al.* 1995: ch. 5). That ditch may originally have been divided into roughly sixty segments, but there were probably only three formal entrances to the enclosure, one of which was blocked at a later stage. Both the main entrances were marked by deposits of cattle bones; radiocarbon dating shows that these were already a century or more old when they were placed in the ditch. There was also evidence for burning at the northern entrance to the monument, and it was here that a major group of antler picks was discovered; a significant proportion of the raw material had been obtained by hunting. It seems possible that behind the bank and running concentric with the ditch was a palisade defined by a series of large posts spaced at approximately equal intervals. Their position in the sequence cannot be established with any certainty, but it is known that a number of large enclosures were built in the same manner around 3000 BC (A. Gibson 1996: 345–7).

This first earthwork at Stonehenge is best considered as a very late causewayed enclosure. Indeed, it was treated as such in Chapter 5. It is a precisely circular monument of a type which is represented on at least two other sites in southern

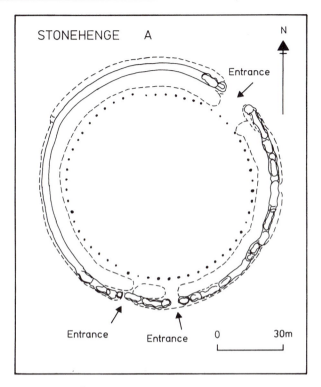

Figure 27. Stonehenge as a causewayed enclosure with an internal palisade. Modified from Cleal *et al.* (1995).

England, and the placing of cattle bones on the ditch bottom at its entrances is in keeping with what is known about other causewayed enclosures in Britain. It was built as the local tradition of long barrows went out of use. Although human bones were not associated with the first monument at Stonehenge, there may well be a link with the commemoration of the dead, for cattle bones were often deposited at mortuary monuments. In fact, in one of the latest long barrows in Wessex a row of three cattle skulls had been deposited along the axis of the mound, one of them in the place normally occupied by human remains (Ashbee *et al.* 1979: 247). There is evidence of domestic artefacts from fieldwork to the east of Stonehenge and particularly on the higher ground above the River Avon. More extensive collections of surface finds recovered closer to the monument may also date from the period in which the enclosure was built, but there is no evidence to suggest that these locations necessarily mark the positions of permanent settlements (J. Richards 1990: ch. 10).

In its second phase, which extended until approximately 2400 BC, Stonehenge changed its character completely (see Figure 28; Cleal *et al.* 1995: ch. 6). The earthwork was substantially remodelled. Large parts of the excavated chalk were

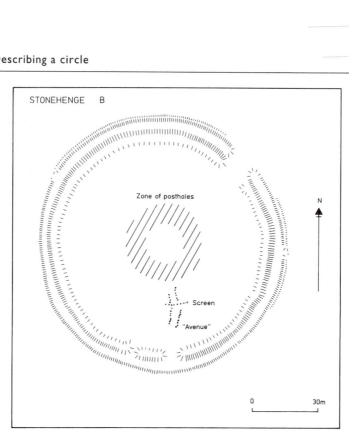

STONEHENGE   B

Zone of postholes

N

Screen

"Avenue"

0   30m

Figure 28. The timber phase at Stonehenge, showing the 'avenue', the 'screen' and the zone of postholes in the central area. Modified from Cleal *et al.* (1995)

levelled into the ditch, although this may not have taken place in one operation, and groups of artefacts and animal bones were deposited in its filling. These were mainly concentrated towards the positions of all three entrances and included a few sherds belonging to a widely distributed ceramic tradition known as Grooved Ware.

As this process developed, a new element is found at Stonehenge. A large number of human cremations were deposited in the uppermost levels of the ditch, and more were placed in small excavations in the bank and along other parts of the perimeter of the monument. A further series were placed in the upper filling of the holes left by the ring of posts ascribed to the first period of activity. These cremations were accompanied by bone pins, and by occasional artefacts, including a fine stone macehead, which have their counterparts on other sites of this period. Although this has been described as a cremation ceme- tery, the fact that equivalent deposits at other monuments include collections of artefacts or animal bones suggests that it may be better to think of these as a series of offerings made around the edge of an earthwork whose significance was rapidly changing.

The interior of Stonehenge also changed its character at this time. I mentioned that all the entrances were emphasised by deposits in and around the ditch: stone, bone and antler artefacts to the south of the site; chalk artefacts around the blocked south-west entrance; and antler tools and human bones, which were found mainly towards the north. Each of the main entrances into the site seems to have taken a more elaborate form. A large series of upright posts in the northern entrance is attributed to this phase and seems to define ten parallel rows of uprights crossing the causeway in the enclosure ditch. The route leading into the enclosure from the southern entrance appears to have been marked by two lines of posts, set only 4 metres apart and interrupted by a more substantial wooden screen, which would have protected the central area from view.

In the middle of the monument, excavation has revealed a considerable concentration of post holes, whose distribution is confined to the area that was later occupied by settings of stones. These postholes are generally earlier in date than the stone-built monument and are normally considered to be all that remains of a substantial timber circle or circles of the type that has been excavated on nearby sites like Durrington Walls and Woodhenge (Wainwright and Longworth 1971).

It is ironic that the closest counterparts for nearly all these features are found in what are described as 'henges', for the term derives from this particular site. Such earthworks are normally defined by an external bank and an internal ditch and date from the Late Neolithic. That hardly describes the situation at Stonehenge, for it is earlier than other earthworks of this kind in southern England and its perimeter takes a quite different form; as we have seen, it is much closer to that of a causewayed enclosure. Even so, the other features observed during the second phase at Stonehenge have affinities with this new tradition. Henge monuments are characteristically associated with structured deposits of artefacts and animal bones, and human cremations are frequently found as secondary deposits in their earthwork boundaries or associated with the postholes in their interior. Generally speaking, the associated artefacts belong to the Grooved Ware tradition. The entrances of these monuments provide a particular focus for symbolic elaboration, as do the timber circles often found within them. The internal structures at Stonehenge – in particular the 'avenue' and 'screen' associated with the southern entrance – are precisely paralleled in a henge monument at Durrington Walls, 3 kilometres from Stonehenge (Wainwright and Longworth 1971). There are other monuments of the same kind nearby, and finds of Grooved Ware occur widely in the surrounding area, although again it is difficult to establish whether they result from sustained occupation (J. Richards 1990: ch. 10). In some ways, there seems to have been an effort to adapt the remains of Stonehenge until they conformed more closely to these new constructions.

We can also make comparisons over a much greater distance, for it seems that many of the features of these sites, including their internal ditches, the timber circles and even the types of artefact associated with them, originated in northern

Britain (Harding and Lee 1987). In this respect, they differ from the markedly southern distribution of most of the causewayed enclosures. The evidence from Stonehenge is by no means clearcut, but it does suggest the remodelling of the existing site into a kind of monument which is found extremely widely. Its stereotyped groundplan has its counterparts at scattered locations throughout the British Isles, suggesting that those who used Stonehenge belonged to a more extensive social network than their predecessors. Instead of the rather local context of the first Stonehenge, this evidence evokes more distant places and beliefs.

The next major change can also be understood in relation to wider developments in Britain. This was the replacement of the timber structures at the centre of the monument in stone (see Figure 29; Cleal *et al.* 1995: ch. 7). This is something that happened at many other sites, from Wessex to the Western Isles, although it must not be mistaken for an invariable sequence, for there are many stone circles without wooden predecessors just as there are also examples built before most of the timber circles were constructed (Barnatt 1989: ch. 4; A. Gibson 1994: 191–223). The settings at Stonehenge went though a history of creation and rearrangement involving at least five successive structures, but the

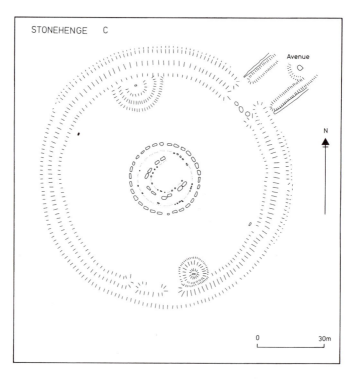

Figure 29. The developed stone structure at Stonehenge, after Cleal *et al.* (1995).

details are less important than the fact that for roughly 900 years, between about 2500 and 1600 BC, the site was subjected to constant reorganisation: a process that must have involved the efforts of a large labour force.

Despite these admittedly important changes of detail, there are two principal elements in the central stone setting: a circle or circles of upright stones and a horseshoe-shaped setting open to the northern entrance to the site. The sequence began with two concentric circles of specially selected stone, built about 2500 BC, and these were replaced by the most impressive features of the monument that we see today: the great circle of upright sarsens, with lintels joining the tops of the stones, and an internal setting facing the entrance, which was built in a similar way. At times, both these arrangements were reinforced by smaller settings of monoliths, one of which may have employed similar lintels, but the basic layout was never radically changed.

Two features are especially important here. Despite a long history of excavation, there is nothing to suggest that the distribution of postholes in the site extended outside the area occupied by the stone circles. This lends weight to the contention that they were intended to replace timber settings at the centre of the monument. At the same time, the recently published radiocarbon dates for the monument show that the great sarsen structure, with its unique arrangement of lintels, was much older than was once believed. This implies that it should really be considered in relation to the timber buildings of the Late Neolithic period, and might explain an observation that was first made many years ago, that the use of mortice and tenon joints in building this monument is a direct reference to the techniques of timber carpentry (A. Gibson 1994: 197, 211; Whittle 1996b).

It was during the period in which stone settings were erected at the heart of Stonehenge that an earthwork avenue was built to link the monument to the River Avon. The final section of this earthwork also followed the alignment of the midsummer sunrise, and it seems as if the axis of the entire monument was adjusted slightly to ensure that this would happen. The construction of the Avenue is important in another way, too, for it was during this period that the surrounding landscape became the focus for an extraordinary concentration of burial mounds. Some of the most conspicuous of these were built on the higher ground, so that to anyone inside the circle they would appear on the skyline. The barrows found near to the site can be unusually large and they tend to be associated with rich burials. The Avenue leads towards Stonehenge through one of the most imposing of all these groups of mounds.

The stone settings inside the monument are linked with the wider landscape in many complex ways. They provide a permeable screen though which partici-pants in the ceremonies carried out in the interior would be able to view the burial mounds distributed across the surrounding landscape. The Avenue linking the monument to the River Avon would have led the visitor through an area in which such barrows might appear even more prominent than the stone settings themselves, which are not visible for most of its course. Yet the link between

Stonehenge and the wider world was also made explicit by the way in which the midsummer sun might seem to travel along the course of that Avenue and light the horseshoe-shaped setting at the centre of the monument.

This event would appear timeless, and the same might be true of the stone settings, which accurately reproduced both the groundplan and most probably the constructional techniques of older timber circles in the surrounding landscape. Yet, again, there is a paradox, for it was this supposedly timeless structure that was built and taken down on so many occasions that it is difficult to believe that it was ever intended to assume a definitive form. Just as the burials in the surrounding area might change their entire configuration as part of the politics played out in the wider community, the appropriate form for this monument was no doubt a contentious issue throughout its lengthy history.

The final phase of Stonehenge was a simpler structure, consisting of two concentric rings of pits enclosing the stone settings erected during the previous phase (see Figure 30; Cleal *et al.* 1995: ch. 7). Their dates are between about 1600 and 1500 BC. These features silted up naturally and cannot have contained uprights, although their profiles are so similar to those of some of the sockets thought to have held bluestones during an earlier phase that it seems quite

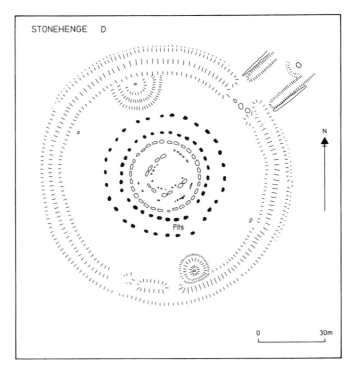

Figure 30. The final structural phase at Stonehenge, emphasising the two rings of pits enclosing the stone circles. Modified from Cleal *et al.* (1995).

possible they mark the position of a further extension to the monument that was never completed. Whatever the correct answer, a number of antlers were placed on the bottoms of these pits before they began to silt up.

The existing stone structure was modified during this final phase, for at least three of the stones in the setting of sarsen trilithons were decorated with carvings of metalwork. There are at least forty-three carvings of unhafted axeheads and one depiction of a dagger complete with its hilt. The axes are of a type normally dated to about 1500 BC, and this is compatible with the age of the dagger carving with which they are associated. It is many years later, however, than the date at which this stone setting is likely to have been erected. Such axes are unusual in graves and are more often found in votive deposits (Needham 1988), but the solitary dagger recalls the examples found in nearby burials. Indeed, the unusual association between such daggers and axes is found in the richest of all the burial mounds visible from Stonehenge: the exceptional assemblage from Bush Barrow.

There may be a direct relationship between the last constructional phases at Stonehenge and the increasingly complex distribution of cemeteries in the surrounding landscape (see Figure 31). Woodward and Woodward (1996) have suggested that this phase saw the development of two concentric rings of barrows in the area around the monument. The mounds in the inner ring are clearly visible from the centre of the stone circle, and their siting seems to echo the organisation of the site itself (Cleal *et al.* 1985: 34–40). Barrett (1990) has suggested that the growth of barrow cemeteries is related to more complex procedures in the staging of funerals and to a growing emphasis on genealogy and inheritance. At all events, the commitment of so much human effort to this monument was followed by a wider transformation. After 1500 BC few, if any, large monuments were built entirely for public rituals, and there is less to suggest that such close ties were maintained with the past. Rather, there is evidence for more obvious changes in the settled landscape, including the creation of field systems (J. Richards 1990: ch. 10), and for episodes of conspicuous consumption of an altogether different kind. The new system had more in common with Sahlins's performative structures. It was based on different considerations and had no place for a monument whose very appearance was a statement of its earlier history.

CONCLUSION

This has been a selective account of a monument whose every interpretation is controversial, but it does serve to illustrate some wider points. The sequence at Stonehenge presents an appearance of massive continuity, but it does so against a background of drastic change. Each of these changes is represented at this site, but the relationship is sometimes indirect. The cross references between the monument and the activities in the wider landscape may seem rather oblique,

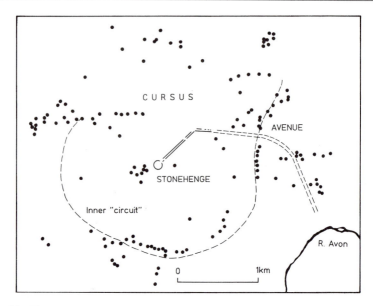

Figure 31. The relationship between Stonehenge and barrow cemeteries in the surrounding landscape, modified from Woodward and Woodward (1996). The monument is ringed by groups of burial mounds but linked to the outer world by its Avenue.

but to some extent this results from the intersection of different time scales. The fascinating feature is that the changes that we recognise at Stonehenge itself are less abrupt than those we can identify in the world about it, as if those broader developments had to be interpreted and assimilated in relation to existing practice. In the end, like the Renaissance Theatre of Memory (Yates 1966: ch. 6), every element referred to something in the past.

To some extent, that is how ritual works, and, as we shall see, it is certainly the way in which the creation and use of monuments reflects wider changes in society at large. The last four chapters of the book extend from the history of this single site to its wider setting among the types of monument in Britain and Ireland. Using the same basic ideas, they seek to trace their history over the same period of time.

Chapter 7

The public interest

Ritual and ceremonial, from passage graves to henges

This chapter uses current controversy over the sequence at Newgrange to introduce a number of issues concerned with the structural development of British and Irish monuments. It contends that nearly all the different 'types' of monument found in the Late Neolithic and Early Bronze Age can be understood as interpretations of a circular archetype which reflects a more general perception of the world. This extends from the settings of pebbles found beneath some of the Irish tombs to the carved decoration associated with these sites, and from the placing of timber circles around their edges to the layout of the burial mounds themselves. It also extends to the massive enclosures created beyond these tombs. This chapter argues that such a development marks a significant threshold in the use of monumental architecture. It involves a change from the essentially private space of the tomb, which few people could enter, to the creation of open arenas as a theatre for more public events.

INTRODUCTION

The starting point for this discussion is provided by the megalithic tombs of the Boyne valley in Ireland. On the inside these are characterised by passage graves of the kind whose origins were discussed in Chapter 4. Externally, they take the form of precisely circular mounds. It is that element of circularity that I shall consider in the remaining chapters of this book.

The best known of these tombs is Newgrange. This is because the excavations here are fully published and because the site has been reconstructed and put on display. Both elements are controversial, as we shall see. There is disagreement over the sequence of monuments on the site, and many people also reject the excavator's reconstruction of the facade of the monument, which is the form in which we view Newgrange today. The purpose of this chapter is not to take sides in these controversies, but to show how the issues that are debated in relation to this one famous site may bear on a more fundamental question in the understanding of monuments: the relationship between the form taken by the architecture and the kind of audience to whom it was addressed.

I find it most revealing that the report on the excavations at Newgrange should have been divided into two volumes, in entirely different formats and issued by different publishers (M. O'Kelly 1982; C. O'Kelly 1983) . At first sight, there is an obvious justification for this procedure, for the first volume to appear was concerned with the megalithic tomb and the structures which accompanied it, whereas the second presented the results of work on a 'settlement' which developed in front of the monument after the tomb had gone out of use. In contrast to the monumental architecture of the passage grave, all the components of this settlement were interpreted in terms of everyday activity.

This radical division between the sacred and secular uses of the site has not proved satisfactory, and even at the time when the supposedly domestic site was published there were problems with this interpretation, for on one side of the entrance to the monument there were concentric arcs of pits, which were not easy to interpret as evidence of a domestic building (C. O'Kelly 1983: 16–21). Subsequent work on the site has shown that these formed part of an enormous circular enclosure built alongside the tomb, which occupied almost the same surface area as the mound itself (Sweetman 1985). Some of the pits contained human cremations, rather like those found in the second phase at Stonehenge. Whatever the controversies surrounding the extraordinary site at Newgrange, it is quite clear that this was a later development than the passage grave. It is associated with a series of radiocarbon dates which fall in the Late Neolithic period and with sherds we can now identify as Grooved Ware. These also have their counterparts at Stonehenge.

The circle of pits at Newgrange does not impinge directly on the tomb itself, although a smaller passage grave is included within its area. It does, however, cut across the course of a circle of massive monoliths which are approximately concentric with the kerb of the original monument (see Figure 32). The relationship between these two circles has generated considerable controversy. The original excavator, O'Kelly, believed that the stone circle at Newgrange was either built before the tomb was constructed, or both were created at the same time as one another. The monoliths were in place before any material slipped from the mound. In some cases that debris seems to have accumulated against the upright stones, demonstrating that they were already in position by that stage. In another instance, one of the monoliths had fallen, but lay directly on the old ground surface, showing that at that point in the sequence the structure of the mound was still intact (M. O'Kelly 1982: ch. 6). The front facing of that mound collapsed before the period of O'Kelly's Beaker settlement, for the structures associated with that phase overlay the fallen material.

Sweetman's subsequent excavation at Newgrange did not support O'Kelly's interpretation. It suggested that one of the upright stones might have been bedded in the filling of a trench that was not dug until that later phase of activity on the site (Sweetman 1985: 214–16). The two interpretations are incompatible. The only way of reconciling these observations is to suggest that the trench itself was not a secondary feature of the monument or that this particular monolith

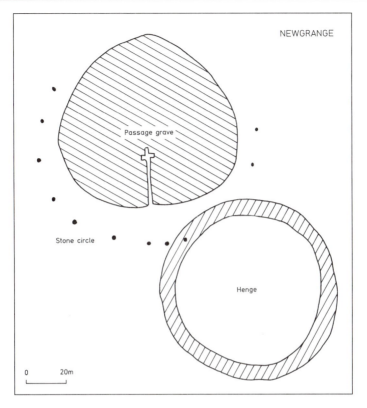

NEWGRANGE

Passage grave

Stone circle

Henge

0   20m

Figure 32. Outline plan of the passage grave and timber circle at Newgrange, after M. O'Kelly (1982) and Sweetman (1985).

had been re-erected. Otherwise, it seems as if one of the excavators must have been mistaken. Sweetman considers that the stone circle was later in date than the ring of posts, but neither could be shown to have cut the other. There does not seem to be any way of resolving the problem.

Apart from the need to document the history of a major site, why should this controversy be so important? It is because the sequence traces two fundamentally different ways of perceiving monuments. In the passage grave, space was extremely restricted. As modern visitors to Newgrange will be aware, the monument can contain only a limited number of people at any one time. If it becomes too crowded it is quite impossible to see some of the carved decoration which was placed at prominent points in its interior. Nor is it possible to observe the way in which the midwinter sunrise lights the central chamber, for the effect can be masked by the presence of too many people. That is why there is a considerable waiting list to view that phenomenon today (Condit 1993). The same kinds of restrictions must have been important in the past, with the result that the monument encapsulated a crucial distinction between those who were allowed to enter its interior and those who remained outside, unable to gain much idea of what was happening within the tomb. They might have been able to hear sounds emanating from the monument, but they would not have been able to see what was going on. Since the chamber is lit by the sun only once a year, even the initiates may have been divided into those who were permitted to observe this event and those who could only enter the chamber at other times.

The stone circle has features in common with many other sites in Britain, Ireland and, to some extent, in north-west France (Burl 1976). The majority of these form entirely open enclosures. At Newgrange the ring of uprights highlights an external area between the monoliths themselves and the decorated kerbstones. This zone is wider towards the entrance to the monument and becomes narrower around the sides of the mound.

This suggests that the area in front of the entrance formed a kind of forecourt, which could accommodate more people than the tomb. The crucial area was emphasised by the presence of massive pieces of quartz against the flanks of the monument (see Figure 32). As the space between the stone setting and the kerb became narrower, the amount of quartz diminished. O'Kelly himself considered that these pieces of quartz were the remains of a revetment wall supporting the edge of the mound on either side of the entrance, and this is how the site has been reconstructed today (M. O'Kelly 1982: 73–4). His view has often been questioned on the grounds that such an arrangement would have been unstable, but it is a product of our own perception of architecture that we expect such structures to last. A striking effect of this kind may have been contrived for one particular occasion, in the knowledge that it would collapse afterwards. Alternatively, the quartz was used as a surface layer, colouring one side of the mound. When it eventually eroded it came to rest against the kerbstones, forming a kind of platform. This may not have been intended, but no attempt was made to clear the debris. Rather, it was on top of the fallen material that the Late Neolithic 'occupation' took place. Whatever the original context of the stone circle, it was only at this stage that the ring of pits and posts was first created (C. O'Kelly 1983: 16–21). By then, if not before, activity had moved right away from the interior of the tomb and focused on the open area beside it. The private world of the ancestors was replaced by a more public arena.

THE CIRCULAR WORLD

In archaeological parlance, the sequence at Newgrange involved the replacement of a passage grave by a henge. The difference between these phases is encapsulated by their publication in separate volumes. I am not convinced that this is the most useful way of thinking about the site.

In Chapter 6 I showed how another famous monument – in this case Stonehenge – was constantly reconstructed, so that it assumed the appropriate form for the rituals that took place there. It was adapted to conform to the architectural conventions that determined how other monuments of the same period should be built. But while those changes might seem rather radical, in another sense it is doubtful whether the site really changed from one 'type' of monument to another. Those developments did not seem to effect a radical break because they were achieved by such subtle modifications. Its basic configuration remained unaltered. From first to last, it was a precisely circular enclosure, with other circular settings of posts and stones inside it.

That suggests another way of thinking about the monuments of the Boyne valley. In fact, the image of the circle is all-pervasive here (see Figure 33). It extends beyond the plan of the monuments themselves and is often found in other media. The gapped circle, with a radial line leading to its centre, is one of the dominant images in Irish rock art, which is generally found in the open air (Bradley 1997). Although there are considerable difficulties in dating this material, it seems to have been current by the time that Newgrange was built. In a recent paper, Jackson (1995) has pointed out that the organisation of space in this design is exactly the same as we find in a passage grave. There is a similar

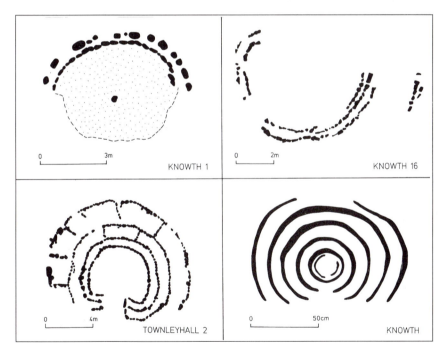

Figure 33. Circular imagery in the Boyne valley. The drawings illustrate a setting of pebbles outside the chambered tomb of Knowth 1, a similar setting on top of the mound of Knowth 16, the arrangement of stones buried beneath the monument at Townleyhall and a circular carving on the principal passage grave at Knowth. After Eogan (1963, 1984, 1986).

emphasis on the circle in Irish megalithic art, although there is not the same use of radial lines (Shee Twohig 1981: ch. 4). Circular motifs are among the elements on the hidden surfaces of the stones at Newgrange and the neighbouring site at Knowth, but they are also found in a much more ornate form associated with the kerbstones and the entrance to the tombs (Eogan 1986: ch. 7).

The same basic design could also be created using small stones, in rather the same manner as we find in Japanese gardens today (Eogan 1986: 47–8, 65, 73–5). These settings have not been discussed in detail, but they occur very widely. On some sites, notably the passage grave at Townleyhall, they were laid out as rings of boulders on the ground surface beneath the mounds (Eogan 1963, 64–79). It is not clear whether any time had elapsed between the creation of these designs and the building of the mound, so we cannot tell whether they were meant to be viewed by the living. What is certain, however, is that boulders of these proportions cannot have been used to retain the finished structure. In no sense did they play a structural role in the tombs.

In other cases, rings of boulders of similar size were built on the surface of the mounds. This happened in the cemetery surrounding the major tomb at Knowth (Eogan 1984: Plate 24b and Figure 53). Again, their role is decorative rather than structural, although it might be better to think in terms of a deeper underlying symbolism which embraced several different elements: the hidden boulder settings buried beneath the mounds; the equally 'hidden' art on the backs of the orthostats; the rings of stone visible on the slopes of the mounds; and the conspicuous carved decoration on major components of the monument. Nor does the variety of such features end there, for outside the kerbs at both Newgrange and Knowth there were other circular or subcircular settings of stones (Eogan 1986: 46–8, 65; M. O'Kelly 1982: 75–7). Often, these were edged by small boulders, and at Knowth one of these features recalls the characteristic designs found on carved surfaces in the tomb and also in the open air. A circular setting of white quartz, similar in conception to a cup mark or a basin, is enclosed by several concentric rings of pebbles (Eogan 1984: 33). At Newgrange there is evidence for the existence of similar features outside the kerb, but true to the prevailing ideas at the time of the excavation, one of these was considered to mark the position of a house (M. O'Kelly 1982: 77). Given the limited but specialised range of artefacts associated with these features – they include carved stone objects with their best parallels on the Continent – it seems more likely that they should all be compared with the stone settings at Knowth and other tombs.

It is not clear where some of the structures at Newgrange lie in the sequence of activity on the site, but at Knowth there is evidence of a succession of different deposits by the entrances to the tomb. The latest was a circle of timber uprights, similar to those found inside henge monuments (Eogan and Roche 1997). There was a more elaborate structure of the same kind outside the kerb at Newgrange, but in this case it was not associated with an entrance (Sweetman 1987). It may be that these buildings were simply the successors of the other circular features created at these sites, and, if so, would imply an even greater degree of equivalence between what are usually regarded as quite separate media: the timber circles, which are sometimes considered as roofed buildings; the boulder settings, which must have played an entirely non-utilitarian role; and the motifs that were carved on the structure of the tombs. All these media made use of a similar basic vocabulary, and it is no surprise that, at the same time, they were echoed on a larger scale by the layout of the passage graves themselves.

The passage grave cemetery at Knowth illustrates virtually all of these features. Before the main tomb was built the site was occupied by at least nine circular houses, whose remains are buried below the later earthwork (Roche 1989; Eogan and Roche 1997). The principal monument is a massive circular mound, entered by two passages which are aligned on the equinoxes, while a series of smaller circular tombs are located around this structure (see Figure 34; Eogan 1986: chs. 1 and 2). They follow the limits of a roughly circular area and for the most part their passages are directed towards its centre. While this provides one image of concentric circles – the ring of satellite tombs is echoed by the kerb of the principal monument – a few of these structures overlie circular settings of boulders or show traces of similar settings built into the mound. The same motif is a particular feature of the decoration found in the principal tomb, where it is mainly associated with the entrances and the kerb. Outside these there are rings of pebbles and a circular area of quartz edged by upright stones. During a later phase a ring of posts was erected outside the entrance of one of the passages.

This poses a dilemma, for if all these media overlapped at Knowth, could the process not have gone even further at Newgrange? Perhaps the enormous pit and post circle identified by Sweetman was just another variant of the same basic idea. Maybe the large embanked enclosures of the Boyne valley that are normally compared with British henges represent part of the same process (Stout 1991). The argument should also extend to the great circle of monoliths surrounding the tomb at Newgrange.

Such similarities are, of course, much more extensive. In Chapter 5 we saw how some of the latest causewayed enclosures assumed a precisely circular outline, while the development of Stonehenge over 1,500 years shows how tenacious that basic design could become once it was first adopted. Such similarities are rarely discussed, but they are not confined to the prehistory of Britain and Ireland. They are present along the Atlantic seaboard from the first development of passage graves, and they continue into later periods through the presence of a tradition of circular houses which extends from Iberia to Ireland. Indeed, the practice of building such structures is so widespread that in Ireland it began during the Neolithic period and did not end until the first millennium AD.

Normally, we would resist the temptation to link these observations together and would regard any such approach as altogether too imaginative (although since these words were first written the subject has finally been broached in print; see Gibson 1994: 192; Cleal et al. 1995; Richards 1996; Woodward and Woodward 1996; Darvill 1996: 249–59). At best we would talk rather vaguely

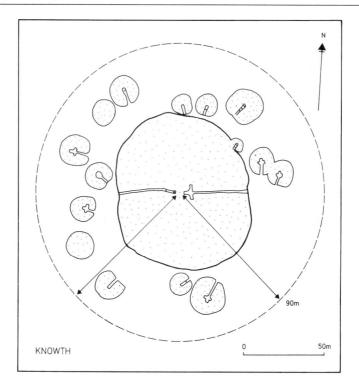

Figure 34. An outline plan of the megalithic cemetery at Knowth, emphasising
its circular layout. Information from Eogan (1986).

about a 'cultural tradition' of circular structures along the western margin of
Europe, contrasting that evidence with the situation further to the east. Yet that
approach might be over-cautious, for, in the light of the studies presented in
Chapters 3 and 5, there seems no reason why one particular way of organising
space should not have been interpreted and reinterpreted over very long periods
of time. Surely, that is the political dimension that is so central to the study of
prehistoric monuments.

I would argue that this constant emphasis on the circle reflects a shared
perception of the world – a prehistoric cosmology. It is all too easy to lose
direction here, but it is quite possible to identify the existence of such a system
without being able to account for the ways in which it was originally interpreted. It is enough to recognise that all communities have their own ways of
perceiving the world, and that these play a fundamental part in shaping the
built environment. As a result, the planning of monuments, and even that of
whole settlements, often encapsulates a more general perception of space: one
which is shaped by mythology as much as topography.

The idea of a circular or spherical cosmos is equally commonplace. Though it can carry an enormous weight of symbolism, it may originate in the experience of the individual inhabiting an increasingly open landscape. He or she is at the centre of a world which recedes towards the horizon, where the land meets the sky (Ingold 1993). The main fixed points on the land may be natural features like hills, while those in the sky are the sun and moon, whose positions can be seen to change in relation to such landmarks. This may be why circular constructions are often subdivided according to the cardinal points, or why they often stand for a cycle in the human or natural worlds; a good example would be the passage of the seasons. Whatever their ultimate meanings, circular constructions reflect a perception of space that extends outwards from the individual and upwards into the sky.

THE ARCHAEOLOGICAL EVIDENCE OF CHANGE

I have used the controversial history of Newgrange to illustrate one fundamental feature of Late Neolithic architecture in these islands; that is, the way in which closed structures like the passage grave seem to have been superseded by more open monuments such as the henge. This is not just a question of who was allowed access to these places; on a more basic level, it also involves the number of people whom they could accommodate. At the same time, I have expressed my doubts over whether it is really appropriate to think of the archaeological sequence in terms of different 'types' of monument at all. This is not because so many of these structures have features that overlap with one another, although this is no doubt true. My objection is altogether more radical, for the evidence from the Boyne Valley, rather like that from Stonehenge, suggests that change was related not to the different ways in which monuments were constructed, but to more profound modifications of the same basic perception of the world. It was this feature that came first, and it may be more important than the debates among archaeologists concerning the classification of field monuments.

In the particular case of the Boyne valley tombs, I suggested that the excavated evidence is less consistent with a straightforward sequence of monuments than it is with a more gradual change in the audience who attended public events at these sites. If the stone circle was a feature of the original monument at Newgrange, then it may have defined a kind of forecourt or stage against the entrance to the tomb, and, if the post circle was built afterwards, it may provide evidence for a further change of emphasis away from the interior of the passage grave. But the case does not depend on that particular site, for there is much wider evidence for changes of this kind, both in Ireland and in northern Britain.

One of the clearest indications of this change of emphasis is easily overlooked: the evidence of megalithic art. It seems to be generally accepted that this tradition of stone carving went through two broad phases, shown by detailed observations made during the excavations of Newgrange, Knowth, Fourknocks and Knockroe. The earlier carvings are of the kind found principally at Loughcrew, while the later style is most common in the Boyne valley (O'Sullivan 1993). If this sequence is correct, it implies that the cemetery at Loughcrew predates the large tombs at Newgrange and Knowth. It would also mean that there was a significant change in the positions in which these carvings were created, for at the earlier monuments the decoration is found almost entirely *inside* the tombs, while in the later phase many of the most elaborate compositions are on the *exterior kerb*. (Shee Twohig 1981: ch. 4). The audience seems to have changed, from the few individuals who were permitted to see the decoration within these tombs to a larger group who were left outside. The bolder, more sculptural designs found on the kerb at Newgrange and Knowth would be easier to recognise from a distance than the early style of carving. In the same way, Bergh has argued that pieces of quartz change their contexts during the sequence of megalithic tombs in Ireland (1995: 156). They are found *inside* the earlier tombs, but towards the other end of the sequence they are employed to embellish the exterior of the monument.

I have also mentioned the possibility that the fallen material against the kerb at Newgrange might have been treated as a kind of platform during the Late Neolithic period (see Figure 35). At one point it seems to have been enhanced by the creation of a clay bank and no fewer than sixteen stone-lined hearths were built on top of this material (M. O'Kelly 1982: 78; C. O'Kelly 1993: 5–40). These have been interpreted as the positions of houses (Cooney and Grogan 1994: 80–1), but it seems very unlikely that domestic buildings would have been placed in such a precarious position. They would have been constructed over a level of broken quartz below a collapsing mound of enormous proportions. The food remains associated with this period of activity include an usually large number of pig bones – a situation that can only be matched at southern English henges – and the distribution of this material suggests that it had been deposited with some formality in front of the tomb (Mount 1994).

The same elements can be recognised quite widely and, again, they are consistent with a growing emphasis on the exterior of these monuments and perhaps with a change in the number of people who were permitted to use them. The evidence take many forms, but these include the construction of platforms outside megalithic tombs and the use of stone circles or earthworks to enclose them (see Figure 36).

The evidence for external platforms is widespread but little understood. It is found in three main areas: Orkney (Davidson and Henshall 1989); the mainland of northern Scotland, where it is a characteristic of the Clava cairns (Henshall 1963: ch. 1); and the west of Ireland, where it has been identified in the Carrowmore complex (Bergh 1995). It can also be recognised at the recently excavated passage tomb at Knockroe in the south-east of Ireland, a site which has many features in common with the decorated tombs of the Boyne valley (O'Sullivan 1996).

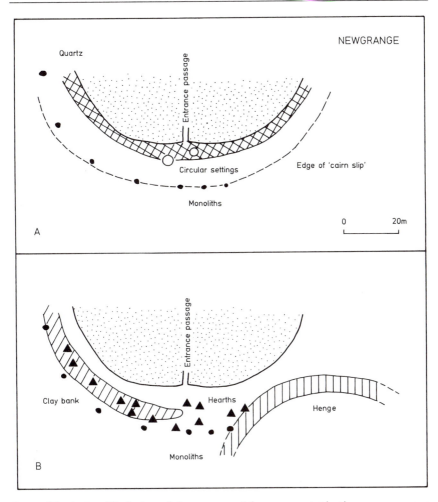

Figure 35. A simplified plan of the structural features outside the passage grave at Newgrange. The information is taken from M. O'Kelly (1982) and C. O'Kelly (1983).

The clearest evidence comes from Scotland, and principally from Orkney. Here, there is no shortage of passage graves with external platforms (Davidson and Henshall 1989: 62). The main problem in interpreting these sites is to decide how and why these features were constructed. They seem to have emphasised the perimeter of the cairn by providing a raised area where the actors were exposed to view. This appears to have happened at Maes Howe, where the edge of one of these structures is marked by a bank and ditch (*ibid.*, pp. 44–51), but there is little to show how such earthworks had been used. At Quoyness, however, the external platform of a large passage grave seems to have provided the focus for a series of distinctive deposits. These have Grooved Ware associations, and their

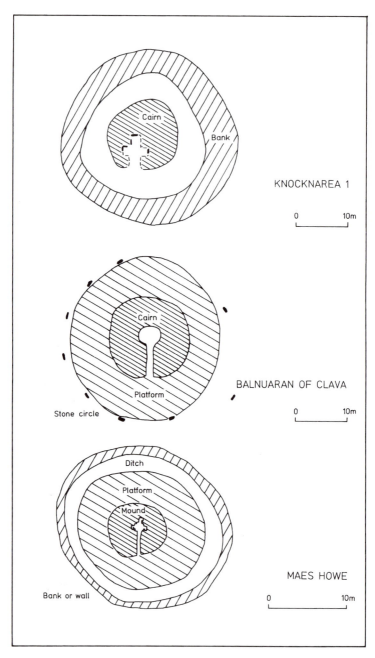

Figure 36. Stone circles and other features enclosing passage graves. The tomb
at Knocknarea is surrounded by a rubble bank. Those at Maes Howe
and Balnuaran of Clava are bounded by platforms. That at Maes
Howe is surrounded by a ditch and its equivalent at Balnuaran of
Clava is ringed by a stone circle. Plans after Bergh (1995), Davidson
and Henshall (1989) and Bradley (1996a) respectively.

contents include animal bones and sea shells (Childe 1952). A similar deposit at Pierowall also contained human bones and polished flint artefacts (Sharples 1984). Sharples has argued that it is only at the latest of the passage graves in Orkney that artefacts are regularly associated with the exterior of the monument (1985: 69).

Elsewhere in northern Scotland, a similar development took place among the Clava cairns (Henshall 1963: ch. 1). Once again, considerable platforms were built against the outer kerbs of a series of passage graves. At Balnuaran of Clava the surface of one of these platforms had originally been paved, and again it seems likely that such structures were used for the deposition of small fragments of cremated bone and seashells: precisely the kinds of material that might also be deposited in the chamber (Bradley 1996b). The limits of these platforms were defined by a ring of monoliths, not unlike the stone circle at Newgrange. In Scotland a closer comparison might be with the setting of slabs that marked the outer edge of the platform at Quoyness (Childe 1952).

The Irish examples present more of a problem. It is uncertain whether a platform of this kind existed outside the entrance to Newgrange, but there certainly was one at Knockroe, where the excavator has argued that it provided a raised area for ceremonies taking place in front of one of the tombs (O'Sullivan 1996). Those in the west of the country are more difficult to interpret. They are associated with three of the four largest cairns in the Carrowmore complex, and on the basis of detailed field survey Bergh (1995) considers them to be original features of the monuments.

In such cases there was an obvious intention to define an area around the edge of a number of mounds or cairns. The major problem is to establish the chronological relationship between the two features. That need not always take the same form. Among the Clava Cairns the passage graves are completely enclosed by a ring of monoliths. These are graded by height, so that the tallest uprights are found opposite the entrance to the tomb, and the same effect is mirrored by the stones used in the kerb. Although the platform provided a kind of stage against the flank of the monument, it also acted as a buttress to hold the kerbstones in position. For that reason, either it was built simultaneously with the cairn or it was added very soon afterwards; in either case, its construction was contemporary with that of the stone circle (Bradley 1996b). An appropriate comparison is with Maes Howe, where the ditch that encloses the entire monument was probably the source of the material used to build the central mound (Childe 1956). Thus at Balnuaran of Clava the *stone circle* seems to have been an integral feature of a passage grave. At Maes Howe the same applies to what was really a *henge*.

In other cases very similar platforms were built *after* the tombs had gone out of use. At Taversoe Tuick the construction of one of these features blocked the entrance passage (Davidson and Henshall 1989: 160–2) and the same happened at Quoyness, where a wall was built on top of the platform and prevented access to the central chamber (Childe 1952). In the same way, at Pierowall the external platform was not built until the cairn had collapsed (Sharples 1984).

It is more difficult to discuss those cases in which a megalithic tomb is actually enclosed within a circular earthwork. Apart from Maes Howe, the best examples of this arrangement are found in Ireland. Several occur in the Carrowmore complex (Bergh 1995), but perhaps the clearest instance of this pattern is Giant's Ring at Ballynahatty in Ulster (Hartwell 1991). There is no doubt that the relationship between these features was carefully worked out. At Ballynahatty the passage grave is found inside a circular embanked enclosure. In plan, the relationship is rather unimpressive, for while the earthwork is extensive, the tomb is not found at its centre. In fact, that is rather deceptive, for the enclosure does not conform to the contours of the site on which it was built: one side of the enclosure is flattened where it meets the edge of the hilltop. On the ground, however, that anomaly is explained. Perhaps the earthwork was supposed to have the tomb towards its centre, yet the design was difficult to put into practice, since the megalithic monument does not seem to have been located with this idea in mind. The tomb was too near the break of slope for a large circular enclosure to fit around it. The implication must be that the henge is a later development.

To sum up, it seems as if the latest passage graves saw a number of significant changes. In some cases these happened after their original construction, or even when access to their chambers was closed, but at other sites composite monuments were built in which new features were added to the traditional design. Large platforms were created against the kerbs of some of these tombs, and in certain instances their outer edges were marked by circular earthworks, or even by rings of monoliths. Existing tombs were perhaps enclosed within structures of this kind, while the area in front of their kerbstones became the focus for a series of offerings of kinds that would previously have been limited to the interior. There is also some evidence that the later tombs were embellished by external decoration in the form of carved motifs and deposits of quartz.

I have dwelt at some length on a range of rather anomalous monuments, for these have largely escaped the prehistorian's predilection for classification. What they do suggest is that any simple duality between enclosures and tombs over-simplifies the available evidence, for there are many indications that a change of emphasis took place during and after the Late Neolithic. This was by no means a unitary process, and that may be why it has not been possible to identify the same sequence on every separate site. At the same time, it seems to have resulted in the creation of open arenas around the closed spaces of the tomb.

This is important, for these circular enclosures are precisely the types of construction that can also be found as monuments in their own right, sometimes in the vicinity of these tombs. Thus there are earthwork enclosures similar to Giant's Ring near to the passage graves of the Boyne valley (Stout 1991), and there are stone circles within sight of the famous tomb of Maes Howe (C. Richards 1996). Such structures are much more common than the features associated with the periphery of passage graves, but the connection is a compelling one. What dating evidence there is suggests that these newly built enclosures may have succeeded the tradition of tomb building altogether. Thus the timber circle, which was one of the last features to be built outside the entrance to the eastern chamber at Knowth, has its counterpart inside these enclosures.

I began with the sequence at Newgrange and will end this chapter with another important sequence, this time on the Mainland of Orkney. Colin Richards's recent work has shown that there is a subtle interplay between the organisation of houses, tombs and henges in this area (C. Richards 1996). The burial chamber at Maes Howe was laid out according to the same principles of order as the domestic buildings on the nearby settlement at Barnhouse. The excavated features inside the later henge monument known as the Stones of Stenness follow some of the same conventions, and Maes Howe is linked with this site through its use of uprights of very similar proportions. The major difference between the two monuments in fact concerns these stones. Those within the henge are very similar to the material used to define the corners of the burial chamber at Maes Howe, but this time they form a structure completely open to the elements: it is as if only the skeleton of the original design were left. The entire construction was visible from outside. This has implications for the nature of the audience and for the ways in which the monument was used. That is why the same site provides the starting point for Chapter 8.

Chapter 8

Theatre in the round

Henge monuments, stone circles and their integration with the landscape

It has often been argued that British henge monuments and stone circles represent the same kind of structure built out of locally available materials. Henges appear in regions in which earthworks would be easy to build and stone circles are found in areas of harder rock. Taking the stone circles of Orkney as its point of departure, this chapter argues that such an interpretation is insufficient. Many circular enclosures were built in places with a continuous horizon of high ground, so that the form of the monument provides a microcosm of the local landscape. A continuous earthwork masks much of that landscape, concealing the surrounding area from view and also restricting visual access to the events taking place within these sites. A stone circle, however, is entirely permeable and its construction can be used to form explicit links between a central enclosure and points in the wider terrain. It was during the period in which such open circles were used that burial mounds were often constructed in the surrounding hills.

INTRODUCTION

The Stones of Stenness are an imposing monument, located not far away from Maes Howe on the Mainland of Orkney. In the last chapter I suggested that the site might even be regarded as the successor of that tomb. Events that had originally been hidden from view in the central chamber at Maes Howe might have taken place within open arenas of this kind.

Like Stonehenge, the Stones of Stenness create problems for the typologist. So does a neighbouring monument, the Ring of Brodgar, which takes a similar form. Both consist of a circular setting of exceptionally tall monoliths, enclosed by a rock-cut ditch with a single entrance (see Figure 37). Although the radiocarbon dates associated with both of these monuments suggest that they were among the earliest henges, their distinctive configuration poses certain problems.

The earthworks have features in common with henge monuments – their size, their groundplan and the presence of at least one entrance – but no sign of a bank survives on either site. One may have existed at the Stones of Stenness, but the

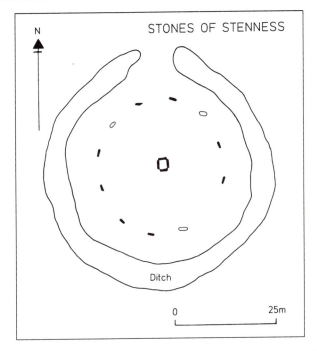

Figure 37. A simplified plan of the Stones of Stenness, after Richards (1996).

excavated evidence is not particularly strong (Ritchie 1976). The Ring of Brodgar, which has also been investigated, lacked an outer bank altogether (Renfrew 1979: ch. 5). This poses problems for the typologist, since it is the presence of an external bank that identifies a circular enclosure as a henge.

The stone settings might seem to present fewer difficulties, since they are a common feature inside such earthworks. On most recently excavated sites, however, they can be identified as a secondary development, for, just as happened at Stonehenge, it seems as if these structures usually replaced timber circles. Extensive excavations at Stenness showed no sign of an older structure of this kind. It is certainly possible to explain away these anomalies – there may not have been much wood in Orkney during the Neolithic period, and, instead of an outer bank, both sites may have had an external wall, the material of which was later reused. But, even if we accept these arguments, the question surely arises as to how we are to explain the relationship between these two different 'types' of monument: the earthwork henge, on the one hand, and the freestanding stone circle, on the other.

On one level, this may seem a sterile pursuit, for in the previous chapter I expressed my doubts over the usefulness of classifications of this kind. In the Boyne valley, for example, it seemed more productive to consider the different structures in the megalithic cemeteries of Newgrange and Knowth as transformations of the same circular image; in this sense, they were not really 'types' of monument at all. This approach allowed us to consider not only the passage graves and the settings of stone and timber found on both these sites, but also the patterned stonework located outside the mounds. All these structures had features in common with the rings of boulders that were associated with some of the smaller tombs and also with the carved decoration applied to the monuments themselves. It was because the same symbolic system incorporated all these elements that the change from closed monuments to open arenas was less abrupt than it might otherwise have seemed. Henges and stone circles have so many features in common that the same approach might be appropriate in this case.

In fact, most authorities are agreed that stone circles and henge monuments were the local equivalents of one another and may have been used in the same ways (Burl 1976; Harding and Lee 1987; Barnatt 1989). This is particularly true of the largest stone circles, for these compare in size with some of the henges. Like them, they may also possess a single clearly defined entrance. The most explicit statement of this view comes from Burl:

> Henges may be found all over Britain, yet only in the east did they proliferate. From Norfolk up to the Moray Firth they were built over a period of perhaps a thousand years. . . . It may be pertinent to enquire why such a continuity is not apparent in the south-west or north-west, in both of which areas the development of henges seems to have been stultified. An answer is that cognate sites do exist but in the megalithic form of stone circles. . . .
>
> The explanation is plain. Even in regions outside the mountainous parts of the Lake District, the digging of ditches and raising of banks cannot have been easy. . . . It is possible to see a gradual change from henge to stone circle as the geology alters from the soft chalks of the east, amenable to the quarrying of ditches and the building of banks, into the more intractable limestones and sandstones of the west, where it would have been easier to transport and erect monoliths than to dig a ditch or even to scrape together material for a bank.
>
> (1976: 26–7)

Thus the differences between these two groups of monuments were the result of practical considerations (see Figure 38). Those sites, like the Stones of Stenness, which included both earthworks and monoliths, were exceptional and are generally found in regions where none of the building materials raised problems. The same arguments have been used to account for the distinction between earthen long barrows and megalithic tombs.

This explanation seems rather unlikely, and it does so for two quite different reasons. We can certainly accept that stone circles are not likely to be found in areas where suitable rocks were absent, but that does not explain why there should be so many freestanding monuments in different areas of Britain and

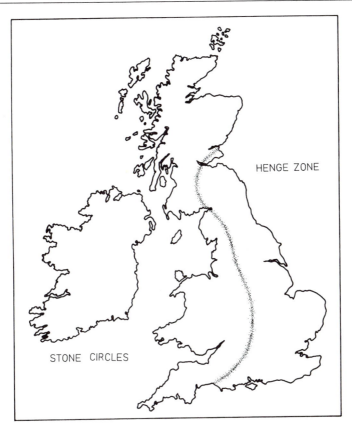

Figure 38. The regions of Britain dominated by henges or stone circles. Simplified from Burl (1976).

Ireland. Even where it was difficult to dig a ditch, as it would have been in many parts of the uplands, sufficient boulders might be available to build a rubble bank. The fact that Early Bronze Age cairns are so often found close to stone circles shows that such an enclosure could have been created without too much difficulty. In fact, that is exactly what happened at Mayburgh in north-west England (Topping 1992: 349–53).

A more serious objection arises if we consider how these monuments might have been experienced by people in prehistory. And that is the question which provides the subject matter for this chapter.

THE SITUATION OF CIRCULAR MONUMENTS

There is something of an imbalance in studies of stone circles and henges. Either they have been analysed on too small a scale, or the scale is too large. The solution to the problems posed by sites like those in Orkney falls between these different approaches.

Traditionally, studies of stone circles have been minutely detailed. This has happened for two reasons. First, there is the entirely proper task of attempting to gain some insight into their regional characteristics and chronology, and this has involved some very useful studies of their changing organisation in different parts of the country (Burl 1976; Barnatt 1989). As a result, we are in a position to recognise a number of regional groups within this kind of architecture, although the problem still remains of deciding what those different traditions meant to the people who created them. The most satisfactory of these studies, like those of megalithic tombs, have helped to define areas in which material culture seems to have been employed in self-consciously local ways. A less satisfactory aspect of some of these studies is the attempt to divide these monuments into a series of apparently independent traits, each of them drawn from another region by procedures that are never explained.

The other reason for the detailed studies of stone circles is the influence of Alexander Thom and his followers, who have argued that some of these apparently circular monuments were laid out by sophisticated surveying methods involving the use of a standard unit of length (Thom 1967; see also Ruggles 1988). Despite the high degree of accuracy with which the remains of these sites have been surveyed, not all this work has been convincing, often because the archaeological features of these monuments have been misunderstood. Nor is it the case that the most complex solutions are necessarily the best ones. Barnatt and Herring, for example, have shown how many of Thom's specialised constructions, which involve a whole series of layouts that diverge from a true circle, could have been arrived at quite by chance in attempting to lay out a ring of stones by eye (Barnatt and Herring 1986).

The result of both approaches has been to compile a substantial corpus of site plans, linked to a complex classification of the details of the stone circles. While this has been valuable as a way of achieving a better understanding of regional variations among these sites, this approach may have gone as far as it can do without the evidence of excavation.

The situation with henge monuments is exactly the opposite, for the basic grouping of sites radically over-simplifies the issues by focusing entirely on the form of the perimeter earthwork. As a result, these sites are normally grouped according to their size and the number of entrances (Atkinson 1951). Most schemes take little account of the wide variety of features found inside them, even those which are apparent without excavation. Differences of size have been noted, but only two regional styles of henges have been defined within a distribution that covers large parts of Britain and Ireland. One consists of embanked enclosures like those in the Boyne valley (Stout 1991), while the other comprises the henge monuments in North Yorkshire, which are typified by two concentric ditches (Atkinson 1951). Because these sites are earthworks and subject to considerable erosion, there has not been the same concern with the principles according to which they were designed, although some attention has been paid to the orientation of their entrances (Harding and Lee 1987: 35–7).

Other studies of both types of monument have been conducted at the regional scale. With certain exceptions, these have been far more impressionistic, for this area of research is less attractive to the archaeological scientist. At a very broad level, it is apparent that the main concentrations of monuments, and especially the largest sites, are found in areas of above-average fertility. These have been described as the 'core areas' of Neolithic and Early Bronze Age Britain (Bradley 1984: ch. 3). This approach has severe limitations. Not only are there regions, like East Anglia, where exceptionally fertile areas contain very few major monuments, but it presupposes that these structures were at the heart of the settlement pattern, so that the scale of these sites provides an indication of the number of people who were living there.

This is an unsatisfactory procedure. Although a number of areas containing monuments have been investigated by field survey, there is little to suggest that the density of human activity was any greater in the surroundings of these monuments than it was in other parts of the local landscape. In south Dorset, where a series of sample areas have been investigated according to the same methods, it even seems as if the density of artefacts in the modern ploughsoil *increased* with distance from the ceremonial sites (P. Woodward 1991: ch. 3). Although the scale of these structures is obviously related to the number of people who built them, there does not seem to be enough evidence of productive land use in the neighbourhood of these monuments to suggest that they were constructed by an entirely local population.

This is also the hidden assumption behind attempts to study the distribution of these monuments as evidence of 'territories' in the past – we simply do not know whether they were central places at all (*pace* Barnatt 1989: ch. 5). In fact, their siting at the local level might well suggest another interpretation, for the larger monuments built during the Late Neolithic were often located near major rivers. It is equally striking how many of them are near to modern roads – or, rather, to the topographical features that account for their position in the landscape. In the same way, some of the smaller stone circles are associated with routes along upland valleys or even with mountain passes. In fact, it seems much more likely that these monuments were sited for accessibility from the surrounding area. They were not necessarily the focus for a concentration of settlements: perhaps they were distributed along routeways.

The problem for any new analysis is to move between these two kinds of study: to integrate the precise surveys that have been carried out of individual monuments with these more impressionistic accounts of their placing in the wider landscape. The only exceptions to the general pattern are those studies that relate the position and layout of these monuments to astronomical alignments. This last approach does pay more attention to the local topography, but in some ways this emphasis on astronomy means that a more striking feature seems to have been overlooked. Many monuments command a view of natural features that might have framed the movements of the sun and moon; but they were often in places with an equally extensive view in other directions as well.

The potential importance of this feature was overlooked until recently when it was recognised by two different people, working entirely independently: by Colin Richards (1996), who was investigating Neolithic monuments in Orkney, and by the present writer. This is the striking similarity that exists between the siting of the monuments in the landscape and the broader configuration of the surrounding country. Thus a well-known stone circle like Castlerigg seems to crystallise the characteristic features of the landscape in which it is built (Burl 1988), with a facade of standing stones confronting a chain of mountains. Likewise, the location of Durrington Walls in a dry valley means that much of the internal area was ringed by the near horizon, so that when the earthwork bank was built it merely reinforced the existing characteristics of that place (Wainwright and Longworth 1971). There is abundant evidence that Neolithic monuments were constructed on sites that had been used before. I suggest that those locations also epitomised a circular perception of space, so that the creation of these monuments would encapsulate the qualities of the surrounding area and might summarise in massive form any existing understandings of that location. Such monuments may appear to be built at the heart of the prehistoric landscape, but at the same time they may also be important symbols: representations of that landscape as a whole.

Richards's interpretation is similar (C. Richards 1996). Not only do the Stones of Stenness and the Ring of Brodgar represent a transformation of the principles of order seen in Orcadian settlements and tombs, they also echo the characteristic features of the surrounding landscape. Each is located on the end of a narrow isthmus with an extensive system of lochs on either side. Behind these there is a mountainous skyline (see Figure 39). Both monuments are completely permeable, with the result that it is possible to look out from the enclosed area across the water to the high ground on the horizon. The features of these monuments copy that basic design. The height of the sandstone monoliths mirrors the height of the distant hills and the circular plan of each of these enclosures reflects their location within a natural bowl, ringed on every side by higher ground. Even the importance of the lochs seems to be reflected in the ditches dug around these enclosures, for these appear to have held water. This may account for the unorthodox character of both of those monuments, and does so in a way that typologies can never explain.

I can illustrate the importance of similar principles at sites in England. Causewayed enclosures provide a useful point of departure, for, as we have seen, some of these sites assume an exactly circular ground plan, while others do not. Their positions also vary, so that Windmill Hill, for example, was built across the contours so that it faced in one direction. This contrasts with the siting of the nearby monument at Avebury, where the greater part of the henge is ringed by a horizon of hills (Woodward and Woodward 1996). It may have been for the express purpose of creating this effect that the earthwork was built within an

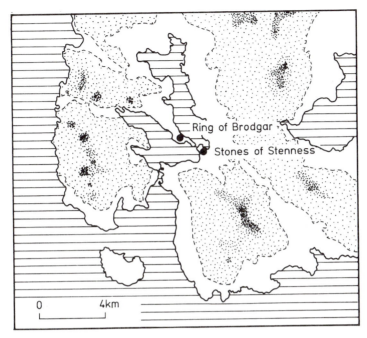

Figure 39. The position of the Orkney henges within a natural basin, after Richards (1996). The higher ground is indicated by stippling.

enormous natural basin. In the north-west something very similar happens at Long Meg and her Daughters (Watson 1994). Here, an early enclosure, known only from crop marks, was replaced by the famous stone circle of that name, but, despite the fact that the two monuments are actually contiguous, they are located according to completely different principles. The ditched enclosure, which may well have been related to sites like Windmill Hill, is half hidden in a shallow valley where visibility is impeded by the local topography (Soffe and Clare 1988). The building of the stone circle, together with its decorated outlier, involved an important change, and this site commands a virtually continuous horizon of hills and mountains. The circle and the standing stone are also aligned on the midwinter sunset (Burl 1988: 197).

Put simply, then, the siting of some of the circular monuments seems to be a reflection of the positions in which they were built. These constructions encapsulated the nature of those places and reproduced them in architectural form. The finished monument might have provided a metaphor for the wider landscape. Moreover, both the location of the monument and its characteristic layout shared a common feature, for each referred to a more general perception of the world.

This is very much the point that I made in discussing the cemeteries of the Boyne valley, but it carries a further implication. As we saw in that case, the same circular archetype might be expressed in many different media. That certainly seems to apply to the ways in which henges and stone circles were employed.

AUDIENCE REACTIONS

We can consider the uses made of both groups of sites from two quite different perspectives: those of the audience observing what was taking place inside these enclosures; and the experience of the participants within the central area of these monuments (see Figure 40).

In Chapter 7 I considered the way in which passage graves were modified to allow a greater number of people to participate in the ceremonies that were carried out there. Although activity no doubt continued in the closed space of the tomb, more provision was made for events happening outside the monument. This might involve the formal definition of an area in front of the entrance, as seems to have happened at Newgrange; it could have led to the creation of raised platforms against the flanks of the tomb; and in certain instances the same principles extended to the creation of circular enclosures with the tomb itself in the centre. These enclosures might be defined by an earthwork or by a ring of standing stones. These developments not only illustrate important changes in the number of people who could have participated in activities on these sites, they also provide some of the sources for the monuments discussed in this chapter.

That emphasis on the growing size of the audience provides a connecting link with the open enclosures which seem to have been created when megalithic tombs themselves were no longer being built. Many features of the new kinds of monument indicate the nature of that process, but they also highlight an important contrast between the ways in which different enclosures were used.

Perhaps the closest links between these different traditions are found at sites like Giant's Ring or Maes Howe, where a passage grave appears to have been encapsulated within an earthwork enclosure, although at the Irish site this was achieved by lowering part of the interior and building a massive embankment, while in Orkney the tomb itself appears to sit on a platform whose outer edge is defined by a ditch. In each case, the effect would have been the same, for it would have highlighted the positions of the people who were permitted to enter the enclosure and would have made their actions easier to watch for an audience outside the monument. That same principle is emphasised even more clearly by the henges found in England and Scotland, for here the division between the interior and exterior space is much more sharply defined. On virtually all these monuments the audience is separated from those inside the enclosure by a ditch, with the result that these sites can be regarded as a kind of circular arena. The bank, which was always on the outside, would be sufficient to accommodate a substantial audience, but there would have been a considerable barrier between them and those within the enclosure itself.

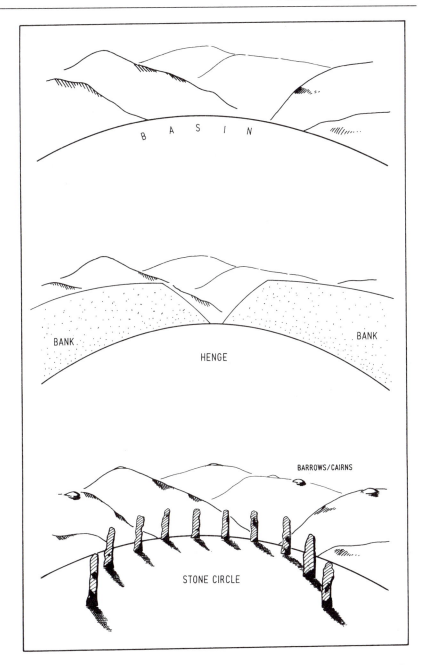

Figure 40. The relationship between henges, stone circles and the surrounding landscape. The drawing depicts the same basin, partly screened by the earthworks of a henge but visible in between the monoliths of a stone circle.

This is a sharper division than we find at the Irish henges, where the ditch is normally absent (Stout 1991), and it is emphasised still further at the entrance(s) to the British monuments. In normal circumstances, henge monuments could be entered at only one or two points along their circuit, with the result that from any distance the nature of the interior might have been screened from view. That same element of 'closure' is found within the entrances themselves, for at some of these sites the bank was heightened in this area (Topping 1992: 262). Thus the nature of the entrances not only imposed a restriction on how these enclosures could be approached from the surrounding area, they imposed additional limitations on how much of the inside could be seen. This suggests a threefold division of space on these sites. Certain people might be allowed access to the interior of these monuments. Another group might look down into the interior from the bank, but would be separated from them by a ditch, while others may not have been permitted to see into the enclosure at all. For them the inside, and the activities that went on there, would have seemed just as secret as any of the rituals undertaken within the tombs.

Stone circles would have the opposite effect, for with the exception of those which were built inside earthwork enclosures, they were entirely permeable monuments. It would be much more difficult to conceal what was happening there, and the limited number of cases in which these structures were cut off by a bank and ditch suggests that this was never intended. Even the stone circles built inside henges have an exceptional character, for only rarely were they new constructions at all. More often, they result from rebuilding other kinds of structure in a more monumental form.

The contrast with henge monuments also extends to the provision of entrances. It is certainly true that some of the largest circles, which most authorities would consider to be among the oldest (Burl 1976: ch. 2; Barnatt 1989: ch. 4), do seem to possess one clearly marked entrance, but the very fact that these are so rare emphasises the point that at many other sites there is no obvious distinction between one gap in the perimeter and another. At times this may have posed problems, and that may suggest the reason why a number of stone circles were approached by avenues. These may have determined the 'correct' way to approach monuments whose boundaries were otherwise easy to transgress. Although some of these avenues led to stone circles that were built inside henges, there are other instances in which they are associated with entirely open sites.

AN INSIDER'S OPINION

I have already argued that a number of circular enclosures epitomise the characteristics of the area in which they were built. Circular monuments might be constructed within circular landscapes. But that perception is very much the outlook of the field archaeologist, who is studying monuments which have substantially decayed and whose perspective is often influenced by the use of maps. It may be true that a monument like Avebury was ringed by a horizon of hills, but could the people who were originally allowed inside the enclosure actually have observed that?

The insider's perception of these places might be different from that of an outsider. At Avebury itself the contrast is obvious. It is true that the site was built at the centre of an enormous bowl within the chalk downland. It is ringed by higher ground extending to the skyline on virtually every side, and along the horizon there are a large number of barrows, many of them of Early Bronze Age date (Woodward and Woodward 1996). They seem to have been located there so that they would achieve that effect in relation to an enclosure that was already an established feature of the landscape. The position of the older earthworks on Windmill Hill can be identified from Avebury, and the summit of Silbury Hill is also visible. Virtually all these effects can be registered from the gigantic bank which marks the outer perimeter of the monument. Within the enclosure, however, the effect is very different, for the sheer size of that earthwork, even after millennia of erosion, hides large parts of the horizon from view. We may *know* that they are there, but unless we leave the interior of the monument many of them are invisible. The contrast is very striking. An 'outsider' occupying a position on the crest of the bank will be aware of the subtle relationship between the layout of the henge and the landscape round about it. He or she will also be able to observe the large number of monuments that had been built along the skyline, although they cannot be seen from one location; it would be necessary to perform a complete circuit of the enclosure in order to identify them all.

The 'insider', however, would have been almost completely cut off from the world. This would have happened not just because the perimeter of the monument was defined by a massive earthwork, but because that structure obscured any visual connection between the interior and the exterior. The only view out would have been through the narrow apertures formed by the entrances to the henge. With that exception, this was a world in itself, remote from the landscape outside.

Such effects are found at the sites of many henges, but they could not have been created through the construction of freestanding stone circles; their articulation with the landscape is entirely different. Just as those outside the monument would enjoy a clear view of the interior, those located inside the circle could see the full extent of the surrounding country. This is especially important as so many burial mounds were built in upland areas. The visual links between these two kinds of monument would have been immediately apparent. Quite as much as any astronomical alignments, these visual cues would have helped to link the monument to the wider landscape. This is particularly important in the light of growing evidence that the distribution of settlement and burial mounds extended into the upland during the currency of this type of structure (Bradley 1978: ch. 6).

The contrast with henge monuments is captured by two well-known sites in north-west England, each associated with stone axes from the Langdale Fells. Mayburgh, which is largest of three henge monuments at Eamont Bridge, is located in a position that has an almost continuous horizon of high ground, much of it a considerable distance away. But the creation of its rubble bank, in a manner more appropriate to an Irish henge, completely concealed this view from those inside the earthwork, which has only one entrance (Topping 1992). Elsewhere in the same region, a large stone setting was created at Castlerigg, but in this case it was a freestanding monument with little or no surrounding bank. Again, it was built in a place that was completely ringed by mountains and hills, but, in complete contrast to the situation at Mayburgh, this physical relationship is also apparent to the onlooker (Burl 1988). Nothing impedes the view from the centre of the circle to the edges of the region within which it was built – the monument is entirely permeable. As if to emphasise that point, its major axis follows a solar alignment. Castlerigg forms a direct equation between the monument and the mountains beyond, among them the source area of Cumbrian axes.

The form of such monuments makes it possible to express two kinds of relationship which would not be so apparent to those inside a henge. First, it allows the people permitted to enter the circle to relate the character and position of that monument to other constructions in the landscape around it. This is less easy to achieve in the case of an earthwork enclosure, even when the same kinds of feature had been created in the vicinity. At the same time, it would be far more difficult to integrate the structure of a henge with the movements of the sun and moon, for the only axis where appropriate observations might be at all easy to achieve would be through the entrance(s). On many sites the features of the horizon would be hidden from view and the external bank would limit the observer's field of vision. There is no evidence for the existence of markers on top of such an earthwork.

THE MATTER OF TIMING

We must consider the question of chronology. For many years it was conventional wisdom to suppose that stone circles were generally later in date than henges, and elements of that interpretation continue to this day (Burl 1976: ch. 2). In itself, the idea was perfectly reasonable and depended on two kinds of evidence. First, most of the artefacts found inside stone circles dated from the Bronze Age, whereas there was considerable evidence to show that henge monuments were a Neolithic development. Second, there was evidence from a number of excavated sites of stone circles replacing timber circles during a phase associated with Beaker pottery. Although most of these observations were made in the course of henge excavations, there are freestanding circles, like those on Machrie Moor, where the same sequence has been recorded (Haggarty 1991).

None the less, there is reason for caution. More than adequate evidence exists that stone circles originated during the Neolithic period, and some evidence that these early sites were not limited to the larger settings that have been treated as the equivalent of henge monuments (Burl 1976; Barnatt 1989). Where stone circles succeeded timber settings there may have been a concern to create a more durable structure, whatever the date of this development from one site to another. It is even possible to envisage composite structures in which both materials were used together, as perhaps happened in the Sanctuary at Avebury (Pollard 1992).

It is certainly true that the artefacts from stone circles seem to have a longer history than the vast majority of those associated with henges. The latest pottery from henges normally belongs to the Beaker phase, while the finds from freestanding monuments built of stone extend at least as late as the end of the second millennium BC. But there is a problem here. Most of the artefacts that were used to date the stone settings come from their interior and were associated with burials; there is no reason to suppose that they relate to the original use of these monuments. As I shall argue in Chapter 9, there is considerable evidence to suggest that this was a secondary development: one that entailed quite major changes to the character of these sites. Stone circles may have remained an important feature of the landscape for a longer period than their earthwork equivalents, but that tells us about their changing history rather than their original construction.

A modified version of the same basic argument is to suggest that it was the larger stone circles that were built in parallel with the henges, and that some of the smaller circles might have been a later development (Burl 1976). It is certainly true that most of the smaller monuments are associated with sites in the uplands, for it was not until the Early Bronze Age that many of these areas were occupied on any scale. This view is supported by environmental evidence, and by the chronology of the burial mounds in these landscapes. Such a sequence has the added advantage that the history of stone-built monuments would run in parallel with that of timber circles, which are easier to date by radiocarbon. A recent paper by Gibson has shown that these decreased in size during this period (1994: 200–7).

A sequence of this kind has important implications for the relationship between stone circles and henges, for it suggests that perceptions of the landscape were changing. The henges may have been located in places with distinctive topographical features. They may even have forged an equation between monumental architecture and the natural landforms among which they were built, but those who were allowed inside them would have been cut off from their surroundings. These sites were a space set apart, which was not accessible to everyone. Although the events taking place in the interior could have been observed from their perimeter, massive earthworks separated those who could enter these arenas from those who were left outside.

I have argued that the freestanding stone circles have quite different properties. Because they are permeable structures they permit a continuous relationship between the sacred space of the interior and the landscape beyond. They also permit closer cross-reference between the circle itself and other monuments in the vicinity; an obvious example is provided by Stonehenge (see Figure 41). If the later examples really were built when the uplands were settled on an increasing scale, this evidence might suggest a new integration between monuments and the wider world. This relationship extended beyond their placing in the natural terrain. It made greater use of other kinds of monument, and it also drew more attention to the sky. These monuments were built in an increasingly open landscape and in the upland areas, where changes of topography were most abrupt, this provided the perfect opportunity for incorporating astronomical alignments into the working of these sites.

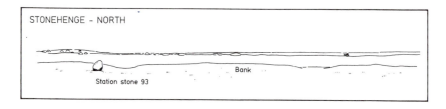

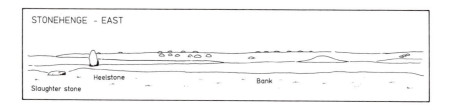

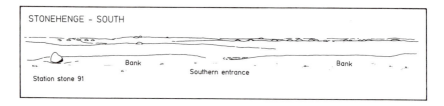

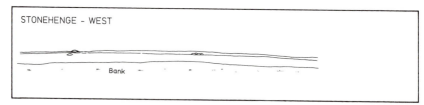

Figure 41. Skyline barrows viewed from inside the monument at Stonehenge. After Cleal et al. (1995) with modifications.

That sequence takes the account to an important turning point in British pre-history, for the subsequent development of these landscapes leads in the opposite direction. In their later phases the open monuments became less accessible, and eventually they went out of use. These enclosures were replaced by farms and the burial mounds by fields. Yet a thread of continuity can still be traced across that great divide. I shall attempt to do so in the two chapters that remain.

Chapter 9

Closed circles

The changing character of monuments, from enclosures to cemeteries

In the course of field survey, archaeologists encounter many different types of monument and try to classify them from their surface remains. A good example is provided by the study of what have been called 'variant circles'. Although this research has resulted in an elaborate classification, it was not until some of these sites were excavated to modern standards that it became apparent how many of the monuments had passed through a complex sequence of construction and reconstruction. Many of the different 'types' encountered during fieldwork might be better thought of as stages in a process which ended at different points on different sites. Two basic patterns are represented, each with its implications for the understanding of Early Bronze Age monuments. In one case, open enclosures were built, which became increasingly inaccessible as their interiors were occupied by burials. In the other instance, enclosures of rather similar form were completely concealed beneath round barrows or cairns. In both situations it seems as if monuments of types which had once served a wider community were being appropriated for the burials of a restricted section of the population.

INTRODUCTION

Virtually all the ceremonial monuments constructed in Britain and Ireland between 3000 and 1500 BC were circles of one kind or another. There are many separate types, and yet their edges are blurred. I discussed the wider significance of some of these structures in Chapters 7 and 8, and two points seemed important then. First, I suggested that the change from tombs to enclosures was a gradual process and that in the north it was set in motion by changes in the audience attracted to such sites. It played on a wealth of circular imagery that extended into the very fabric of those monuments. My second observation concerned the relationship between henges and stone circles. Most archaeologists had played down the differences between these various enclosures and considered that they all shared the same significance. They argued that any distinction between the two classes of monument was due to the materials out of which they were built.

I argued that this interpretation overlooked important contrasts in the ways in which these places were used and in their articulation with the wider landscape.

There remains a third possibility: that certain 'types' of monument may represent stages in a process curtailed at different points on different sites. This is an argument that Barrett has advanced for the Bronze Age burial mounds of Wessex, contending that their appearance today is the product of a lengthy history (1994: ch. 5). During the development of such a site it might have assumed several different forms. Thus bowl barrows might develop into bell barrows, small circular enclosures might be rebuilt as mounds and the positions of flat graves could be redefined until they were marked by massive earthworks. Such changes sometimes accompanied the re-excavation of the existing graves or took place as other burials were introduced. By the end of that sequence, however, the sites had assumed a new identity.

The same may be true of some of the circular enclosures, for many sites do not conform to the simple divisions that have been considered so far. As well as the classic henges and stone circles, there are other sites, which go under the rather unhelpful title of 'variant circles'. These exist in a bewildering variety, and the obvious temptation is to try to introduce some order into the confusion by devising a simple classification. In most cases this must be based on their surface topography. The majority of this work has been done in Wales and Scotland (Lynch 1972; Ritchie and Maclaren 1972), although comparable phenomena have been observed in other areas, in particular, in Ireland (Lynch 1979) and in north-east England (Barnatt 1990). At first sight, the variety of forms seems quite bewildering (see Figure 42). To the simple division between henges and stone circles we must add a whole range of subtypes: *ring cairns*, *complex ring cairns*, *embanked stone circles*, *cairn circles* and *kerb circles*. This scheme was originally devised for monuments in Wales, but seems to have a wider application. It depends on four main features: the sizes of the different circular monuments; the presence or absence of an entrance to these sites; the height of any ring of upright stones; and the relationship, where there is one, between these features and the material of a cairn. Sites may be entirely open, or they may be concealed to varying extents beneath a mound of earth or rubble. Similarly, the uprights may form a feature in their own right, they may protrude from the material of the monument or they may provide the outer kerb of a cairn.

In 1984, Leighton argued that such classifications were inappropriate, given the damage suffered by many of these sites. It was no longer possible to interpret their surface remains with any confidence, and the creation of typologies, he claimed, was a pointless exercise. Yet the fact remains that such schemes are frequently supported by modern excavation. Of course, much does depend on the condition of these sites, but even more important is the skill of the individual excavator. Projects such as Lynch's investigation of the Early Bronze Age cemetery at the Brenig or Scott's at Temple Wood have done much to show that the classification of variant circles is worth undertaking (Scott 1989; Lynch 1993).

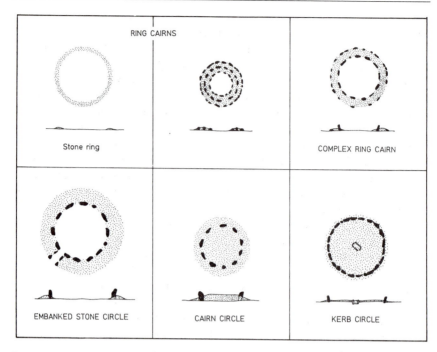

Figure 42. The typology of 'variant circles' according to Lynch (1972).

The results of such excavations have also introduced a new flexibility into the interpretation of these monuments. It is not that the surface evidence is impossible to interpret. Rather, recent excavations have shown that those remains were the end product of a lengthy history. Like the round barrows studied by Barrett, such sites had often taken very different forms before they assumed their final configuration. The separate 'types' of monuments might have some validity but they were not necessarily fixed at all. The actual sequence was much more fluid, and in some cases the forms that particular monuments assumed are better regarded as stages in a lengthy process. That sequence came to an end at different points in the sequence.

It seems that there were two basic processes at work. In one case that process involved the use of an open arena, and in the other it resulted in the construction of a mound or cairn. The two concepts could hardly be more different from one another, although sometimes they shared the same point of departure. In one instance the development of the monument ended with the building of a circular enclosure which was apparently inaccessible to the living population. In the other sequence, the remains of the dead were covered by a considerable mound and were cut off completely from the world outside.

Taking the variant circles as its point of departure, this chapter will trace the history of these monuments through the Early Bronze Age. The accessibility of these constructions remains an important question, but during this period there is the added complication that a significant number of these enclosures were used for burying the dead. This raises the intriguing possibility that as the forms of these monuments changed from one period of use to another, their functions may also have altered in material ways.

CLOSING TIMES

One of the fullest sequences is provided by the stone circles at Temple Wood, in the west of Scotland (Scott 1989). This site has the added advantage that in its earliest phase it is directly comparable with the monuments discussed in Chapter 8. There were originally two monuments at Temple Wood, standing side by side (see Figure 43). They are located towards the bottom of a wide valley communicating with the sea and, like so many others, they would have been ringed on almost every side by a horizon of higher ground. Within the surrounding area, there is a major concentration of monuments. These include the possible sites of

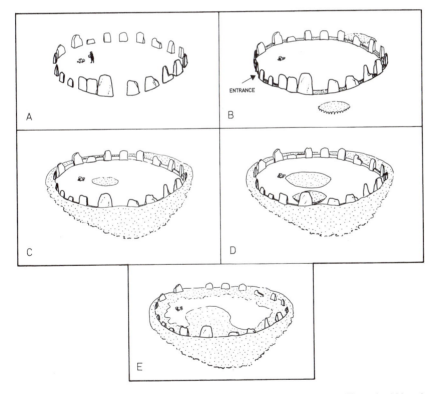

Figure 43. Outline drawings of the successive monuments at Temple Wood, modified from Scott (1989). What was originally a stone circle became increasingly inaccessible as it was reused for burial.

two more stone circles, an earthwork henge, a row of Early Bronze Age round barrows, cist burials, menhirs and a variety of stone settings, some of which are difficult to parallel in other areas. The outer edge of the lowland basin where all these monuments are found is marked by a number of unusually complex rock carvings (RCAHMS 1988).

There were two circles at Temple Wood, and though the radiocarbon dates from the site are not particularly helpful, there seems little doubt that the first monuments belong to the Neolithic period. One was a timber circle, which was replaced on precisely the same site by a freestanding circle of monoliths. The other, a larger setting of uprights, lacked a timber first phase and, again, consisted of a ring of spaced monoliths, unconstrained by a surrounding bank and ditch. Two of these monoliths were carved, one with a distinctive motif, which has been found in a number of other contexts dated to the later part of the Neolithic period (Bradley 1997: ch. 4). Among these was a decorated rock outcrop at Achnabreck within the same monument complex as Temple Wood. Nothing is known about what took place inside these early circles.

From this point in the sequence only the larger of the stone circles at Temple Wood remained in use. The first major alteration to this monument involved the building of a low stone wall joining the base of the original uprights. This enclosure was probably broken by a single entrance to the east. It marks the beginning of a most distinctive process by which what was originally a permeable monument was gradually closed off. That process gathered pace, for in the next period of rebuilding the gaps between the uprights were completely filled by the addition of stone slabs and the entrance seems to have been blocked. Although it was still possible to see into the interior of the enclosure, the area was no longer accessible.

At about the same time (it is difficult to relate the interior features to the changing structure of the enclosure itself) it seems that the monument began to be used for burials. The earliest of these is associated with Beaker pottery, but the sequence extends down to the Middle or Late Bronze Age. Some of the first burials were in massive stone cists and each of these was covered by a small circular cairn with a kerb of slabs set on edge in rather the same manner as the rebuilt perimeter of the monument; another was built just outside the enclosure. Cremation burials were added later, and, at a stage which is difficult to define exactly, the entire perimeter wall was buried below a broad bank of rubble, which also extended across large parts of the interior. It seems likely that the tops of the original stone circle still protruded above this level, but by this stage the form of the monument had departed entirely from the original conception. What had once been an open enclosure, set within a 'circular' landscape, was now a funerary monument. Its original features were obscured and its perimeter was effectively buried.

If we were to use the 'correct' terminology, Temple Wood might have to be characterised not as one 'type' of monument, but as several successive types. It began with a freestanding timber circle and then with two stone circles of the conventional kind. It was apparently converted into some form of *embanked stone circle* or even a *complex ring cairn*, and inside it there were two *kerb cairns*. In its final phase, depending on how much of the interior had been filled with rubble, it might even fulfil the criteria for what Lynch (1972) calls a *kerb circle*.

A simpler way of presenting the same sequence would be to say that what had once been an open monument was closed off and eventually was almost concealed, while the sacred space that it had originally defined was used as the burial place for a small number of people. The cists in which they are buried are just like those found beneath the large round cairns in the surrounding area, and it seems quite possible that two of these monuments overlay the remains of other stone circles (Scott 1989: 100, 107; Bradley 1993: 92–3).

This particular sequence is unusually detailed, perhaps because the entire monument was not exposed to damage until its chance discovery below a deposit of peat. The individual elements in this sequence, however, are found at other monuments.

The first of these features is the treatment of the perimeter. At Temple Wood the character of the monument changed from an open to a closed circle. The same process can be traced on other sites, although not all these cases can be illustrated in the same amount of detail. Something rather similar has been observed with the stone circle at Berrybrae in north-east Scotland, although in this case the treatment of the original structure seems to have been even more drastic (Burl 1979: 26–30). This was a monument with one recumbent stone and a ring of nine uprights set in the outer edge of a bank. The site had been erected on a platform that was created for the purpose and appears to have been laid out on a solar alignment. The recumbent stone was the major feature of the monument, for beside it was a setting of white quartz.

Inside the circle there was a small ring cairn associated with a deposit of cremated bone. It is not clear whether such cairns are an original feature of recumbent stone circles or whether they were added afterwards. Certainly, it was during a later period of use that the form of this site was altered. Some of the uprights were pushed over and the tops of the others were broken. The remains of the ring cairn were demolished and the perimeter of the circle was replaced by a drystone wall. This concealed all the original monoliths apart from the recumbent stone and its neighbours, which seem to have resisted this onslaught.

Berrybrae was originally conceived as a stone circle, a monument that would have been relatively permeable, although the site had no formal entrance. In each case the uprights were the main feature of the original design, yet these were largely destroyed. A concerted effort was made to demolish the primary stone circle and the ring cairn that had been built inside it before the original monument was concealed below a drystone wall. As we shall see, the perimeter of other monuments may have been changed just as radically.

A second issue raised by the sequence at Temple Wood is the way in which the interior of what had been conceived as an entirely open monument was increasingly taken up by burials. Again that happens widely, but this development is difficult to interpret.

Perhaps the most important point is also the simplest of all. For many years it was supposed that stone circles originated during the Early Bronze Age rather than the Neolithic period. This was because burials of that date were so often found inside them. In the absence of stratigraphy or any method of absolute dating, it was reasonable enough to infer that these were primary deposits and reflected the original purpose of these sites. Not until it became apparent that stone circles might have developed in parallel with henges was this view seriously questioned, and even now it seems possible that some of the smaller stone circles built in the uplands were Bronze Age funerary monuments.

Some indication of the frequency with which burials have been found on these sites is provided by Burl (1972), who estimates that in Britain 23 percent of the stone circles include the remains of the dead or small cairns of the type used to mark their graves. Such figures are not without their difficulties, for many of these monuments are in areas of acid soil, where unburnt bones would not survive. Unless the dead had been buried in cists or accompanied by distinctive artefacts, inhumations are unlikely to have been identified. On the other hand, so sure were early excavators that stone circles were burial sites that any pit containing burnt material was identified as a mortuary deposit. This introduces some uncertainty, but, even making allowance for these problems, there is more evidence for formal burials inside stone circles than there is from henges.

There is a problem with many finds of human remains from stone circles, for, though these deposits can often be dated, it is rarely possible to relate their chronology to the monument itself. There are too few sites like Temple Wood where we can study the stratigraphic relationship between the perimeter and features in the interior, and stone circles are notoriously difficult to date by conventional means. The best contexts are probably the sockets in which the stones had been set, but on unthreatened monuments it is difficult to contemplate their excavation in the interests of research. Timber circles, on the other hand, are more easily dated because their postholes are accessible for study. Moreover, where the posts had been burnt or charred they provide excellent radiocarbon samples.

On the other hand, there is one very striking clue to the changing role of these monuments: where the interior space is occupied by burial cairns. We saw a good example of this development at Temple Wood. There seems little doubt that stone circles were originally intended as open arenas but there are many sites where the internal area is occupied by cairns. In some cases they take up so much of the available space that it would be difficult to enter the enclosure at all. Moreover, there are a small number of circles which seem to incorporate basic astronomical alignments which simply could not have been observed once those cairns had been built. This point has been argued most forcibly in the case of the recumbent stone circles of north-east Scotland (Shepherd 1987), but the same idea may have a wider application.

In fact, the invasion of stone circles by burial cairns did not occur on every site, although this is not to deny that the two forms of monument generally occur in close proximity to one another. It is most often observed in two areas, Cumbria and the Peak District, where many of these sites have been investigated in detail (Waterhouse 1985; Barnatt 1990).

The evidence from these regions is of unusually high quality and the combination of excavated information and field survey certainly supports the notion that many of the burial cairns found in association with stone circles and related monuments may be a secondary development (see Figure 44). This is most obvious where such monuments were superimposed on elements of the original construction, but the same point can probably be made where a cairn occupies most of the internal space inside an enclosure of this kind. It may also account for the apparently haphazard placing of cairns within these enclosures. This point is particularly striking, since the evidence from both regions shows a clear relationship between the creation of stone monuments with entrances and the addition of burial cairns, most probably during a later phase. It seems as if it was the *open* enclosures that were sought out for reuse rather than those which appear to have been closed from the outset, and this point is only emphasised by the siting of later cairns on top of the banks of several ring cairns. Again, a very similar relationship can be recognised in other parts of the country, although the nature of the surface remains are rarely recorded in so much detail.

BURYING MONUMENTS

At Temple Wood most of these processes took place together. The perimeter was modified until the main circle was cut off from the outside world and its interior was occupied by an increasing number of burials, some of them in specially constructed cairns. Yet even when this process had reached its full extent the outline of the enclosures was still apparent, and at least part of the interior may have remained free of rubble. There are other sites where the same process went still further.

A good example is a site at Dun Ruadh in County Tyrone, where the remains of a substantial ring cairn appear to be enclosed by a ditch with an external bank. Recent excavation has confirmed the long-held suspicion that this monument had been through a long sequence of changes (Simpson *et al.* 1992). In its original form it was a single-entrance henge, but during a later phase of activity part of the interior was enclosed by a low stone wall. This feature was broken by an entrance aligned with that of the henge. Within the stone setting there were a series of cists containing cremations associated with Early Bronze Age Food Vessels, and overlying the entire construction was an unusually high ring cairn, the interior of which was defined by an area of cobbling. It was during the Bronze Age phases of this monument that further cist burials were dug into the bank of the henge.

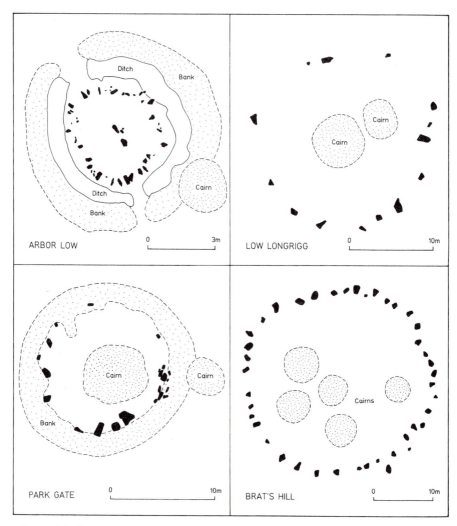

Figure 44. Stone circles and related monuments associated with round cairns in the Peak District and Cumbria, after Waterhouse (1985) and Barnatt (1990).

A broadly comparable sequence is known from Cairnpapple, near Edinburgh (see Figure 45; Piggott 1948). Again, the starting point for the sequence is provided by the earthworks of a henge. This monument was sited on a hilltop, which enjoyed a wide view over the surrounding area. Within this enclosure were two successive settings of posts or stones. The first of these did not form a complete circuit. Rather, it defined a semicircular area focusing on a roughly oval setting of upright stones of a kind known at other monuments of this period and sometimes described as a 'cove'. In the fillings of these sockets were a number of

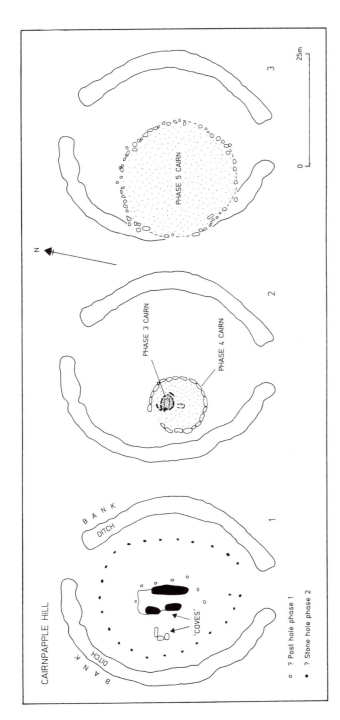

Figure 45. The excavated sequence at Cairnpapple Hill, according to the interpretation in Piggott (1948). What began as a sequence of open enclosures was increasingly taken over for the construction of burial cairns.

human cremations, and others were found on the old land surface alongside them. This setting was replaced by a ring of some twenty monoliths, which may have contained a second, rather larger feature of the same type. This setting was concentric with the inner ditch of the enclosure, suggesting that Cairnpapple saw the change from a timber monument to a stone circle that is so common around the middle of the third millennium BC. Although we cannot tell quite when the earthwork was constructed – it may have been built to enclose either of these settings – the final monument exemplifies many of the features discussed in Chapter 8. The stone circle itself is an entirely permeable construction, but the presence of the earthwork hides the interior from view. At the same time, the entire monument is located at the centre of what I have called a 'circular' landscape, although this time it looks across lower ground and does not rise up to the usual horizon of hills.

Again, all that was to change during the Early Bronze Age, for the monument went through as many as three phases of rebuilding during this period. The first involved the creation of a small kerb cairn within the interior of the stone circle. This structure is very similar to those found inside the enclosed area at Temple Wood and was associated with an inhumation burial containing Beaker pottery.

There followed the construction of a much more massive rubble cairn, revetted by a kerb of upright stones, and this was subsequently enlarged until the finished monument occupied much of the inside of the original enclosure and overlay part of its ditch and bank. By now there was very little open ground within the enclosure and the form of the original earthwork had been largely obscured. Again, this phase of rebuilding was marked by the construction of cists. The associated artefacts suggest that this process ran in parallel with the developments that I have described at Temple Wood and Dun Ruadh.

The excavator faced certain problems in interpreting the sequence on this site for the simple reason that each successive phase of construction did so much damage to the remains of its predecessors. For that reason, none of the monoliths remained *in situ*. But he did observe that the number of large stones required to revet the Early Bronze Age cairn was virtually the same as the number that had been employed in the stone circle. Economy of hypothesis suggested that the original monoliths had been taken down and reused. There was even the suggestion that one of these fragments could be matched with the cast left within its original socket.

At Cairnpapple, then, even more drastic changes were made to an existing stone circle than those we have observed on other sites. The surrounding earthwork was partly obliterated by the construction of an enormous burial mound – on a much smaller scale we see the same development at Arbor Low in the Peak District (Barnatt 1990: 31–9). The treatment of the original stone-built monument, however, was more drastic than what happened there or at Temple Wood, for it was completely demolished. This time the appropriate comparison is with Berrybrae. At Cairnpapple the monoliths were then reused in a quite different kind of monument. The original enclosure had occupied an unusual position for a henge, but in its final phase Cairnpapple was only one of many large funerary monuments to be built on prominent hilltops.

Much the same sequence is repeated at another site, 45 kilometres away at Glenrothes. Here, two different monuments are involved: the main henge monument at Balfarg and the neighbouring stone circle of Balbirnie. There are two henge monuments at Balfarg (Mercer 1981; Barclay and Russell-White 1993). One of these has been fully excavated and has revealed the same basic sequence as the first enclosure at Cairnpapple. A timber circle or circles seems to have been succeeded by a ring of monoliths. At the centre of the site there was a flat grave containing a Beaker burial. As at Cairnpapple, it is not clear at what stage the earthwork enclosing these features was constructed.

To some extent this development overlaps with the sequence at Balbirnie (Ritchie 1974), where the earliest feature on the site was a circle of ten stones (see Figure 46). In contrast to its counterpart at Balfarg, this was not enclosed by any earthwork. It had a rectangular stone setting at its centre, which has a close counterpart at the Stones of Stenness, where it might have acted as a monumentalised version of the kind of stone-lined hearth found in nearby houses or even among the features outside the kerb at Newgrange. There are sherds of Grooved Ware from Balbirnie, and there is evidence that cremated bones had been placed around the bases of the monoliths of the stone circle: a feature that recalls some of the deposits found in the first phase at Cairnpapple.

In between that central setting and the ring of monoliths a series of cists were constructed, not unlike those found at Temple Wood. There were five of these in all and their creation took up much of the available space in the interior of the monument. They were associated with a series of burials and with a variety of pots and other artefacts dating from the Early Bronze Age. One of the vessels from the site, a late Beaker, is of the same general date as the example accompanying the grave in the centre of the Balfarg henge. The final transformation of the monument at Balbirnie was into a single cairn. The monoliths of the original stone setting were linked together by a wall and the internal area, including the cist burials, was covered by a deposit of boulders. Among the stonework were scatters of cremated human bone and pottery that probably belong towards the end of the Early Bronze Age.

If the large monument at Balfarg recalls the earlier stages of the sequence at Cairnpapple, the history of the stone circle at Balbirnie has more in common with the later part of that sequence, for this was another open monument that was effectively buried beneath a burial cairn during the Early Bronze Age. Burl (1976) has compared the treatment of the Balbirnie stone circle with that of the circle at Berrybrae, while the use of the internal area for such a concentration of cist burials also has much in common with developments at Dun Ruadh and Temple Wood.

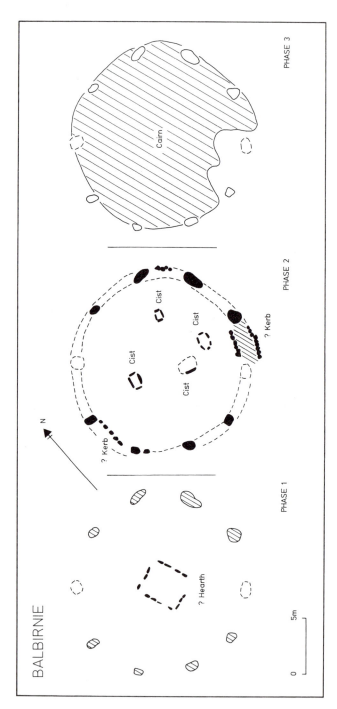

BALBIRNIE

? Hearth

PHASE 1

? Kerb

Cist

Cist

Cist

Cist

? Kerb

PHASE 2

Cairn

PHASE 3

N

0 ___ 5m

Figure 46. The excavated sequence at Balbirnie, according to the interpretation in Ritchie (1974). What was originally an open enclosure became less accessible until it was entirely buried beneath a cairn.

TOWARDS THE END

I have emphasised the evidence from a few well-excavated sites rather than attempt to interpret evidence of poorer quality. I have also relied on the results of surface observation only where the fieldwork has been of the same high standard. This results in something of an imbalance in our knowledge of these developments. It places more emphasis on sites in northern Britain than those in the south-west, where a similar development is suggested by the surface remains, and it emphasises the sequence on stone-built monuments rather than those with timber circles. That is because the excavated evidence is easier to interpret and because the sequences would appear to be spread over longer periods of time.

Even with these limitations, there is enough information to suggest that a remarkable change may have happened towards the end of the period in which stone circles were in use. Far from being created as Early Bronze Age funerary monuments, as prehistorians once supposed, these enclosures underwent a profound change in the manner in which they were utilised. It is because their uses altered in so many ways that their surface remains have been so difficult to classify in the field.

In Chapter 8 I emphasised the special properties of what I called 'permeable' monuments. I distinguished between the stone circles and the inward-looking world of the henge. I suggested that it was no coincidence that so many stone circles should have been created as the extent of the settled landscape changed towards the middle of the third millennium BC. The increasing use of the uplands in many parts of Britain made it possible to create quite new effects through the use of monumental architecture. It allowed structures to be built whose organisation provided a microcosm of the landscapes in which they were made. It allowed people outside the monuments to observe what was happening within, and it permitted those who were inside these structures to relate their configuration to a wider world beyond. That was not possible at many of the henges.

That ability to draw connections between the sacred space of the monuments and the features of the natural topography can be connected with two other elements. It seems to have been during the later use of stone circles that places in the uplands were marked by an increasing array of funerary monuments, some of the most impressive of them located along the skyline. At the same time, the building of such permeable enclosures in such a varied topography made it possible for the features of these monuments to refer directly to the world around them. This is what seems to have happened through the use of astronomical alignments in the planning of some of these sites. They located the newly built monuments within a wider sacred geography, but the key point is that the system depended on visual cross-references between these different elements.

It was during the Early Bronze Age that many of the largest monuments in Britain began to go out of use. This may have happened for many reasons, but during the course of that period it is clear that more effort was devoted to the construction of mounds than to the creation of other kinds of structures. More important, the richest burials could draw on a much wider range of grave goods than the assemblage of the Late Neolithic, so that the artefacts deposited with the dead might be made from exotic materials and evoke associations with widely scattered areas of Continental Europe. The burial of such objects in the grave made one kind of statement about the position of the dead and the expectations of their successors. The choice of location for the funeral became significant in another way.

We see this from the increasingly complex organisation of Early Bronze Age burials, in which different graves and even different mounds seem to have been carefully located in relation to one another, but we also see it in attitudes to history, for many of the richest graves and largest cemeteries were created near the monuments of the distant past (Barrett 1994: ch. 5; Woodward and Woodward 1996). This may have provided a vital source of legitimacy, for it offered a stability otherwise absent in the workings of Bronze Age society.

It may be in precisely this context that the later use of stone circles is to be understood. The structural evidence reviewed in this chapter can be interpreted in terms of three basic processes: a process of closure, by which what had originally been open arenas were made increasingly inaccessible; an appropriation of the past for the commemoration of a few individuals; and an attempt to harness the special properties of sacred places. All three developments had one common end, for each allowed an increasing identification between particular people and particular locations in the landscape. By implication, there is also evidence that others must have been excluded. Nowhere are these processes more evident than at a monument like Cairnpapple, where the last traces of the stone circle were erased and buried with the dead themselves.

Chapter 10

An agricultural revolution

The domestication of ritual life during later prehistory

Earlier chapters have traced the evolution of circular monuments through a succession of distinctive forms. This chapter completes this discussion by considering the ways in which the same ideas were interpreted as the character of land use changed towards the middle of the second millennium BC. It was at this stage that settlements, cemeteries and field systems developed in close proximity to one another, and it was then that there was an increase in the importance of arable farming. The first part of this chapter explores the complex interrelationship between the organisation of the last round barrows and the use of round houses in the neighbouring settlements. Taking the results of recent fieldwork in Cranborne Chase as its point of departure, it reconsiders the relationship between the 'ritual' landscapes of earlier prehistory and the agricultural landscapes that developed out of them.

The second part of the chapter looks forward to developments in the Late Bronze Age and Iron Age, and also offers a retrospect on the character of the lengthy sequence considered in this book. It contends that the creation and use of monuments was one of the main ways in which human experience was changed after the first adoption of domesticates. In many areas it was only as the role of such monuments lapsed that most of the elements associated with the 'Neolithic revolution' are found for the first time.

ROUND BARROWS AND ROUND HOUSES

One of the many problems experienced by archaeologists investigating 'variant circles' such as those discussed in Chapter 9 is in distinguishing between the remains of ring cairns and the foundations of prehistoric houses. This is considered as an inconvenience, a matter to be resolved by excavation, and a more important issue is overlooked. How were the forms of domestic buildings related to the those of funerary monuments? Having considered this question in relation to the first long mounds, we must explore the same issue as it applies to the last round barrows.

The general sequence in prehistoric Britain and Ireland underwent a considerable change from the middle of the second millennium BC. The timing of this development varies from one region to another. Thus the process was under way towards the end of the Early Bronze Age on Dartmoor and in parts of East Anglia, it was apparent on the chalk downland of Wessex and Sussex during the Middle Bronze Age, and is most obvious on the gravels of the south Midlands in the Late Bronze Age (Bradley 1996b). Despite these differences of chronology, the main features remain much the same. Monuments of the types discussed in Chapters 6 to 9 finally went out of use, and some of these sites were destroyed. There is a new emphasis on land division and the creation of field systems; there is more evidence of arable farming than there is in earlier periods; and, almost for the first time, settlement sites become archaeologically visible. These settlements are identified by the remains of substantial timber houses, storage pits, waterholes and, in some cases, earthwork enclosures. The distinction seemed so clear that in 1980 it was used to mark an important time of change in British prehistory (Barrett and Bradley 1980). The Earlier Bronze Age could be characterised as the period of the barrow cemeteries, while the Later Bronze Age witnessed an agricultural revolution with virtually all the characteristics once sought in the Neolithic.

More recent research has shown that these developments happened over a longer period of time. Any notion that they marked a horizon of change has had to be abandoned. Even so, the fact that such similar changes came to affect virtually all areas of the country did identify two significant questions for research. How was the transition effected from a landscape of monuments to a landscape of fields? And was the change as drastic as it had appeared in 1980? To this we can add a third, deceptively simple, question. How is it that the remains of the houses built at this time can be mistaken for those of funerary monuments?

This chapter is perhaps unusual in one respect. All the others have offered new interpretations of the significance of particular monuments or groups of monuments and, where possible, they have focused on sites which have been investigated by excavation. Although these examples were often chosen because of the high quality of the fieldwork, my interpretation often differed in significant ways from the discussion provided by the original investigator. The present chapter follows the same format, but in this case some of the fieldwork to be reconsidered is my own.

Between 1977 and 1984 I attempted to investigate the changing history of a region of Wessex called Cranborne Chase. The project was conducted together with John Barrett and Martin Green, and the results of this work were published by all three of us in 1991. The title of the book, 'Landscape, monuments and society', gives some indication of its aims (Barrett et al. 1991). It sought to interpret the earthwork monuments built in this region between about 4000 and 1500 BC and to study the transition to a landscape of settlements, houses and fields that happened after that time. In the book we considered each of these systems separately, but attempted to identify those features of the older landscape which still retained their importance during the crucial period of change – in this case, the Middle Bronze Age. In Cranborne Chase the only features that fitted this criterion were the round barrows built throughout this phase. At the same time, we also looked for evidence that some of the settlements, cemeteries and fields had already played a role before that period. The results of the research were inconclusive. There were fragments of earlier pottery on many of these sites but they did not seem to be linked with any structural evidence. Despite the excavation of a wide range of monuments, including a henge, several round barrows, two settlements, their cemeteries and their fields, it seemed as if there were few points of contact between the two systems, and there were even cases in which older monuments had been ploughed out during the period of change. Maybe the conventional wisdom was right after all. Perhaps we were condemned to interpret each kind of landscape in a completely different way.

I now consider that our approach was too cautious, for at a deeper level these different elements were more closely related than is often supposed. As we have seen, British prehistorians have devoted considerable efforts to defining different classes of monuments and to tracing their development over time and space. They have even used this evidence to show how different insular society was from its counterparts on the Continent. As I argued in Chapter 6, one of the features they emphasise is the long-standing tradition of circular monuments in Britain – from henge monuments to stone circles, and from round barrows to round houses. Yet they do not seem to have considered that there is anything interesting about the way in which the same groundplan was chosen for so many different structures. In fact, the problem is more serious than it seems at first, for we now know that some of these circular monuments emphasise simple lunar or solar axes, whereas others are organised according to the cardinal points.

I considered some of this evidence in an earlier chapter, and at this point it is enough to suggest that these different elements form part of the same symbolic system. That may be just as relevant to the late prehistoric houses as it was to stone circles and tombs, but there has been a curious reluctance to consider why so many different structures assumed a similar layout. In contrast to those studying the archaeology of the Neolithic and Early Bronze Age, specialists on later prehistory have sought a practical explanation for their material. Those prehistoric round houses, for example, are supposed to be oriented towards the south-east so that they will catch the light of the morning sun. This seems entirely plausible, but in fact many of them are slightly misaligned. They face in the general direction required by this hypothesis but the placing of their doors often misses the position of the sunrise. In fact, their planning may be governed by symbolic considerations (Parker Pearson 1996: 127).

The same interpretation is suggested by some of the Early Bronze Age round barrows in southern England. It is obviously difficult to talk about the orientation of monuments that possess a continuous perimeter, but there are quite a number of examples whose quarry ditch is broken by one or more causeways. These have recently been discussed by Ashbee (1976: 55–6). Although he considers their chronology, nowhere does he mention that their entrances are generally to the south or south-east. This reflects the alignment of Bronze Age round houses, but in a context in which a 'functional' explanation is impossible.

A rather similar significance may attach to some of the pottery vessels used during the Early Bronze Age. The larger of these were often associated with cremation burials: indeed, it is sometimes suggested that Collared Urns were employed in funerary rituals rather than everyday life. It has never been easy to explain how such ungainly vessels were used, and still less why they should have been inverted over the remains of the dead. One possible explanation has been suggested by Lynn (1993), who has commented on the striking resemblance between these inverted pots and the round houses that were a feature of the landscape from the Late Neolithic period onwards (see Figure 47). Although all too little is known about the Early Bronze Age pattern of settlement, this observation suggests that a symbolic connection existed between the dwellings of the living and the 'house urns' buried with the dead.

It would be possible to consider other connections of this kind, but that is not the purpose of this chapter. My basic point is a simple one. The same circular archetype accounts for the organisation of many different kinds of structure. It is not necessary to know its original meanings for us to recognise that supposedly different types of monument were related to the same organisation of space. While they share one ideal groundplan, we must remember that they could also have been transformations of one another.

This has important implications, for it means that some of the characteristic features of the later prehistoric landscape employed the same symbolic code as earlier forms of monument. In that sense the change from a landscape dominated by burial mounds to one dominated by round houses might not appear as abrupt as it has seemed. The same applies to the translation of ritual activity between these two domains. On another level, this suggests that in discussing prehistoric perceptions of the world archaeologists have made an unwarranted distinction between domestic landscapes, with their evidence of food production, and what they call ritual landscapes, with their more specialised monuments. In fact, both were built out of the very same elements. Instead of basing our analysis on the positions of different monuments in the landscape of Cranborne Chase, we should have begun by recognising the fundamental importance of cosmology.

How does this help us to reinterpret the archaeology of that region? The problem has always been to relate the Middle Bronze Age barrows, with their echoes of earlier monuments, to the settlements and houses, which seem to be a largely new development. Two features are quite clear: it is in the Middle Bronze Age that cemeteries are first found in close proximity to the settlements, and both kinds of site share the same range of pottery. These links are supported by neutron-activation analysis of the ceramics and by radiocarbon dating (Bradley 1981). At one site in southern England, Itford Hill, parts of the same vessel were divided between one of the houses and one of the burials (Holden 1972).

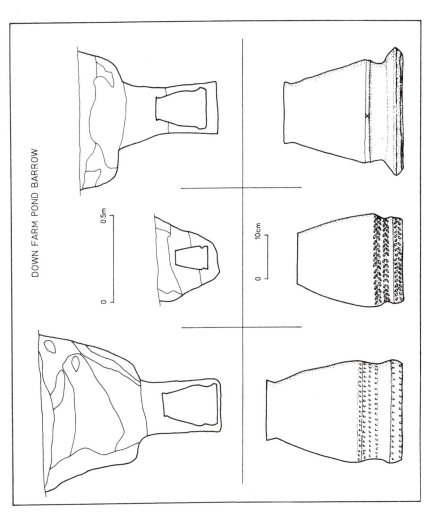

DOWN FARM POND BARROW

Figure 47. Early Bronze Age ceramics as 'house urns'. The illustration shows outline sections of three of the burials in the Down Farm pond barrow, after Barrett *et al.* (1991), together with detailed drawings of the inverted pots, after Barrett (1991b).

A useful starting point is provided by two pairs of cemeteries and settlements. The first of these cemeteries is associated with South Lodge Camp, where the Cranborne Chase Project began its work (Barrett *et al.* 1991: 144–83). The settlement is a ditched enclosure set within an already established field system. A hundred metres away is a cemetery of small barrows, one of which may have originated during the Early Bronze Age. At least two of the other mounds are contemporary with the enclosure, while the third is probably later in date than one element of its field system. The two barrows with Middle Bronze Age cremations both have shallow ditches, interrupted by a causeway to the south. The smaller of these, Barrow Pleck Site C, is virtually the same size as the smaller of the buildings inside South Lodge Camp (House 1). This barrow contained a central cremation and a series of burials which clustered around the ditch terminals. The house, on the other hand, contained an animal burial in the equivalent position to the primary burial beneath the mound (see Figure 48).

The resemblance between these two structures might be dismissed as coincidental, but in fact it is repeated not only in Cranborne Chase but in another region with a detailed settlement record. It was at Itford Hill on the chalk hills of Sussex that one of the first associations between a Middle Bronze Age settlement and its cemetery was recognised, and in this case the mound took a rather similar form to Barrow Pleck Site C, with a shallow ditch interrupted to the south (Holden 1972). A series of upright posts had been bedded in that feature (I am not convinced by the recent claim that these elements belong to a

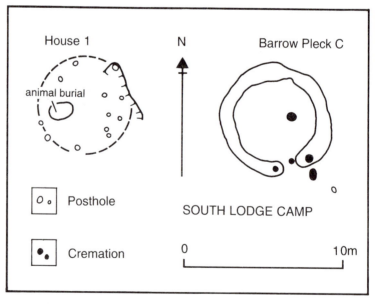

Figure 48. Outline plan of a round house at South Lodge Camp compared with that of a barrow in the nearby cemetery, after Barrett *et al.* (1991).

reused henge, see M. Gibson 1996). Again, there was one central cremation and a further concentration of burials outside the 'entrance' to this monument. The houses in the nearby settlement were of two kinds. The larger of these were equipped with porches, which projected from the main ring of roof supports to meet an outer screen that supported the eaves. Again, these structures showed the same organisation of space as the round barrows, with their porches oriented towards the south. In one case a phallus had been deposited in the equivalent position to the main group of cremations. The use of upright posts to define the edge of the round barrow may emphasise the link between these separate structures (see Figure 49).

It is worth remaining with the Sussex sites a little longer, as these present further points of interest. Itford Hill is not the only completely excavated Middle Bronze Age round barrow. There was another on Steyning Round Hill, and this repeats the characteristic layout in which a shallow ditch is open to the south (Burstow 1958). Again, there may have been a central burial, but in this case there were two clusters of cremations. One followed the edge of the mound or cairn to the north, while the other occupied the equivalent position to the south. It was the latter group that included the only item of metalwork (see Figure 50).

This find is particularly interesting because similar artefacts can be found in the excavation of Middle Bronze Age settlements. A particularly valuable project was at Blackpatch, also in Sussex, where the excavator plotted the positions of all

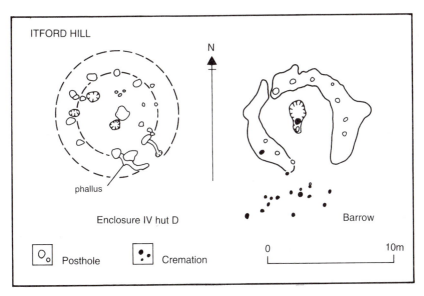

Figure 49. Outline plan of a round barrow on Itford Hill compared with that of a house in the nearby settlement. Modified from Burstow and Holleyman (1957) and Holden (1972).

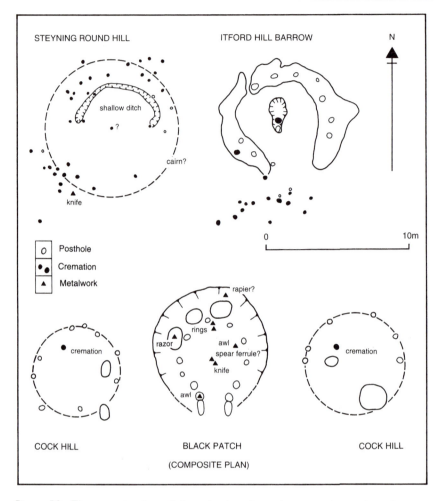

Figure 50. The organisation of deposits in selected cemeteries and settlements in Sussex. The information is drawn from Burstow (1958), Ratcliffe-Densham and Ratcliffe-Densham (1961), Holden (1972) and Drewett (1982).

the artefacts discovered inside the houses (Drewett 1982). He interpreted these as evidence for the distribution of activities within and between the different buildings, but in the case of the metal artefacts this does not seem likely. It is hard to accept that they were lost by chance, least of all two finger rings which were found together on the floor. Given the number of metal artefacts and their size – they even include part of a rapier – it seems more likely that they were deposited deliberately, perhaps when the houses were abandoned. This might also explain why the range of metal items was almost exactly the same as we find in the cemeteries of the same period.

The distribution of these items within these houses is revealing too. Since the major structures are almost identical to one another, I am illustrating a composite structure, within which I have plotted the distribution of all the metal finds (see Figure 50). Two of these were found in the centre of the building, one was associated with its porch, and the others were towards its outer edge. Each of these locations has its counterpart in the organisation of the cemeteries. There is normally a central burial beneath the mound or cairn and a second focus of activity is at the entrance to the south. On Steyning Round Hill a third concentration of deposits follows the northern perimeter of the monument. Again, this suggestion is open to the objection that such similarities could have arisen by chance, but this comparison between barrows and houses works the other way round, for two of the excavated buildings on the Sussex site of Cock Hill have human cremations beneath their floors (see Figure 50; Ratcliffe-Densham and Ratcliffe-Densham 1961).

To return to our original starting point in Cranborne Chase, how did the sequence develop? I mentioned that our work was structured around two pairs of cemeteries and settlements. What of the other site? This was at Down Farm, Woodcuts (Barrett *et al.* 1991: 183–214). The cemetery was a reused barrow originally constructed during the Neolithic period and it was located 110 metres from an enclosed settlement rather like South Lodge Camp. Again, the Middle Bronze Age burials were generally located to the south of the monument, but in this case the dead were treated in several different ways. The main group of deposits included seven cremations, but just beyond these there were three inhumation burials. On the north side of the monument was a scatter of unburnt human bones. All these deposits were in the same stratigraphic context and should be contemporary with one another (see Figure 51). This is rather revealing as the inhumations recall the burial practices of the Early Bronze Age. The urned cremations are a characteristic feature of the Middle Bronze Age, while the scatter of unburnt bones anticipates the treatment of the dead during the Late Bronze Age and Iron Age. At Down Farm, however, the relevant context provides radiocarbon dates which agree with those from the settlement.

The cremation cemetery shows a similar organisation of space to the houses found nearby. It also recalls the plan of a rather larger building at South Lodge Camp. But that does not exhaust the comparisons we can make. Some time after our project had ended, Martin Green discovered another small group of mounds in Cranborne Chase and excavation showed that two of these were linked by an avenue of paired posts which ended in a timber circle (see Figure 52; Green 1994). At the time it seemed likely that this was a Neolithic feature, but recent radiocarbon dates exclude this possibility entirely. Although one of those mounds originated during the Late Neolithic, the post setting that surrounds it was erected during the Late Bronze Age. Such a find is unprecedented in Wessex, but it has interesting implications. It means that at least one round barrow in Cranborne Chase was still the focus of attention when others were being

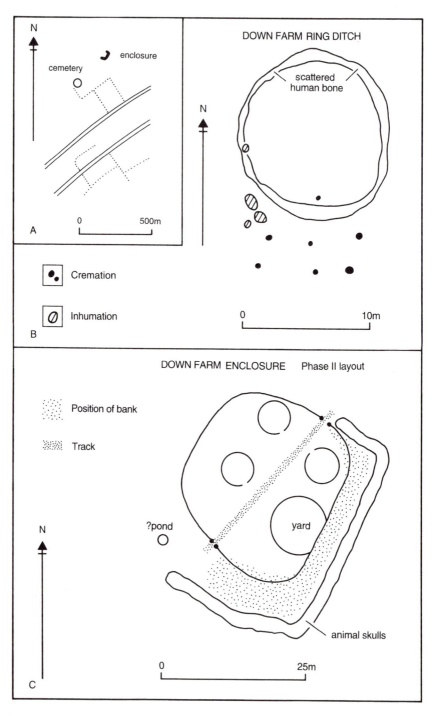

Figure 51. The relationship between the Middle Bronze Age cemetery and settlement at Down Farm, after Barrett *et al.* (1991).

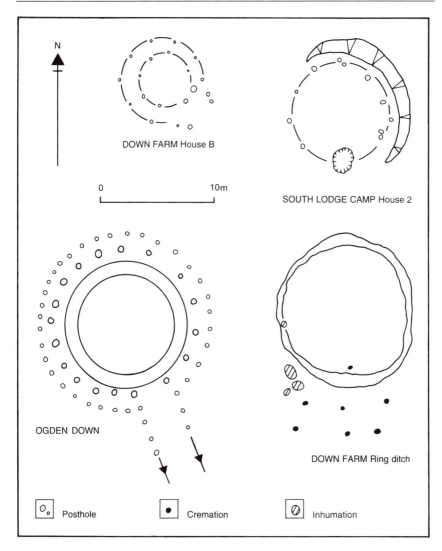

Figure 52. The structural organisation of selected cemeteries and round houses in Cranborne Chase. The plans of the round houses and the Down Farm cemetery are modified from Barrett *et al.* (1991). The plan of the Ogden Down round barrow and post alignment is taken from an unpublished original kindly provided by Martin Green.

ploughed out. It may be more than a coincidence that the round barrow selected for reuse was of approximately the same size as the houses built during the Middle Bronze Age and that the avenue approached it from the south-east. Despite the unusual character of this structure, it conformed to established principles that governed the ordering of space.

I have mentioned how the deposit of unburnt bones found in the Down Farm cemetery anticipates the ritual practices of the Late Bronze Age and Iron Age when round barrows were little used. The location of this material is very interesting, for it is found in the sector of the barrow ditch which faces towards the settlement. In the equivalent position in the ditch enclosing that settlement there was another unusual group of material (see Figure 51). This consisted of a complete cow skull together with the skulls of five dogs. This is the kind of deposit we might anticipate on a rather later site where human remains might also be found. A similar connection was recognised by John Barrett at South Lodge Camp, where a series of bronze artefacts were found in the enclosure ditch at its closest point to the barrows. As he pointed out, these artefacts are of types which in an earlier period would have been buried with the dead (Barrett *et al.* 1991: 183). Indeed, there are the remains of twisted wire ornaments from both of these contexts.

These arguments are enough to indicate that those two landscapes in Cranborne Chase were linked to one another in more ways than we originally thought possible. It would be misleading to distinguish too sharply between the 'ritual' landscape that formed in earlier prehistory and the agricultural landscape that seems to have taken its place, for even the most practical activities, such as building a house or enclosing a settlement, drew on a symbolic code of considerable antiquity. It was the fact that changes were expressed though modifications of an established cosmology that made it possible to contemplate new developments in the pattern of settlement. It was precisely because the successive landscapes of Cranborne Chase were organised according to similar principles of order that changes could be accomplished so rapidly.

LOOKING FORWARD

The vantage point provided by this study commands a view in two directions. First, I shall consider how these relationships were worked out during the Late Bronze Age and Iron Age, and then I shall conclude this account of monuments and their influence by reflecting on the ways in which their creation had helped to shape human experience over the previous 2,500 years.

The Middle Bronze Age of Cranborne Chase was a period of transition from one kind of system to another, and even though some of the same ideas may have been retained they appear to have been expressed in entirely different ways. Apart from the changes in the subsistence economy which I have already described, there were other major developments. One was the gradual disuse of burial mounds. The Middle Bronze Age examples considered in the first part of this chapter came at the very end of a long tradition and were without obvious successors. Although the same period saw the development of flat cemeteries or urnfields, we know less about how the dead were treated after that time (Brück 1995). By the early Iron Age, however, it seems that their remains were often placed within settlement sites (Hill 1995). This practice entirely eclipsed the older tradition of building funerary monuments. A variety of human remains extending from articulated bodies to isolated fragments came to be associated with occupation sites, where they might often be deposited together with animal bones and a variety of domestic artefacts. There were some changes in the contexts where this took place, and these may have shifted over time from the outer boundaries of the settlements to their interior, where a particularly favoured context was the grain-storage pit. At the same time, there may have been a parallel development away from the deployment of isolated bones to the burial of entire bodies. In both these ways the dead seem to have been integrated into the domestic sphere. The use of storage pits for so many of these deposits suggests that a further link may have existed between death, regeneration and fertility, as symbolised by the storage and growing of grain (Barrett 1989; Brück 1995; see also Bloch and Parry 1982).

If that is so, it may be less surprising that a greater emphasis was placed on the symbolic role of the boundaries around these settlements. We have already seen how their earthworks might provide a focus for deposits of human remains. Other specialised deposits could also be made in this area (Hingley 1990; Hill 1995). This is important because recent work has emphasised that the planning of some of these sites was itself attended by symbolism. This is true on two different levels. In many parts of later prehistoric Britain the enclosed sites followed an almost precisely circular outline. This applies whether the perimeter was defined by a fence, a simple bank and ditch or by the more massive barriers usually described as defences. Examples of such traditions include the Late Bronze Age ringworks of eastern England, the palisaded enclosures of the Scottish borderland and the 'defended' farmsteads found in western Britain. Although these sites have been considered in functional terms, the placing of their entrances sometimes suggests that they were laid out in relation to a complex symbolic scheme. That may be why the enclosures of the Wessex Iron Age generally had their entrances to the east. The same is true of the more massive monuments described as hillforts (Hill 1996). This tradition was sufficiently tenacious to survive into the first millennium AD, when it influenced the planning of Irish ringforts.

That characteristic layout in turn recalls the organisation of the houses, which usually conformed to a circular groundplan. Again, the entrances were generally to the south or east, and where the sites are sufficiently well preserved it is clear that their doorways were the focus of symbolic elaboration. There may also have been a significant distinction between the left- and right-hand sides of these buildings, again suggesting that the importance of the circular archetype was still maintained (Fitzpatrick 1994). The origins of these practices are worth considering here, for we have seen how the houses of the Middle Bronze Age were organised according to similar principles to the mounds in the nearby cemeteries. Again, the focus for ritual activity seems to have changed over time, from specially constructed monuments into the domestic sphere. This may explain why circular shrines have been identified inside a number of later prehistoric settlements – they merely made explicit a development that had happened much more widely. Domestic life had become a major focus for symbolic elaboration (Barrett 1989; Parker Pearson 1996).

We can sum up these developments by emphasising a series of similarities and contrasts. Monumental architecture changed its character over time, and structures which had lain outside domestic life altogether were abandoned or destroyed in favour of enclosures and hillforts. These were integrated more directly into the everyday life of the community. Yet, while this may look like a radical development, these new constructions provided the focus for a series of structured deposits, some of which may be the direct successors of those found on earlier sites. Moreover, the very form of many of the 'domestic' enclosures still echoed the principles of order expressed by specialised monuments in the past. The treatment of the dead echoes these distinctions too, for it was a process that became closely integrated into the cycle of food production. By the middle of the Iron Age the dead were frequently placed in storage pits amidst the houses of the living, yet it is well to remember that even the organisation of those buildings had features in common with the structure of burial monuments last used many centuries before.

LOOKING BACK

It is a curious paradox that so many features of later prehistory are precisely the ones that are supposed to be the outcome of the 'Neolithic' revolution. This is true not only of Britain and Ireland but of most of the regions that were outside the area that experienced the first wave of agricultural settlement. There is evidence of what seems to be defensive architecture, and weaponry was produced on an increasing scale. There are signs that craft production intensified during the same period and indications of greater social inequality. According to one interpretation of the concentrations of granaries inside southern English hillforts, social transactions may also have involved the administration of surplus grain (Gent 1983). Of all the developments that can be identified during this period, only one was shared with the communities of the Neolithic: the mobilisation of human labour for building public monuments.

In fact, the prehistory of European agriculture went through not one but two major periods of change and these have more in common than we often suppose. The first accompanied the extension of Bandkeramik culture through central and north-west Europe and continued in a modified form among neighbouring communities as far as western France and southern Scandinavia. To a certain extent the second can be related to the rise of the Urnfield complex, elements of which are found across large parts of the Continent from the late second millennium BC. Its interpretation has raised many problems, not least the way in which it brings together some very different elements: the flat cemeteries that give the group its name; the early development of hillforts and the reorganisation of cereal farming. At one time archaeologists supposed that these changes were the result of a migration from central to western Europe, but today more attention is being paid to the changes in ritual practice that took place at this time. The transmission of these new ideas has been compared with the spread of religious beliefs (Alexander 1979). Such beliefs may even have extended to new ways of thinking about fertility and the natural world. Thus the rapid expansion of farming in many different parts of Europe may have been facilitated by ideological change.

This idea is naturally a controversial one, but it is striking how much it is echoed in recent discussions of the Neolithic period. Andrew Sherratt talks of a process analogous to religious conversion taking place at that time; Whittle (1996a) writes about 'the creation of new worlds'; and , as we saw in Chapter 2, Thomas suggests that 'the appropriation of nature may have been conceptual as much as it was physical' (1991a: 181). These new conceptions first arose among people who most certainly were farmers, but many were adopted across a wider area, in which hunter gatherers contributed more to the population. In that case, such ideas were expressed most eloquently through the building of monuments.

If there were some similarities between the adoption of Neolithic material culture and the spread of the Urnfield complex, there are important problems that need to be addressed. Both involved major changes in attitudes to food production, but it was between about 1300 and 800 BC that we first recognise the political changes that are so often considered to result from the adoption of agriculture. We must ask ourselves why they did not occur very widely in northern and western Europe before that time. Why were people prepared to commit themselves to intensive mixed farming at this stage, when their ancestors had rejected a similar opportunity?

In Chapter 2 I put forward the suggestion that farming might have seemed inconsistent with the attitudes shared by hunter gatherers in many different parts of Europe. I also suggested that such inhibitions took a long time to break down and that this may account for the rather gradual adoption of domesticates. In most cases the result was a dispersed pattern of settlement and an economy in which the use of livestock was probably more important than cereal farming. In many regions this was to remain the case until the later part of the Bronze Age. But that is not to say that attitudes remained unchanged, for, as I have argued in previous chapters, human experience of place and time had seen subtle shifts over that period, so that the new ideas associated with the Urnfield complex were easier to accept than those accompanying the first Neolithic expansion. The all-important changes of attitude came about not only through a growing familiarity with domesticated plants and animals. Above all, they may have required that new sense of time and place. The development of this particular way of thinking may have been influenced by the presence of monuments.

I have said something of how and why those monuments were created, but why should they have had such a profound impact on human consciousness? Part of the answer may be suggested by the ways in which the long barrows developed. The original prototypes may have been the abandoned houses of the dead and the idea of building a mound might have been suggested by seeing the ways in which such buildings decayed. That is to say, the basic conception arose from the day-to-day experience of living in a world steeped in symbolic significance. These different levels of meaning would be learnt in the course of social life, and they would eventually be taken for granted. They would form part of the lived experience of people in the past and would mould their perceptions and conduct as effectively as any explicit rules. Changes would generally be easier to institute if they conformed to those expectations, and over a long period of time such conventions might change their significance as much by accident as design.

Monuments acted as mnemonics, as ways of recalling an otherwise vanished past, so that the almost instinctive process of reading the significance of material culture was extended over time in a way that had only rarely been possible before the Neolithic period. This meant that in some cases traditional practices were carried through into a new social setting, where their significance was altered. In other instances, where the population had a less stable history, the presence of older monuments posed a problem that people needed to interpret in ways that had meaning for themselves. In each case the result might be very much the same. They maintained a rigid adherence to traditional principles of design in a world that was changing.

The stability of stone and earthwork monuments stands in total contrast to the flux of daily life and even transcends the passing of the generations. Stone monuments might last longer than timber structures, and one was often built to replace the other, but a still more important development concerned the treatment of the dead and cut across any differences of raw materials. The first mortuary monuments separated the dead from the world of the living, while later monuments often allowed continuous access between them. This is evidenced by the addition and rearrangement of the bones, but the decision to build such structures has a more profound implication, for it involved not only continuous contacts between the past and the present, but suggests that the same process was to extend into the future as well. The same may have been true of Early Bronze Age burial mounds, where it seems as if the deposition of the primary burial was understood as only the first stage in a lengthy process (Mizoguchi 1993).

The history of enclosures took a rather similar form. Those with causewayed ditches may originally have been associated with groups of houses, but, as the nature of the settlement pattern changed, these earthworks retained their original design in a setting that was completely different. The form of the perimeter earthwork became increasingly stereotyped, and there is far more evidence of rituals taking place at these sites, including feasting, the treatment of the dead and the deposition of specialised artefacts. In one sense these places stood for the nucleated settlements that existed only as a memory. Their earthworks seem to have provided a symbolic centre for a community, whose members may have been dispersed across large areas of the landscape: such ties to place retained their ideological importance although they were less evident in daily life.

This is even more obvious in the case of the circular monuments. Whether these were passage graves, henges or stone circles, they may all have reflected a common symbolic scheme. The siting of henges and stone circles suggests that the same ideas extended to the landscape as a whole, so that these monuments could be considered as the centre of a world. The visual cross-references between these sites and other monuments, some of them extending as far as the horizon, united these different places in a complex sacred geography. It was not only the enclosures that had their place in the scheme of things, for the graves of specific people were located in direct relationship to these sites, until what had originally been open arenas, capable of containing large congregations, became the burial places of a few individuals. Conceptions of place and time held firm despite these changes. These sites had been used for many generations and it seems to have been unthinkable to depart from their original outlines. When burial cairns were constructed within older stone circles they were located in conformity to a long-established sense of what was appropriate in these places. Even when their original roles had been modified profoundly, the fabric of these structures was often paid some respect. Thus when an enclosure like Cairnpapple was buried beneath an enormous barrow, both the choice of location and the outline of that mound acknowledged its long-standing significance.

Thus it was into a very different world from that of Mesolithic hunter gatherers that the ritual and economic system associated with the Urnfield complex began to be assimilated. It was a world which knew its own antiquity and had its own conception of a future: a world in which particular locations had become the pivot of communal life and in which particular people were buried according to their understanding of that scheme. As a result, without anyone intending it, this was also a world in which the extended time scale of agricultural production was no more incomprehensible or alien than the appropriation of places in the landscape. That may be why it was possible for a second agricultural revolution to take place in so many different parts of Europe and over a surprisingly short period.

The evidence from southern Britain illustrates the limits of this sequence more effectively than the situation anywhere else. Here, the first monuments to be built were mounds that seem to have referred back to a distant tradition of longhouses in the agricultural settlements of the loess. The last funerary monuments in this area were small circular mounds which illustrate the same kind of relationship, for they are organised according to the same principles as the domestic buildings found near to them. From the Middle Bronze Age onwards it was those houses that provided one of the principal foci in the ritual life of the community. As one kind of sequence ended, another had already begun. This sums up the peculiar character of a process that in different ways had extended across large parts of the Continent. Between the houses of the living and the houses of the dead there was a mixing of identities that contributed as much as anything to the shaping of human experience in Neolithic and Bronze Age Europe.

References

Abrams, E. 1989. Architecture and energy: an evolutionary perspective. In M. Schiffer (ed.) *Archaeological method and theory*, 1, 47–87. Tucson: University of Arizona Press.

Adam, B. 1990. *Time and social theory*. Oxford: Polity Press.

Ahlbäck, T. 1987. *Saami religion*. Uppsala: Donner Institute for Research in Religious and Cultural History.

Alexander, J. 1979. Islam in Africa: the archaeological recognition of religion. In B. Burnham and J. Kingsbury (eds) *Space, hierarchy and society*, 215–28. Oxford: British Archaeological Reports.

Andersen, S. 1993. Early and Middle Neolithic agriculture in Denmark: pollen spectra from soils in burial mounds of the Funnel Beaker Culture. *Journal of European Archaeology* 1, 153–80.

Ashbe, P. 1976. Amesbury Barrow 51: excavation, 1960. *Wiltshire Archaeological Magazine* 70/71, 1–60.

Ashbee, P., Smith, I. and Evans, J. 1979. The excavation of three long barrows near Avebury, Wiltshire. *Proceedings of the Prehistoric Society* 45, 207–300.

Atkinson, R. 1951. The henge monuments of Great Britain. In R. Atkinson, C. M. Piggott and N. Sandars, *Excavations at Dorchester, Oxon*, 81–107. Oxford: Ashmolean Museum.

Bailey, G. 1983. Concepts of time in quaternary prehistory. *Annual Review of Anthropology* 12, 165–92.

Bamford, H. 1985, *Briar Hill excavations 1974–1978*. Northampton: Northampton Development Corporation.

Bang-Andersen, S. 1983. On the use of ochre among prehistoric hunter gatherer groups in southern Norway. *Mesolithic Miscellany* 4.2, 10–12.

Barclay, G. and Russell-White, C. 1993. Excavations in the ceremonial complex of the fourth to second millennia BC at Balfarg/Balbirnie, Glenrothes, Fife. *Proceedings of the Society of Antiquaries of Scotland* 123, 42–210.

Barker, G. 1985. *Prehistoric farming in Europe*. Cambridge: Cambridge University Press.

Barnatt, J. 1989. *Stone circles of Britain*. Oxford: British Archaeological Reports.

Barnatt, J. 1990. *The henges, stone circles and ring cairns of the Peak District*. Sheffield: Sheffied University Department of Archaeology and Prehistory.

Barnatt, J. and Herring, P. 1986. Stone circles and megalithic geometry: an experiment to test alternative design practices. *Journal of Archaeological Science* 13, 431–49.

Barrett, J. 1988. The living, the dead and the ancestors: Neolithic and Early Bronze Age mortuary practices. In J. Barrett and I. Kinnes (eds) *The archaeology of context in the Neolithic and Early Bronze Age: recent trends*, 30–41. Sheffield: Sheffield University Department of Archaeology and Prehistory.

Barrett, J. 1989. Food, gender and metal: questions of social reproduction. In M. L. S. Sørensen and R. Thomas (eds) *The Bronze Age – Iron Age transition in Europe*, 304–20. Oxford: British Archaeological Reports.

Barrett, J. 1990. The monumentality of death: the character of Early Bronze Age mortuary mounds in southern Britain. *World Archaeology* 22, 179–89.

Barrett, J. 1991a. Towards an archaeology of ritual. In P. Garwood, D. Jennings, R. Skeates and J. Toms (eds) *Sacred and profane*, 1–9. Oxford: Oxford University Committee for Archaeology.

Barrett, J. 1991b. Bronze Age pottery and the problem of classification. In J. Barrett, R. Bradley and M. Hall (eds) *Papers on the prehistoric archaeology of Cranborne Chase*, 201–30. Oxford: Oxbow.

Barrett, J. 1994. *Fragments from antiquity*. Oxford: Blackwell.

Barrett, J. and Bradley, R. (eds) 1980. *Settlement and society in the British Later Bronze Age*. Oxford: British Archaeological Reports.

Barrett, J., Bradley, R. and Green, M. 1991. *Landscape, monuments and society*. Cambridge: Cambridge University Press.

Becker, C. J. 1947. Mosefunde Lerkar fra yngre Stenalder. *Aarbøger*, 1947 (whole volume).

Beeching, A., Coudart, A. and Lebolloch, M. 1982. Concevreux (Aisne): Une enceinte chalcoloithique et la problématique des 'camps'. In Vallée de l'Aisne: cinq années de fouilles protohistoriques. *Revue Archéologique de Picardie* numéro spécial, 149–69.

Benike, P. and Ebbesen, K. 1986. The bog find from Sigersdal. *Journal of Danish Archaeology* 5, 85–115.

Bergh, S. 1995. *Landscape of the monuments*. Stockholm: Riksantikvarieämbet Arkeologiska Undersöknigar.

Bernaldó de Quirós, F. 1995. El naciamiento de la muerte. In R. Fábregas Valcarce, F. Pérez Losada and C. Fernández Ibáñez (eds) *Arqueoloxía da Morte*, 35–59. Xinzo da Lima: Concello da Xinzo da Lima.

Bernhardt, G. 1986. Die linearbandkeramische Siedlung von Köln-Lindenthal, *Kölner Jahrbuch* 18/19: 7–165.

Biel, J. 1991. Auf den Spuren der Michelsberger Kultur. *Archäologie in Deutschland* 4 (October–December 1991), 26–9.

Binant, P. 1991. *Les sepultures du Palaeolithique*. Paris: Errance.

Bird-David, N. 1990. The giving environment. Another perspective on the economic system of hunter gatherers. *Current Anthropology* 31, 183–96.

Bird-David, N. 1993. Tribal metaphorization of human-nature relatedness: a comparative analysis. In K. Milton (ed.) *Environmentalism: the view from anthropology*, 112–25. London: Routledge.

Blanchet, J.-C. 1993. Ile-de-France. *Gallia Informations* (1993), 1–175.

Bloch, M. 1974. Symbols, songs, dances and features of articulation: is religion an extreme form of traditional authority? *Archives Européen de Sociologie* 15, 55–81.

Bloch, M. 1977. The past and the present in the present. *Man* 12, 278–92.

Bloch, M. 1985. From cognition to ideology. In R. Fardon (ed.) *Power and knowledge*, 21–48. Edinburgh: Scottish Academic Press.

Bloch, M. 1986. *From blessing to violence*. Cambridge: Cambridge University Press.

Bloch, M. and Parry, J. 1982. Introduction: death and the regeneration of life. In M. Bloch and J. Parry (eds) *Death and the regeneration of life*, 1–44. Cambridge: Cambridge University Press.

Boelicke, U. 1976. Das Neokithische Erdwerk Urmitz. *Acta Praehistorica et Archaeologica* 7, 73–121.

Boelicke, U., Von Brandt, D., Lüning, J., Stehli, P. and Zimmerman, A. 1988. *Der bandkeramicsche Siedlungsplatz Langweiler 8*. Bonn: Rheinisches Ausgrabungen 28.

Bogucki, P. 1988. *Forest farmers and stockbreeders. Early agriculture and its consequences in north-central Europe*. Cambridge: Cambridge University Press.

Boujot, C. and Cassen, S. 1992. Le developpement des premières architectures funeraires monumentales en France occidentale. In C.-T. Le Roux (ed.) *Paysans et batisseurs*, 195–211. Rennes: Revue Archéologique de l'Ouest, supplément 5.

Bourdieu, P. 1990. *The logic of practice*. Cambridge: Polity Press.

Bradley, R. 1978. *The prehistoric settlement of Britain*. London: Routledge.

Bradley, R. 1981. Various styles of urn: cemeteries and settlement in southern Britain, 1400–1000 BC. In R. Chapman, I. Kinnes and K. Randsborg (eds) *The archaeology of death*, 93–104. Cambridge: Cambridge University Press.

Bradley, R. 1984. *The social foundations of prehistoric Britain*. Harlow: Longman.

Bradley, R. 1989. Darkness and light in the design of megalithic tombs. *Oxford Journal of Archaeology*, 8, 251–9.

Bradley, R. 1990. *The passage of arms*. Cambridge: Cambridge University Press.

Bradley, R. 1991. Ritual, time and history. *World Archaeology* 23, 209–19.

Bradley, R. 1993. *Altering the earth*. Edinburgh: Society of Antiquaries of Scotland.

Bradley, R. 1996a. Excavations at Clava. *Current Archaeology* 148, 136–42.

Bradley, R. 1996b. Rethinking the Later Bronze Age. In O. Bedwin (ed.), *The archaeology of Essex: proceedings of the Writtle conference*, 38–45. Chelmsford: Essex County Council.

Bradley, R. 1997. *Rock art and the prehistory of Atlantic Europe*. London: Routledge.

Bradley, R. and Edmonds, M. 1993. *Interpreting the axe trade*. Cambridge: Cambridge University Press.

Braudel, F. 1969. *Écrits sur l'histoire*. Paris: Flammarion.

Brinch Petersen, E. 1974. Gravene ved Dragsholm. *Nationamuseets Arbeidsmark* (1974), 112–20.

Brück, J. 1995. A place for the dead: the role of human remains in Late Bronze Age Britain. *Proceedings of the Prehistoric Society* 61, 245–77.

Burl, A. 1972. Stone circles and ring cairns. *Scottish Archaeological Forum* 4, 31–47.

Burl, A. 1976. *The stone circles of the British Isles*. New Haven, CT: Yale University Press.

Burl, A. 1979. *Rings of stone*. London: Weidenfeld & Nicholson.

Burl, A. 1988. 'Within sharp north . . . ' Alexander Thom and the great stone circles of Cumbria. In C. Ruggles (ed.) *Records in stone*, 175–205. Cambridge: Cambridge University Press.

Burstow, G. P. 1958. A Late Bronze Age urnfield on Steyning Round Hill. *Proceedings of the Prehistoric Society* 24, 158–64.

Burstow, G. P. and Holleyman, G. 1957. The Late Bronze Age settlement on Itford Hill, Sussex. *Proceedings of the Prehistoric Society* 23, 167–212.

Buttler, W. and Haberey, W. 1936. *Die bandkeramische Ansiedlung bei Köln-Lindenthal*. Berlin: De Gruyter.

Buus Eriksen, L. 1992. Ornehus frå Stevns- en tidligneolitisk hustomt. *Aarbøger* (1992), 7–19.

Carsten, J. and Hugh-Jones, S. 1995. Introduction. In J. Carsten and S. Hugh-Jones (eds) *About the house*, 1–46. Cambridge: Cambridge University Press.

Case, H. 1969. Neolithic explanations. *Antiquity* 43, 176–86.

Caulfield, S. 1978. Neolithic fields: the Irish evidence. In C. Bowen and P. Fowler (eds), *Early land allotment in the British Isles*, 137–43. Oxford: British Archaeological Reports.

Chapman, J. 1994. The living, the dead and the ancestors: life cycles and the mortuary domain in later European prehistory. In J. Davies (ed.) *Ritual and remembrance: responses to death in human societies*, pp. 40–85. Sheffield: Sheffield Academic Press.

Chapman, R. 1981. The emergence of formal disposal areas and the 'problem' of megalithic tombs in prehistoric Europe. In R. Chapman, I. Kinnes and K. Randsborg (eds) *The archaeology of death*, 71–81. Cambridge: Cambridge University Press.

Chapman, R. 1995. Ten years after: megaliths, mortuary practices and the territorial model. In L. A. Beck (ed.) *Regional approaches to mortuary analysis*, 29–51. New York: Plenum Press.

Childe, V. G. 1949. The origin of Neolithic culture in Northern Europe. *Antiquity* 23, 129–35.

Childe, V. G. 1952. Re-excavation of the chambered tomb at Quoyness. *Proceedings of the Society of Antiquaries of Scotland* 86, 121–39.

Childe, V. G. 1956. Maes Howe. *Proceedings of the Society of Antiquaries of Scotland* 88, 155–72.

Clark, G. and Neeley, M. 1987. Social differentiation in European Mesolithic burial data. In P. Rowley-Conwy, M. Zvelebil and H. P. Blankholm (eds) *Mesolithic north-west Europe: recent trends*, 121–7. Sheffield: Sheffield University Department of Archaeology and Prehistory.

Cleal, R., Walker, K. and Montague, R. 1995. *Stonehenge in its landscape: twentieth century excavations*. London: English Heritage.

Clutton-Brock, J. 1984. Dogs. In L. Mason (ed.) *Evolution of domesticated animals*, 198–210. Harlow: Longman.

Condit, T. 1993. On the outside looking in. *Archaeology Ireland* 7.4, 15.

Connerton, P. 1989. *How societies remember*. Cambridge: Cambridge University Press.

Cooney, G. and Grogan, E. 1994. *Irish prehistory: a social perspective*. Dublin: Wordwell.

Coudart, A. and Demoule, J.-P. 1982. Le site néolithique de Menneville. *Revue Archéologique de Picardie*, numéro spécial, 119–47.

Criado, F. 1989. We, the post-megalithic people. In I. Hodder (ed.) *The meanings of things*, 79–89. London: Unwin Hyman.

Darvill, T. 1996. *Prehistoric Britain from the air*. Cambridge: Cambridge University Press.

Da Cruz, D. J. 1995. Chronologia dos monumentos com tumulus do noroeste Penninsular e da Beira Alta. *Estudios Pré-historicos* 3, 81–119.

Davidson, J. and Henshall, A. 1989. *The chambered tombs of Orkney*. Edinburgh: Edinburgh University Press.

Dennell, R. 1983. *European economic prehistory*. London: Academic Press.

Drewett, P. 1982. Later Bronze Age downland economy, and excavations at Blackpatch, East Sussex. *Proceedings of the Prehistoric Society* 48, 321–400.

Duhamel, P. and Prestreau, M. 1991. La nécropole monumentale néolithique de Passy dans le contexte du gigantisme-funéraire euopéen. *Actes du 14e Colloque Interrégionale sur le Néolithique*, 103–117. Orléans: Société Archéologique Scientifique et Litteraire du Vendômois.

Edmonds, M. 1993. Interpreting causewayed enclosures in the past and the present. In C. Tilley (ed.) *Interpretative archaeology*, 99–142. Oxford: Berg.

Eogan, G. 1963. A Neolithic habitation site and megalithic tomb at Townleyhall townland, Co Louth. *Journal of the Royal Society of Antiquaries of Ireland* 93, 37–81.

Eogan, G. 1984. *Excavations at Knowth, 1*. Dublin: Royal Irish Academy.

Eogan, G. 1986. *Knowth and the passage-tombs of Ireland*. London: Thames & Hudson.

Eogan, G. and Roche, H. 1997. *Excavations at Knowth, 2*. Dublin: Royal Irish Academy.

Evans, C. 1988. Acts of enclosure: a consideration of concentrically-organised causewayed enclosures. In J. Barrett and I. Kinnes (eds) *The archaeology of context in the Neolithic and Bronze Age: recent trends*, 85–96. Sheffield: Sheffield University Department of Archaeology and Prehistory.

Farrugia, J.-P. 1992. *Les outils et les armes en pierre dans le rituel funéraire du Néolithique Danubien*. Oxford: British Archaeological Reports.

Fitzpatrick, A. 1994. Outside in: the structure of an Early Iron Age house at Dunston Park, Thatcham, Berkshire. In A. Fitzpatrick and E. Morris (eds) *The Iron Age of Wessex: recent work*, 68–72. Salisbury: Wessex Archaeology.

Fleming, A. 1972, Vision and design: approaches to ceremonial monument typology. *Man* 7, 57–73.

Fleming, A. 1973. Tombs for the living. *Man* 8, 177–93.

Gamble, C. 1986. *The Palaeolithic settlement of Europe*. Cambridge: Cambridge University Press.

Gell, A. 1992. *The anthropology of time*. Oxford: Berg.

Gent, H. 1983. Centralised storage in later prehistoric Britain. *Proceedings of the Prehistoric Society* 49, 243–67.

Gibson, A. 1994. Excavations at the Sarn-y-bryn-caled cursus complex, Welshpool, Powys, and the timber circles of Great Britain and Ireland. *Proceedings of the Prehistoric Society* 60, 143–223.

Gibson, A. 1996. A Neolithic enclosure at Hindwell, Radnorshire, Powys. *Oxford Journal of Archaeology* 15, 341–8.

Gibson, M. 1996. *A re-assessment of the Bronze Age cemetery-barrow on Itford Hill, East Sussex*. Bournemouth: Bournemouth University School of Conservation Sciences.

Giddens, A. 1984. *The constitution of society*. Cambridge: Polity Press.

Gosden, C. 1994. *Social being and time*. Oxford: Blackwell.

Green, M. 1994. Down Farm. *Current Archaeology* 138, 216–25.

Grogan, E. 1996. Neolithic houses in Ireland. In T. Darvill and J. Thomas (eds) *Neolithic houses in northwest Europe and beyond*, 41–60. Oxford: Oxbow.

Haggarty, A. 1991. Machrie Moor, Arran: recent excavations at two stone circles. *Proceedings of the Society of Antiquaries of Scotland* 121, 51–94.

Harding, A. and Lee, G. 1987. *Henge monuments and related sites of Great Britain*. Oxford: British Archaeological Reports.

Harding, J. 1995. Social histories and regional perspectives in the Neolithic of lowland England. *Proceedings of the Prehistoric Society* 61, 117–36.

Härke, H. 1995. 'The Hun is a methodical chap'. Reflections on the German tradition of pre- and proto-history. In P. Ucko (ed.) *Theory in archaeology: a world perspective*, 46–60. London: Routledge.

Hartwell, B. 1991. Ballynahatty – a prehistoric ceremonial centre. *Archaeology Ireland* 5.4, 12–15.

Hayden, B. 1990. Nimrods, piscators, pluckers and planters: the emergence of food production. *Journal of Anthropological Archaeology* 9, 31–69.

Healy, F. 1997. Site 3. Flagstones. In R. Smith, F. Healy, M. Allen, E. Morris, I. Barnes and P. Woodward, *Excavations along the route of the Dorchester by-pass, Dorset, 1986–8*. Salisbury: Wessex Archaeology.

Hensel, W. and Milisauskas, S. 1985. *Excavations of Neolithic and Early Bronze Age sites in south eastern Poland*. Warsaw: Poliska Akademia nauk Instytut Historii Kultury Materialnej.

Henshall, A. 1963. *The chambered tombs of Scotland*, volume 1. Edinburgh: Edinburgh University Press.

Hill, J. D. 1995. *Ritual and rubbish in the Iron Age of Wessex*. Oxford: British Archaeological Reports.

Hill, J. D. 1996. Hillforts and the Iron Age of Wessex. In T. Champion and J. Collis (eds) *The Iron Age in Britain and Ireland: recent trends*, 95–116. Sheffield: J. R. Collis Publications.

Hingley, R. 1990. Iron Age 'currency bars': the archaeological and social context. *Archaeological Journal* 147, 91–117.

Hodder, I. 1984. Burials, houses, women and men in the European Neolithic. In D. Miller and C. Tilley (eds) *Ideology, power and prehistory*, 51–68. Cambridge: Cambridge University Press.

Hodder, I. 1988. Material culture texts and social change: a theoretical discussion and some archaeological examples. *Proceedings of the Prehistoric Society* 54, 67–75.

Hodder, I. 1990. *The domestication of Europe: structure and contingency in Neolithic societies*. Oxford: Blackwell.

Hodder, I. 1991. *Reading the past*. Second edition. Cambridge: Cambridge University Press.

Hodder, I. 1994. Architecture and meaning: the example of Neolithic houses and tombs. In M. Parker Pearson and C. Richards (eds) *Architecture and order: approaches to social space*, 73–86. London: Routledge.

Holden, E. 1972. A Bronze Age cemetery-barrow on Itford Hill, Beddingham. Sussex: *Sussex Archaeological Collections* 110, 70–117.

Ingold, T. 1984. Timescales, social relationships and the exploitation of animals: anthropological reflections on prehistory. In J. Clutton-Brock and C. Grigson (eds) *Animals and archaeology: 3: early herders and their flocks*, 3–12. Oxford: British Archaeological Reports.

Ingold, T. 1993. Globes and spheres: the topology of environmentalism. In K. Milton (ed.) *Environmentalism; the view from anthropology*, 31–42. London: Routledge.

Iversen, J. 1941. *Landnam i Danmarks Stenalder*. Copenhagen: C. A. Reitzels Forlag.

Jackson, P. 1995. A continuing belief system? In K. Helsgog and B. Olsen (eds) *Perceiving rock art*, 396–4–6. Oslo: Novus forlag.

Jacobs, K. 1995. Return to Oleni' ostrov: economic and skeletal dimensions of a Boreal Forest Mesolithic cemetery. *Journal of Anthropological Archaeology* 14, 335–50.

Jarman, M., Bailey, G. and Jarman, H. 1982. *Early European agriculture*. Cambridge: Cambridge University Press.

Jennbert, K. 1984. *Den productiva Gåvan*. Lund: Acta Archaeologica Lundensia.

Johnson, M. 1989. Conceptions of agency in archaeological interpretation. *Journal of Anthropological Archaeology* 8, 189–211.

Joussaume, R. and Pautreau, J.-P. 1990. *Le préhistorie du Poitou*. Tours: Ouest-France.

Juel Jensen, H. 1994. *Flint tools and plant working*. Aarhus: Aarhus University Press.

Karsten, P. 1994. *Att kasta yxan i siön*. Lund: Acta Archaeologica Lundensia.

Kayser, O. 1990. Sur les rites funéraires des derniers chasseur-collecteurs d'Europe de l'ouest et du nord-ouest à la fin du Mésolithique. *Revue Archéologique de l'Ouest*, supplément 2, 75–80.

Kayser, O. and Bernier, P. 1988. Nouveaux objets decorés du Mésolithique armoricain. *Bulletin de la Société Préhistorique Française* 85.2, 45–7.

Keeley, L. and Cahen, D. 1989. Early Neolithic forts and villages in north-east Belgium. *Journal of Field Archaeology* 16, 157–66.

Kopytoff, I. 1986. The cultural biography of things: commoditisation as process. In A. Appadurai (ed.) *The social life of things*, 64–91. Cambridge: Cambridge University Press.

Kuper, R., Lüning, J., Stehli, P. and Zimmerman, A. 1977. *Der bandkeramische Siedlungsplatz Langweiler 9*. Bonn: Rheinishe Ausgrabungen 18.

Lalic, I. 1996. *A rusty needle*, trans. F. R. Jones. London: Anvil Press.

Larsson, L. 1982. A causewayed enclosure and a site with Valby pottery at Stävie, Western Scania. *Meddelanden fran Lunds Universitets Historiska Museum* 1981–2, 65–114.

Larsson, L. 1983. *Ageröd V. An Atlantic site in Central Scania*. Lund: Acta Archaeologica Lundensia.

Larsson, L. 1988. A construction for ceremonial activities from the Late Mesolithic. *Meddelanden fran Lunds Universitets Historiska Museum* 1987–8, 5–18.

Larsson, L. 1989. Late Mesolithic settlements and cemeteries at Skateholm, southern Sweden. In C. Bonsall (ed.) *The Mesolithic in Europe*, 367–78. Edinburgh: John Donald.

Larsson, L. 1990. Dogs in fraction – symbols in action. In P. Vermeersch and P. van Peer (eds) *Contributions to the Mesolithic in Europe*, 153–60. Leuven: Leuven University Press.

Larsson, L., Meikeljohn, C. and Newell, R. 1981. Human skeletal material from the Mesolithic site of Ageröd, Scania, southern Sweden. *Forvännen* 76, 161–7.

Larsson, M. 1986. Bredasten – an Early Ertebølle site with a dwelling structure in South Scania. *Meddelanden från Lunds Universitets Historiska Museum* 6, 25–51.

Lecornec, J. 1994. *Le Petit Mont, Arzon-Morbihan*. Rennes: Documents Archéologiques de l'Ouest.

Leighton, D. 1984. Structured round cairns in west central Wales. *Proceedings of the Prehistoric Society* 50, 319–50.

Le Rouzic, Z. 1932. *Tumulus du Mont St-Michel*. Vannes: Lafoyle and De Lamarzelle.

Lévi-Strauss, C. 1966. *The savage mind*. London: Weidenfeld & Nicholson.

L'Helgouac'h, J. 1983. Les idoles qu'on abat. *Bulletin de la Société Polymathique du Morbihan* (1983), 57–68.

Lichardus, J. 1986. Le rituel funéraire dans la culture de Michelsberg dans la région du Rhin supérieur et moyen. In Demoule, J.-P. and Guilaine, J. (eds) *Le Néolithique en France*, 243–58. Paris: Picard.

Liversage, D. 1992. *Barkaer long barrows and settlements*. Copenhagen: Akademisk Forlag Universitetsforlag, København.

Lombardo, J.-C., Martinez, R. and Verret, D. 1984. Le Chasséen de Culfroid à Boury-en-Vexin dans son contexte historique et les apports de la stratigraphie de son fossée. *Revue Archéologique de Picardie* 1(2), 269–92.

Lüning, J. 1967. Die Michelsberg Kultur. Ihre Funde in zeitlicher und räumlicher Gliederung. *Bericht der Römisch-Germanischen Kommission* 48, 1–350.

Lüning, J. 1982. Research into the Bandkeramik settlement of the Aldenhoven Platte in the Rhineland. *Analecta Praehistorica Leidensia* 15, 1–30.

Lüning, J. 1988. Zur Verbreitung und Datierung bandkeramischer Erdwerk. *Archäologisches Korrespondenzblatt* 18, 155–8.

Lüning, J. and Stehli, P. (eds) 1994. *Die Bandkeramik im Merzbachtal auf der Aldenhoven Platte*. Bonn: Rheinische Ausgrabungen 36.

Lynch, F. 1972. Ring cairns and related monuments in Wales. *Scottish Archaeological Forum* 4, 61–80.

Lynch, F. 1979. Ring cairns: their design and purpose. *Ulster Journal of Archaeology* 42, 1–19.

Lynch, F. 1993. *Excavations in the Brenig valley*. Bangor: Cambrian Archaeological Association.

Lynn, C. 1993. House-urns in Ireland? *Ulster Journal of Archaeology* 56, 70–7.

Madsen, T. 1982. Settlement systems of early agricultural societies in East Jutland, Denmark. *Journal of Anthropological Archaeology* 1, 197–236.

Madsen, T. 1988. Causewayed camps in south Scandinavia. In C. Burgess, P. Topping, C. Mordant and M. Maddison (eds) *Enclosures and defences in the Neolithic of western Europe*, 301–36. Oxford: British Archaeological Reports.

Mallory, J. and Hartwell, B. 1984. Donegore. *Current Archaeology* 92, 271–5.

Manby, T. G. 1976. Excavations at Kilham long barrow, East Riding of Yorkshire. *Proceedings of the Prehistoric Society* 42, 111–59.

Marguerie, D. 1992. *Evolution de la végetation sous l'impact humain en Armorique du Néolithique aux périodes historiques*. Rennes: Université de Rennes.

Marolle, C. 1989. Le village Michelsberg des Hautes Chanvières à Mairy (Ardennes). *Gallia Préhistoire* 31, 93–117.

Masset, C. 1993. *Les dolmens. Sociétés néolithiques, pratiques funéraires*. Paris: Errance.

Mazingue, B. and Mordant, D. 1982. Fonctions primaires et secondaires des fosses du site néolithique de Noyen-sur-Seine et les enceintes de la Bassées (Seine-et-Marne). In *Le Néolithique de l'est de la France*, 129–34. Sens: Société Archéologique de Sens.

Meikeljohn, C. 1986. Old bones, new dates. Recent radiocarbon results from Mesolithic skeletal remains. *Mesolithic Miscellany* 7(1), 9–16.

Meillassoux, C. 1972. From reproduction to production. *Economy and Society* 1, 93–105.

Mellars, P. 1987. *Excavations on Oronsay*. Edinburgh: Edinburgh University Press.

Mercer, R. 1980. *Hambledon Hill: a Neolithic landscape*. Edinburgh: Edinburgh University Press.

Mercer, R. 1981. The excavation of a late Neolithic henge-type enclosure at Balfarg,

Markinch, Fife, Scotland, 1977–1978. *Proceedings of the Society of Antiquaries of Scotland* 111, 63–171.

Midgley, M. 1985. *The origin and function of the earthen long barrows of northern Europe.* Oxford: British Archaeological Reports.

Midgley, M. 1992. *TRB culture.* Edinburgh: Edinburgh University Press.

Mithen, S. 1991. 'A cybernetic wasteland'. Rationality, emotion and Mesolithic foraging. *Proceedings of the Prehistoric Society* 57(3), 9–14.

Mizoguchi, K. 1993. Time in the reproduction of mortuary practices. *World Archaeology* 25, 223–35.

Møhl, U. 1978. Els Dyrskeletterne fra Skottemarke og Favrbo. Skik go brug ved borealtidens jagter. *Aarbøger* 1978, 5–32.

Mount, C. 1994. Aspects of ritual deposition in the Late Neolithic and Beaker periods at Newgrange, Co Meath. *Proceedings of the Prehistoric Society* 60, 433–43.

Mordant, D. and Mordant, C. 1977. Habitat néolithique de fond de vallée alluviale à Noyen-sur-Seine (Seine-et-Marne): etude archéologique. *Gallia Préhistoire* 20, 229–69.

Needham, S. 1988. Selective deposition in the British Early Bronze Age. *World Archaeology* 20, 229–48.

Nicardot, J.-P. 1974. Structures d'habitat à caractère défensif dans le Centre Est de la France. *Antiquités Nationales* 6, 32–45.

O'Kelly, C. 1983. Newgrange, C. Meath, Ireland. *The Late Neolithic/Beaker period settlement.* Oxford: British Archaeological Reports.

O'Kelly, M. 1982. *Newgrange: archaeology, art and legend.* London: Thames & Hudson.

O'Shea, J. and Zvelebil, M. 1984. Oleneostrovski Mogilnik: reconstructing the social and economic organisation of prehistoric foragers in northern Russia. *Journal of Anthropological Archaeology* 3, 1–40.

O'Sullivan, M. 1993. *Megalithic art in Ireland.* Dublin: Country House.

O'Sullivan, M. 1996. A platform to the past: Knockroe passage tomb. *Archaeology Ireland* 10(2), 11–13.

Parker Pearson, M. 1996. Food, fertility and front doors in the first millennium BC. In T. Champion and J. Collis (eds) *The Iron Age in Britain and Ireland: recent trends,* 117–32. Sheffield: J. R. Collis Publications.

Patton, M. 1993. *Statements in stone: monuments and society in Neolithic Brittany.* London: Routledge.

Pavlu, I., Rulf, J. and Zápatocká, M. 1986. Theses on the Neolithic site at Bylany. *Památky Archeologické* 57, 288–412.

Piggott, S. 1948. Excavations on Cairnpapple Hill, West Lothian. *Proceedings of the Society of Antiquaries of Scotland* 82, 68–123.

Piggott, S. 1954. *The Neolithic cultures of the British Isles.* Cambridge: Cambridge University Press.

Pollard, J. 1992. The Sanctuary, Overton Hill, Wiltshire: a re-examination. *Proceedings of the Prehistoric Society* 58, 213–26.

Pryor, F. 1984. Personalities of Britain: two examples of long-term regional contrast. *Scottish Archaeological Review* 3.1, 8–15.

Raetzel-Fabian, D. 1991. Zwischen Fluchtburg und Kultstätte. *Archäologie in Deutschland* 4 (October–December 1991), 22–5.

RCAHMS (Royal Commission on the Ancient and Historical Monuments of Scotland) 1988. *Argyll, volume 6.* Edinburgh: HMSO.

Ratcliffe-Densham, H. B. A. and Ratcliffe-Densham, M. M. 1961. An anomalous earthwork of the Late Bronze Age on Cock Hill. *Sussex Archaeological Collections* 99, 78–101.

Renfrew, C. 1973. *Before civilisation.* London: Cape.

Renfrew, C. 1976. Megaliths, territories and populations. In S. De Laet (ed.) *Acculturation and continuity in Atlantic Europe*, 198–220. Bruges: De Tempel.

Renfrew, C. 1979. *Investigations in Orkney.* London: Society of Antiquaries.

Richards, C. 1996. Monuments as landscape: creating the centre of the world in late Neolithic Orkney. *World Archaeology* 28, 190–208.

Richards, J. 1990. *The Stonehenge environs project.* London: English Heritage.

Ritchie, G. 1974. Excavations of the stone circle and cairn at Balbirnie, Fife. *Archaeological Journal* 131, 1–32.

Ritchie, G. 1976. The Stones of Stenness, Orkney. *Proceedings of the Society of Antiquaries of Scotland* 107, 1–60.

Ritchie, G. and Maclaren, A. 1972. Ring cairns and related monuments in Scotland. *Scottish Archaeological Forum* 4, 1–17.

Roche, H. 1989. Pre-tomb habitation found at Knowth, C. Meath, spring 1989. *Archaeology Ireland* 3, 101–3.

Rowlands, M. 1993. The role of memory in the transmission of culture. *World Archaeology* 25, 141–51.

Rowley-Conwy, P. 1984. The laziness of the short distance hunter: the origins of agriculture in Western Denmark. *Journal of Anthropological Archaeology* 3, 300–24.

Rozoy, J.-G. 1978. *Les derniers chasseurs.* Charleville: Bulletin de la société archéologique champenois, numéro spécial.

Ruggles, C. (ed.) 1988. *Records in stone. Papers in memory of Alexander Thom.* Cambridge: Cambridge University Press.

Sahlins, M. 1985. *Islands of history.* Chicago: Chicago University Press.

Scarre, C. 1992. The Early Neolithic of western France and megalithic origins in Atlantic Europe. *Oxford Journal of Archaeology* 11, 121–54.

Schulting, R. 1996. Antlers, bone points and flint blades: the Mesolithic cemeteries of Téviec and Hoëdic, Brittany. *Antiquity* 70, 335–50.

Scott, J. 1989. The stone circles at Temple Wood, Kilmartin, Argyll. *Glasgow Archaeological Journal* 15, 53–124.

Shanks, M. and Tilley, C. 1987a. *Re-constructing archaeology.* Cambridge: Cambridge University Press.

Shanks, M. and Tilley, C. 1987b. *Social theory and archaeology.* Oxford: Polity Press.

Sharples, N. 1984. Excavations at Pierowall quarry, Westray, Orkney. *Proceedings of the Society of Antiquaries of Scotland* 114, 75–125.

Sharples, N. 1985. Individual and community: the changing role of megaliths in the Orcadian Neolithic. *Proceedings of the Prehistoric Society* 51, 59–74.

Shee Twohig, E. 1981. *The megalithic art of western Europe.* Oxford: Clarendon Press.

Shepherd, I. 1987. The early peoples. In D. Omand (ed.) *The Grampian book*, 119–30. Gospie: The Northern Times.

Sherratt, A. 1990. The genesis of megaliths: monumentality, ethnicity and social complexity in Neolithic north-west Europe. *World Archaeology* 22, 147–67.

Sherratt, A. 1995. Instruments of conversion? The role of megaliths in the Mesolithic/Neolithic transition in north-west Europe. *Oxford Journal of Archaeology* 14, 245–60.

Simpson, D., Weir, D. and Wilkinson, J. 1992. Excavations at Dun Ruadh, Crouck, Co Tyrone. *Ulster Journal of Archaeology* 55, 36–47.

Skaarup, J. 1993. Megalithic graves. In S. Haas and B. Storgaard (eds) *Digging into the past: 25 years of archaeology in Denmark*, 104–9. Aarhus: Jutland Archaeological Society.

Soffe, G. and Clare, T. 1988. New evidence of ritual monuments at Long Meg and her Daughters, Cumbria. *Antiquity* 62, 552–7.

Soudsky, B. 1973. Higher level archaeological entities – models and reality. In C. Renfrew (ed.) *The explanation of culture change*, 195–207. London: Duckworth.

Soudsky, B. and Pavlu, I. 1972. The Linear Pottery Culture settlement pattern in Central Europe. In P. Ucko, R. Tringham and G. Dimbleby (eds) *Man, settlement and urbanism*, 317–28. London: Duckworth.

Srejovic, D. 1972. *Europe's first monumental sculpture: new discoveries at Lepenski Vir.* London: Thames & Hudson.

Srejovic, D. and Letica, Z. 1978. *Vlasac: a Mesolithic settlement on the Iron Gates.* Belgrade: Serbian Academy of Sciences and Arts.

Startin, W. and Bradley, R. 1981. Some notes on work organisation and society in prehistoric Wessex. In C. Ruggles and A. Whittle (eds) *Astronomy and society during the period 4000–1500 BC*, 289–96. Oxford: British Archaeological Reports.

Stout, G. 1991. Embanked enclosures of the Boyne region. *Proceedings of the Royal Irish Academy* 91C, 254–84.

Sweetman, D. 1985. A Late Neolithic/Early Bronze Age pit circle at Newgrange, Co Meath. *Proceedings of the Royal Irish Academy* 81C, 195–221.

Sweetman, D. 1987. Excavation of a Late Neolithic/Early Bronze Age site at Newgrange, Co Meath. *Proceedings of the Royal Irish Academy* 87C, 283–98.

Tackenberg, K. 1951. *Die Beusterburg. Ein jungsteinzeitliches Erdwerk in Niedersachsen.* Hildesheim: August Lax.

Tarlow, S. 1994. Scraping the bottom of the barrow: an agricultural metaphor in Neolithic/Bronze Age European burial practice. *Journal of Theoretical Archaeology* 3/4, 123–44.

Thom, A. 1967. *Megalithic sites in Britain.* Oxford: Clarendon Press.

Thomas, J. 1988a. Neolithic explanations revisited: the Mesolithic–Neolithic transition in Britain and south Scandinavia. *Proceedings of the Prehistoric Society* 54, 59–66.

Thomas, J. 1988b. The social significance of Cotswold–Severn burial sites. *Man* 23, 540–59.

Thomas, J. 1990. Monuments from the inside: the case of the Irish megalithic tombs. *World Archaeology* 22, 168–78.

Thomas, J. 1991a. *Rethinking the Neolithic.* Cambridge: Cambridge University Press.

Thomas, J. 1991b. The hollow men? A reply to Steven Mithen. *Proceedings of the Prehistoric Society* 57.2, 15–20.

Thomas, J. 1993. Discourse, totalisation and 'the Neolithic'. In C. Tilley (ed.), *Interpretative archaeology*, 357–94. Oxford: Berg.

Thomas, J. 1996. *Time, culture and identity.* London: Routledge.

Thrane, H. 1989. Danish ploughmarks from the Neolithic and Bronze Age. *Journal of Danish Archaeology* 8, 111–25.

Tilley, C. 1996. *An ethnography of the Neolithic.* Cambridge: Cambridge University Press.

Topping, P. 1992. The Penrith henges: a survey by the Royal Commission on the Historical Monuments of England. *Proceedings of the Prehistoric Society* 58, 249–64.

Tringham, R. 1991. Households with faces: the challenge of gender in prehistoric architectural remains. In J. Gero and M. Conkey (eds) *Engendering archaeology*, 93–131. Oxford: Blackwell.

Trnka, G. 1991. *Studien zu mittelneolitischen Kreisgrabenanlagen.* Vienna: Akademie der Wissenschaften.

Van Bergh, P.-L. 1991. Géometrie de quelques enceintes fossoyés du Rubané récent rhéno-mosan. *Actes du quinzième Colloque interrégionale sur le Néolithique*, 25–32. Voirpreux: Association Régional pour la Protection et l'Etude du Patrimonie Préhistorique.

Vaquer, J. 1990. *Le Néolithique en Languedoc occidental.* Paris: Editions du CNRS.

Veit, U. 1993. Burials within settlements of the Linienbandkeramik and Stichbandkeramik cultures of Central Europe, and the social construction of space in early Neolithic society. *Journal of European Archaeology* 1, 107–40.

Wainwright, G. and Longworth, I. 1971. *Durrington Walls excavations 1966–1968.* London: Society of Antiquaries.

Waterhouse, J. 1985. *The stone circles of Cumbria.* Chichester: Phillimore.

Watson, A. 1994. Stones from the sky: monuments, mountains and people in Neolithic Cumbria. Unpublished BA dissertation, Reading University.

Whittle, A. 1977. Earlier Neolithic enclosures in north-west Europe, *Proceedings of the Prehistoric Society* 43, 329–48.

Whittle, A. 1986. *Scord of Brouster. An early agricultural settlement on Shetland.* Oxford: Oxford University Committee for Archaeology.

Whittle, A. 1988a. *Problems in Neolithic archaeology.* Cambridge: University Press.

Whittle, A. 1988b. Contexts, activities, events – aspects of Neolithic and Copper Age enclosures in Central and Western Europe. In C. Burgess, P. Topping, C. Mordant and M. Maddison (eds) *Enclosures and defences in the Neolithic of western Europe*, 1–19. Oxford: British Archaeological Reports.

Whittle, A. 1996a. *Europe in the Neolithic: The Creation of new worlds.* Cambridge: Cambridge University Press.

Whittle, A. 1996b. Eternal stones: Stonehenge completed. *Antiquity* 70, 463–5.

Woodman, P. and O' Brien, M. 1993. Excavations at Ferriter's Cove, Co Kerry: an interim statement. In E. Shee Twohig and M. Ronayne (eds) *Past perceptions: the prehistoric archaeology of south-west Ireland*, 25–34. Cork: Cork University Press.

Woodward, A. and Woodward, P. 1996. The topography of some barrow cemeteries in Bronze Age Wessex. *Proceedings of the Prehistoric Society* 62, 275–91.

Woodward, P. 1991. *The South Dorset Ridgeway: survey and excavations 1977–1984.* Dorchester: Dorset Natural History and Archaeological Society.

Wyszomirska, B. 1984. *Figurplastik och gravskick hos Nord-och Nordösteuropas neolitisiska fangstkulyurer.* Lund: Acta Archaeologica Lundensia.

Yates, F. 1966. *The art of memory.* London: Routledge & Kegan Paul.

Zilhão, J. 1993. The spread of agro-pastoral economies across Mediterranean Europe: a view from the far west. *Journal of Mediterranean Archaeology* 6.1, 5–63.

Zvelebil, M. and Rowley-Conwy, P. 1986. Foragers and farmers in Atlantic Europe. In M. Zvelebil (ed.) *Hunters in transition*, 67–93. Cambridge: Cambridge University Press.

Index

Compiled with the assistance of Howard Williams